J. V. CUNNINGHAM, professor of English at Brandeis University, received his A.B. and Ph. D. degrees from Stanford University. He is the author of *The Helmsman*, published in 1942; *The Judge Is Fury*, 1947; *Doctor Drink*, 1950; *Woe or Wonder*, 1951; *The Exclusions of a Rhyme*, 1960; *Tradition and Poetic Structure*, 1960; *To What Strangers, What Welcome*, 1964; *The Journal of John Cardan*, 1964; *The Renaissance in England*, 1966.

LITERATURE AND IDEAS SERIES

Irving Howe, General Editor

The Problem of Style

Edited by
J. V. CUNNINGHAM

A FAWCETT PREMIER BOOK
Fawcett Publications, Inc., Greenwich, Conn.
Member of American Book Publishers Council, Inc.

Library of Congress Catalog Card Number: 66-27489

First Fawcett Premier printing, October 1966

Published by Fawcett World Library
67 West 44th Street, New York, N. Y. 10036

Printed in the United States of America

8207

Contents

VI   NEW THRESHOLDS, NEW ANATOMIES

VII   EPILOGUE

A student unacquainted with the attempts of former adventurers is always apt to overrate his own abilities; to mistake the most trifling excursions for discoveries of moment, and every coast new to him, for a new-found country. If by chance he passes beyond his usual limits, he congratulates his own arrival at those regions which they who have steered a better course have long left behind them.

The productions of such minds are seldom distinguished by an air of originality: they are anticipated in their happiest efforts; and if they are found to differ in anything from their predecessors, it is only in irregular sallies and trifling conceits. The more extensive therefore your acquaintance is with the works of those who have excelled, the more extensive will be your powers of invention; and what may appear still more like a paradox, the more original will be your conceptions.

Sir Joshua Reynolds
Discourses on Art, II

Introduction

THIS IS A book intended to ask questions, though most of the authors represented have given answers. But the answers are sometimes different, and often enough to different questions. For different answers: Aristotle, as Cicero points out, does not distinguish between the two figures of thought, metaphor and metonymy (by which a word associated with the expected word is used instead of it); to Jakobson they are polar opposites. And for different questions: anyone who has taken a course in English composition knows about clichés, how awful they are and how he should avoid them. He will be amused at Frank Sullivan's "Cliché Expert." Yet the late Milman Parry, as Professor Page explains, showed that the *Iliad* and the *Odyssey* are composed very largely of formulaic phrases, that is, of clichés, yet for twenty-five centuries they have been justly regarded as summits of the Western tradition. And Raleigh quietly points out that clichés are part of our public civilization, not to be lightly set aside. And so an answer becomes a question.

The initial question is, Is there such a thing as style? To the believer in organic form there cannot be. He will hold, with Croce, that how a thing is expressed is indistinguishable from the expression, that a difference in manner is a difference in meaning. And so anyone who wishes to consider style must premise that something may be said in different ways and that the ways may be compared. He may even hold, what is something else again, that manner is a potentiality looking for and limiting a meaning, that style precedes any realized expression. For him, then, style is an absolute.

But if there is such a thing as style, what sort of a thing is it? Is it a Platonic Idea, as Cicero holds, an "unsurpassable ideal which seldom appears throughout a whole work but does shine forth at some times and in some places, more frequently in some speakers, more rarely perhaps in others," and so, like the Sublime of Longinus, that striking distinction in speech that bowls one over. Or is it a neutral concept, so that everything has style, though one may contrast various styles and find this good and that bad. Or good and bad for this purpose or that, and so invoke the criterion of decorum, of appropriateness. It is curious that Aristotle, the interminable definer, does not define style, but proceeds at once to characterize the qualities of good style, and then of bad.

And if there is such a thing as style, what sorts of things have it? The notion was first applied to speech, and particularly to written composition. In recent centuries it has been applied to art and artifacts, and defined, as Professor Schapiro defines it, as "the constant form" "in the art of an individual or group." Other historians seek to divine in these constant forms the inner forms of a personality or civilization as represented in their art, artifacts, and sometimes literature. But is a linguistic composition an artifact in the sense that a Pueblo Indian pot is? Or only by metaphor? And if style is a form of form, is not the inner form of the cultural historian a contradiction, since form is external? But if it is a contradiction, is it a purposeful and useful one, enabling the historian to intuit or posit some pervasive principle, some formal cause, that will account for and supplant in value the observable external forms? Some spirit of the age, perhaps, or some oscillating or developing principle of the human spirit or of human history.

Again, is style rather a process, as Stevenson and Raleigh suggest, so that the realization of the design transforms the design? And, if it is a process, can language be regarded as material the speaker shapes as the potter shapes clay? If so, then the result is form, of which style may be taken as a species; it is then both process and shape. But the material itself may have its own inherent style, as Newman shows of a language. Then the style of a particular work, if linguistic, will be only a sub-language, a dialect so to speak, of the larger language, and describable by the methods of linguistics. And does it then have itself a history, as languages have?

Finally, does it have an opposite? And is that opposite thought or matter, or bad style, or lack of style? Such are the questions that definition raises.

After definition comes division: Are there kinds of style?

Certainly actual speech and speech in writing differ, for writing abstracts part of a speech situation and records it in repeatable form. It is possible to abstract more than conventional writing does, as Professor Sledd shows in his phonetic transcriptions, and, indeed, some linguists are now attempting to record intonation and gesture by a system of signs. Nevertheless, an actual utterance is not repeatable except by disc or tape. But is not this, too, an abstraction? And if it is, is it an abstraction of the same order as writing?

Another distinction is between styles that are unnoticeable and those that are noticeable. The first, according to Aristotle, gives clarity, the second weight. And from this comes the Ciceronian distinction between low, middle, and high style, and all the ancient and traditional lore of the figures of speech. For language, at least as abstracted in writing, is noticeable in detail either in its components or in its arrangement. The diction may be unusual, let us say that sort characterized as poetic, or, though not in itself unusual, unusually used. The various describable ways in which words may be unusually used comprise the tropes or figures of thought of traditional rhetoric, of which metaphor and metonymy are most commonly discussed. Yet these discussions are not always conducted with proper tact. If you are thinking of bridge cables as "swinging places where birds alight," you may translate this by metonymy into "The agile precincts of the lark's return." This is figurative since the retranslation requires inference. But if there is a certain slant of light, winter afternoons, that

> When it goes 'tis like the distance
> On the look of death.

look is not figurative for *face* since it is precisely the look that is being referred to. So, too, the Ancient Mariner's "At one stride comes the dark" is not metaphorical, for we all are making great strides these days. But the famous Gorgianic figure, that vultures are "living graves," is metaphorical, whether a good or, as Aristotle and Longinus think, a bad metaphor.

What is noticeable in arrangement is either unusual syntax, such as inversion or asyndeton (omission of connectives), or obtrusive repetition. The lack of conjunctions in "I came, I saw, I conquered," is not usual in speech and hence is noticeable. The figures of repetition, though they occasionally occur by chance in casual utterance, have generally the appearance of design and attract attention: "We have nothing to fear but fear itself." Since repetition is form, it gives to an utterance a form other than and concurrent with grammatical form, and hence tends, as verse does, to make a saying memorable. Since opposites imply each other, antithesis is a form of repetition: "Good is what we can do with evil." Finally, repetition is rhythm,[1] for "it is number that limits all things," and to number is to count, to note repetitions, either exact or approximate. And since numerical recurrence can be anticipated, its completion gives finality, as in metrical lines which consist of speech-segments of equal length.

The transfer from verse to prose of the figures of arrangement marks the beginning of the history of style in the Western tradition as a conscious subject of discussion, as something to be taught and to be learned. The event can be plausibly dated 427 B.C., if truth may be tied to particular occasions. "This year the Leontines," writes an ancient annalist, "dispatched ambassadors to Athens":

> The leader of the embassy was Gorgias the rhetorician, who in eloquence far surpassed all his contemporaries. He was the first man to devise rules of rhetoric and so far excelled all other men in the instruction offered by the sophists that he received from his pupils a fee of one hundred minas. Now when Gorgias had arrived in Athens and been introduced to the people in assembly, he discoursed to them upon the subject of the alliance, and by the novelty of his speech he filled the Athenians, who are by nature clever and fond of dialectic, with wonder. For he was the first to use the rather unusual and carefully devised structures of speech, such as antithesis, sentences with equal members or balanced clauses or similar endings, and the like, all of which at that time was enthusiastically

[1] There have been many attempts to describe the rhythms of English prose, and how successful they have been becomes clear when we notice that scarcely anyone builds on the work of his predecessors. Yet, the ancients write clearly and securely about prose rhythm, and there is much evidence that not only did speakers consciously employ certain rhythms but also that their audiences explicitly recognized them. Such an open employment of recognizable rhythmical patterns is not in our tradition, certainly not in prose, and it is becoming somewhat rare in poetry. This discrepancy between ancient and contemporary experience calls for explanation.

received because the device was exotic, but is now looked upon as laboured and to be ridiculed when employed too frequently and tediously.[2]

The effect of such speech, by all the testimony of Antiquity, and indeed of the Middle Ages and Renaissance, is astonishment, open-mouthed wonder at the gift of gab. But if it fails it seems frigid, bombastic, artificial. It is both offensive and impersuasive. And so the problem arises of hedging against failure, employing the art that conceals art, or alternatively, of developing an unrhetorical plain style whose "careful negligence" may yet permit distinction.

Such are some of the themes of this book and their attendant questions. You may write the answers in the margin.

[2] Diodorus Siculus, 12.53.2-4, tr. C.H. Oldfather (London, 1950).

I. STYLE

Style

THE CENTURY DICTIONARY AND CYCLOPEDIA

style (stil), *noun.* [Formerly also, and properly, *stile*; from Old French *style, stile,* French *style* = Spanish Portuguese *estilo* = Italian *stilo,* from Latin *stilus,* in medieval Latin also, improperly, *stylus,* a stake, pale, a pointed instrument used about plants, the stem or stalk of a plant, and especially for scribing on a waxen tablet, hence writing, manner of writing, mode of expression in writing or speech style. The word is properly written *stile;* the spelling *style* is in simulation of the Greek *stulos,* a pillar, which is not connected.] 1. An iron instrument, in the form of a bodkin tapering to a point at one end, used, in one of the methods of writing practised in ancient and medieval times, for scratching the letters into a waxed tablet, the other end being blunt for rubbing out writing and smoothing the tablet; figuratively, any writing-instrument.

But this my *style* no living man shall touch,
If first I be not forced by base reproach;
But like a sheathed sword it shall defend
My innocent life.
            Ben Jonson, Poetaster, v.i.

Some wrought in Silks, some writ in tender Barks;
Some the sharp *Stile* in waxen Tables marks.
            Cowley, Davideis, i.

2. Something similar in form to the instrument above described, or in some respect suggestive of it. A pointed or needle-like tool, implement, or attachment, as the marking-point in the telegraph or phonograph, a graver, or an etching-needle. 3. Mode of expression in writing or speaking; characteristic diction; a particular method of expressing thought by selection or collocation of words, distinct in some

respect from other methods, as determined by nationality, period, literary form, individuality, etc.; in an absolute sense, appropriate or suitable diction; conformity to an approved literary standard: as, the *style* of Shakespere or of Dickens; antiquated or modern *style*; didactic, poetic, or forensic *style*; a pedantic *style*; a nervous *style*; a cynical *style*.

Stile is a constant & continuall phrase or tenour of speaking and writing, extending to the whole tale or processe of the poeme or historie, and not properly to any peece or member of a tale.
Puttenham, Arte of English Poesie, p. 123.

Proper words in proper places make the true definition of a *style*.
Swift

Jeffreys spoke against the motion in the coarse and savage *style* of which he was a master.
Macaulay, History of England, vi.

If thought is the gold, *style* is the stamp which makes it current, and says under what king it was issued.
Dr. J. Brown, Spare Hours, 3rd series, p. 277.

4. Distinctive manner of external presentation; particular mode or form (within more or less variable limits) of construction or execution in any art or employment; the specific or characteristic formation or arrangement of anything. In this sense the applications of the word *style* are coextensive with the whole range of productive activity. Styles in the arts are designated according to subject, treatment, origin, school, period, etc.: as in painting, the landscape, genre, or historical *style*; the *style* of Titian or of Rubens; the Preraphaelite or the Impressionist *style*; in architecture, the Greek, medieval, and Renaissance *styles*, the Pointed or the Perpendicular *style*; the Louis-Quatorze or the Eastlake *style* of furniture; the Florentine *style* of wood-carving; carpets and rugs in the Persian *style*; *styles* in dress.

I don't know in what *style* I should dress such a figure and countenance, to make anything of them.
Cooper, Lionel Lincoln, iii.

It [a bed-chamber] is fitted up in the *style* of Louis XVI.

Thackeray, Newcomes, xlvi.
Monteverde, Claudio (1568-1643), the inventor of the "free *style*" of musical composition, was born at Cremona in 1568.
Encyclopedia Brit. (9th edition), XVI. 785

5. Particular mode of action or manifestation; physical or mental procedure; manner; way: as, *styles* of rowing, riding, or walking; *styles* of acting, singing, or bowing. 6. Mode, as of living or of appearing; distinctive or characteristic manner of fashion, with reference to appearance, bearing, social relations, etc; in absolute use, an approved or prevalent mode; superior manner; noticeable elegance; the fashion: as, to live in *style; style* of deportment or of dress.

There are some very homely women who have a *style* that amounts to something like beauty.
H.B. Stowe, Oldtown, p. 68.

That otherwise impalpable quality which women call *style*.
Howells, Indian Summer, ii.

7. Hence, in general, fine appearance; dashing character; spirited appearance: as a horse that shows *style*. 8. Mode of designation or address; a qualifying appellation or title; an epithet distinctive of rank, office, character or quality.

With one voice, sir,
The citizens salute you with the *style*
Of King of Naples.
Fletcher, Double Marriage, v. 4.

Give unto God his due, his reverend *style*.
Middleton, Solomon Paraphrased, i

9. In *chronology*, a mode of reckoning time with regard to the Julian and Gregorian calendars. See *calendar*. Style is *Old* or *New*.

Style

PAUL VALÉRY

STYLE—SO PURE IS the word in sound and aspect, it would be a delightful name for some choice being, a rare bird, a character in a fairy tale. It is one of those names whose musical quality suggests a language whose words would sound out their meaning.

But not at all. *Style* was first of all an engraving tool. In the hands of a Virgil or a Tacitus it incised in thin black wax the illustrious verses, the celebrated prose, a part of which has miraculously come down to us. Later, the stylus became a pen and the wax became paper. But even before the hard, cutting point had given way to the supple tip of a sharpened quill, the name *style* had passed from the instrument to the hand that guides it, and from the hand to the man from whom the hand derives its way of doing, and power to do, whatever it does.

It is these successive transitions of one and the same term from idea to idea that imperceptibly develop the intrinsic poetry of language.

Thus *style* signifies the manner in which a man expresses himself, *regardless of what he expresses,* and it is held to reveal his nature, quite apart from his actual thought—for thought has no style. It is in the act of expression that the man distinguishes himself. Here we find his characteristic rhythms, the temperamental constants of his character, his verbal resources which may or may not be very original, his habitual methods, and the enthusiasms or doubts that recur amid the diversity of his written or spoken discourse. All these elements constitute his *style.* But in among them, it should not be forgotten, there slips the curiously insinuating and active faculty of simulation or dissimulation which sometimes becomes dominant.

Thus what makes the style is not merely the mind applied to a particular action; it is the *whole* of a living system expended, imprinted, and made recognizable in expression. It is compounded of consciousness and unconsciousness, of spontaneity and effort; and sometimes calculation enters in. A work of art or an action may be executed with science or skill without disclosing style. A certain negligence does no harm in the matter of style; but neither does care, even excessive care, do away with it. In some men the will breaks through and reveals the sustained energy of their designs; in others indifference is manifest and it too is style; and there are still others who cultivate their carelessness, not unaware that it can take on the value of a style.

But a man's characteristic manner of doing things, *his style*, is not always praiseworthy. There are bad styles. Properly, the word means something more than manner of being or doing, and this "something" is not easily defined. I believe that a good style implies a kind of *organization of originality*, a harmony that excludes the excesses of the imagination. Extravagance and eccentricity burst the bounds of a good style. Untempered caprice is unbecoming to it. Everyone agrees that a tiger has a very different style from a monkey: it has magnificent balance; the monkey is all instability, futile gambols, aimless leaps.

Good style should suggest a very perceptible but indefinable law, which tempers the individual character of acts or works and lends them the dignity of a type or model. A personality then acquires the interest of an original, of a unique specimen which stands out from among the collection of similar beings that is the human race; it becomes a kind of deviation toward the ideal.

Nothing is more devoid of style than a product of mechanical or imitable fabrication. Consequently I deplore (though it is too late) the use of our word to designate an epoch or a school of architecture or of ornamental art, for styles of this kind are definable and imitable; commercial abuse of this verbal abuse has even given us the expression *"meubles de style"* (period furniture), and we know what that means.

Style

MEYER SCHAPIRO

BY STYLE IS meant the constant form—and sometimes the constant elements, qualities, and expression—in the art of an individual or a group. The term is also applied to the whole activity of an individual or society, as in speaking of a "life-style" or the "style of a civilization."

For the archaeologist, style is exemplified in a motive or pattern, or in some directly grasped quality of the work of art, which helps him to localize and date the work and to establish connections between groups of works or between cultures. Style here is a symptomatic trait, like the nonaesthetic features of an artifact. It is studied more often as a diagnostic means than for its own sake as an important constituent of culture. For dealing with style, the archaeologist has relatively few aesthetic and physiognomic terms.

To the historian of art, style is an essential object of investigation. He studies its inner correspondences, its life-history, and the problems of its formation and change. He, too, uses style as a criterion of the date and place of origin of works, and as a means of tracing relationships between schools of art. But the style is, above all, a system of forms with a quality and a meaningful expression through which the personality of the artist and the broad outlook of a group are visible. It is also a vehicle of expression within the group, communicating and fixing certain values of religious, social, and moral life through the emotional suggestiveness of forms. It is, besides, a common ground against which innovations and the individuality of particular works may be measured. By considering the succession of works in time and space and by matching the variations of style with historical events and with the varying features of other fields of culture, the historian of art attempts, with the help of common-sense psychology and social theory, to account for the changes of style or specific traits. The historical study of individual and group styles also discloses typical stages and processes in the development of forms.

For the synthesizing historian of culture or the philoso-

From **Anthropology Today**, edited by A. L. Kroeber. Copyright 1953 by The University of Chicago Press. Reprinted by permission of The University of Chicago Press.

phers of history, the style is a manifestation of the culture as a whole, the visible sign of its unity. The style reflects or projects the "inner form" of collective thinking and feeling. What is important here is not the style of an individual or of a single art, but forms and qualities shared by all the arts of a culture during a significant span of time. In this sense one speaks of Classical or Medieval or Renaissance Man with respect to common traits discovered in the art styles of these epochs and documented also in religious and philosophical writings.

The critic, like the artist, tends to conceive of style as a value term; style as such is a quality and the critic can say of a painter that he has "style" or of a writer that he is a "stylist." Although "style" in this normative sense, which is applied mainly to individual artists, seems to be outside the scope of historical and ethnological studies of art, it often occurs here, too, and should be considered seriously. It is a measure of accomplishment and therefore is relevant to understanding of both art and culture as a whole. Even a period style, which for most historians is a collective taste evident in both good and poor works, may be regarded by critics as a great positive achievement. So the Greek classic style was, for Winckelmann and Goethe, not simply a convention of form but a culminating conception with valued qualities not possible in other styles and apparent even in Roman copies of lost Greek originals. Some period styles impress us by their deeply pervasive, complete character, their special adequacy to their content; the collective creation of such a style, like the conscious shaping of a norm of language, is a true achievement. Correspondingly, the presence of the same style in a wide range of arts is often considered a sign of the integration of a culture and the intensity of a high creative moment. Arts that lack a particular distinction or nobility of style are often said to be style-less, and the culture is judged to be weak or decadent. A similar view is held by philosophers of culture and history and by some historians of art.

Common to all these approaches are the assumptions that every style is peculiar to a period of a culture and that, in a given culture or epoch of culture, there is only one style or a limited range of styles. Works in the style of one time could not have been produced in another. These postulates are supported by the fact that the connection between a style and a period, inferred from a few examples, is confirmed by objects discovered later. Whenever it is possible to locate a work through nonstylistic evidence, this evidence points to the same time and place as do the formal traits, or to a culturally associated region. The unexpected appearance of the style in another region is explained by migration or trade. The style is therefore used with confidence as an independent clue to the time and place of origin of a work of art. Building upon these assumptions, scholars have constructed a systematic, although not complete, picture of the temporal and spatial distribution of styles throughout large regions of the globe. If works of art are grouped in an order corresponding to their original positions in time and space, their styles will show significant relationships which can be co-ordinated with the relationships of the works of art to still other features of the cultural points in time and space.

2

Styles are not usually defined in a strictly logical way. As with languages, the definition indicates the time and place of a style or its author, or the historical relation to other styles, rather than its peculiar features. The characteristics of styles vary continuously and resist a systematic classification into perfectly distinct groups. It is meaningless to ask exactly when ancient art ends and medieval begins. There are, of course, abrupt breaks and reactions in art, but study shows that here, too, there is often anticipation, blending, and continuity. Precise limits are sometimes fixed by convention for simplicity in dealing with historical problems or in isolating a type. In a stream of development the artificial divisions may even be designated by numbers—Styles I, II, III. But the single name given to the style of a period rarely corresponds to a clear and universally accepted characterization of a type. Yet direct acquaintance with an unanalyzed work of art will often permit us to recognize another object of the same origin, just as we recognize a face to be native or foreign. This fact points to a degree of constancy in art that is the basis of all investigation of style. Through careful description and comparison and through formation of a richer, more refined typology adapted to the continuities in development, it has been possible to reduce the areas of vagueness and to advance our knowledge of styles.

Although there is no established system of analysis and writers will stress one or another aspect according to their viewpoint or problem, in general the description of a style refers to three aspects of art: form elements or motives, form relationships, and qualities (including an all-over quality which we may call the "expression").

This conception of style is not arbitrary but has arisen from the experience of investigation. In correlating works of art with an individual or culture, these three aspects provide the broadest, most stable, and therefore most reliable criteria. They are also the most pertinent to modern theory of art, although not in the same degree for all viewpoints. Technique, subject matter, and material may be characteristic of certain groups of works and will sometimes be included in definitions; but more often these features are not so peculiar to the art of a period as the formal and qualitative ones. It is easy to imagine a decided change in material, technique, or subject matter accompanied by little change in the basic form. Or, where these are constant, we often observe that they are less responsive to new artistic aims. A method of stone-cutting will change less rapidly than the sculptor's or architect's forms. Where a technique does coincide with the extension of a style, it is the formal traces of the technique rather than the operations as such that are important for description of the style. The materials are significant mainly for the textural quality and color, although they may affect the conception of the forms. For the subject matter, we observe that quite different themes—portraits, still lifes, and landscapes—will appear in the same style.

It must be said, too, that form elements or motives, although very striking and essential for the expression, are not sufficient for characterizing a style. The pointed arch is common to Gothic and Islamic architecture, and the round arch to Roman, Byzantine, Romanesque, and Renaissance buildings. In order to distinguish these styles, one must also look for features of another order and, above all, for different ways of combining the elements.

Although some writers conceive of style as a kind of syntax or compositional pattern, which can be analyzed mathematically, in practice one has been unable to do without the vague language of qualities in describing styles. Certain features of light and color in painting are most conveniently specified in qualitative terms and even as tertiary (intersensory) or physiognomic qualities, like cool and warm, gay and sad. The habitual span of light and dark, the intervals between colors in a particular palette—very important for the structure of a work—are distinct relationships between ele-

ments, yet are not comprised in a compositional schema of
the whole. The complexity of a work of art is such that the
description of forms is often incomplete on essential points,
limiting itself to a rough account of a few relationships. It is
still simpler, as well as more relevant to aesthetic experience,
to distinguish lines as hard and soft than to give measurements of their substance. For precision in characterizing a
style, these qualities are graded with respect to intensity by
comparing different examples directly or by reference to a
standard work. Where quantitative measurements have been
made, they tend to confirm the conclusions reached through
direct qualitative description. Nevertheless, we have no doubt
that, in dealing with qualities, much greater precision can be
reached.

Analysis applies aesthetic concepts current in the teaching,
practice, and criticism of contemporary art; the development
of new viewpoints and problems in the latter directs the
attention of students to unnoticed features of older styles. But
the study of works of other times also influences modern
concepts through discovery of aesthetic variants unknown in
our own art. As in criticism, so in historical research, the
problem of distinguishing or relating two styles discloses
unsuspected, subtle characteristics and suggests new concepts
of form. The postulate of continuity in culture—a kind of
inertia in the physical sense—leads to a search for common
features in successive styles that are ordinarily contrasted as
opposite poles of form; the resemblances will sometimes be
found not so much in obvious aspects as in fairly hidden ones
—the line patterns of Renaissance compositions recall features of the older Gothic style, and in contemporary abstract
art one observes form relationships like those of Impressionist
painting.

The refinement of style analysis has come about in part
through problems in which small differences had to be dis-
engaged and described precisely. Examples are the regional
variations within the same culture; the process of historical
development from year to year; the growth of individual
artists and the discrimination of the works of master and
pupil, originals and copies. In these studies the criteria for
dating and attribution are often physical or external—matters
of small symptomatic detail—but here, too, the general
trend of research has been to look for features that can be
formulated in both structural and expressive-physiognomic
terms. It is assumed by many students that the expression

terms are all translatable into form and quality terms, since the expression depends on particular shapes and colors and will be modified by a small change in the latter. The forms are correspondingly regarded as vehicles of a particular affect (apart from the subject matter). But the relationship here is not altogether clear. In general, the study of style tends toward an ever stronger correlation of form and expression. Some descriptions are purely morphological, as of natural objects—indeed, ornament has been characterized, like crystals, in the mathematical language of group theory. But terms like "stylized," "archaistic," "naturalistic," "mannerist," "baroque," are specifically human, referring to artistic processes, and imply some expressive effect. It is only by analogy that mathematical figures have been characterized as "classic" and "romantic."

3

The analysis and characterization of the styles of primitive and early historical cultures have been strongly influenced by the standards of recent Western art. Nevertheless, it may be said that the values of modern art have led to a more sympathetic and objective approach to exotic arts than was possible fifty or a hundred years ago.

In the past, a great deal of primitive work, especially representation, was regarded as artless even by sensitive people; what was valued were mainly the ornamentation and the skills of primitive industry. It was believed that primitive arts were childlike attempts to represent nature—attempts distorted by ignorance and by an irrational content of the monstrous and grotesque. True art was admitted only in the high cultures, where knowledge of natural forms was combined with a rational ideal which brought beauty and decorum to the image of man. Greek art and the art of the Italian High Renaissance were the norms for judging all art, although in time the classic phase of Gothic art was accepted. Ruskin, who admired Byzantine works, could write that in Christian Europe alone "pure and precious ancient art exists, for there is none in America, none in Asia, none in Africa." From such a viewpoint careful discrimination of primitive styles or a penetrating study of their structure and expression was hardly possible.

With the change in Western art during the last seventy years, naturalistic representation has lost its superior status. Basic for contemporary practice and for knowledge of past art is the theoretical view that what counts in all art are the elementary aesthetic components, the qualities and relationships of the fabricated lines, spots, colors, and surfaces. These have two characteristics: they are intrinsically expressive, and they tend to constitute a coherent whole. The same tendencies to coherent and expressive structure are found in the arts of all cultures. There is no privileged content or mode of representation (although the greatest works may, for reasons obscure to us, occur only in certain styles). Perfect art is possible in any subject matter or style. A style is like a language, with an internal order and expressiveness, admitting a varied intensity or delicacy of statement. This approach is a relativism that does not exclude absolute judgments of value; it makes these judgments possible within every framework by abandoning a fixed norm of style. Such ideas are accepted by most students of art today, although not applied with uniform conviction.

As a result of this new approach, all the arts of the world, even the drawings of children and psychotics, have become accessible on a common plane of expressive and form-creating activity. Art is now one of the strongest evidences of the basic unity of mankind.

This radical change in attitude depends partly on the development of modern styles, in which the raw material and distinctive units of operation—the plane of the canvas, the trunk of wood, toolmarks, brushstrokes, connecting forms, schemas, particles and areas of pure color—are as pronounced as the elements of representation. Even before nonrepresentative styles were created, artists had become more deeply conscious of the aesthetic-constructive components of the work apart from denoted meanings.

Much in the new styles recalls primitive art. Modern artists were, in fact, among the first to appreciate the works of natives as true art. The development of Cubism and Abstraction made the form problem exciting and helped to refine the perception of the creative in primitive work. Expressionism, with its high pathos, disposed our eyes to the simpler, more intense modes of expression, and together with Surrealism, which valued, above all, the irrational and instinctive in the imagination, gave a fresh interest to the products of primitive fantasy. But, with all the obvious resemblances, modern paintings and sculptures differ from the primitive in structure and content. What in primitive art belongs to an established world of collective beliefs and symbols arises in modern art as an individual expression, bearing the marks of a free, experimental attitude to forms. Modern artists feel, nevertheless, a spiritual kinship with the primitive, who is now closer to them than in the past because of their ideal of frankness and intensity of expression and their desire for a simpler life, with more effective participation of the artist in collective occasions than modern society allows.

One result of the modern development has been a tendency to slight the content of past art; the most realistic representations are contemplated as pure constructions of lines and colors. The observer is often indifferent to the original meanings of works, although he may enjoy through them a vague sentiment of the poetic and religious. The form and expressiveness of older works are regarded, then, in isolation, and the history of an art is written as an immanent development of forms. Parallel to this trend, other scholars have carried on fruitful research into the meanings, symbols, and iconographic types of Western art, relying on the literature of mythology and religion; through these studies the knowledge of the content of art has been considerably deepened, and analogies to the character of the styles have been discovered in the content. This has strengthened the view that the development of forms is not autonomous but is connected with changing attitudes and interests that appear more or less clearly in the subject matter of the art.

4

Students observed early that the traits which make up a style have a quality in common. They all seem to be marked by the expression of the whole, or there is a dominant feature to which the elements have been adapted. The parts of a Greek temple have the air of a family of forms. In Baroque art, a taste for movement determines the loosening of boundaries, the instability of masses, and the multiplication of large contrasts. For many writers a style, whether of an individual or a group, is a pervasive, rigorous unity. Investigation of style is often a search for hidden correspondences explained by an organizing principle which determines both the character of the parts and the patterning of the whole.

This approach is supported by the experience of the student in identifying a style from a small random fragment. A bit of carved stone, the profile of a molding, a few drawn lines, or a single letter from a piece of writing often possesses for the observer the quality of the complete work and can be dated precisely; before these fragments, we have the conviction of insight into the original whole. In a similar way, we recognize by its intrusiveness an added or repaired detail in an old work. The feel of the whole is found in the small parts.

I do not know how far experiments in matching parts from works in different styles would confirm this view. We may be dealing, in some of these observations, with a microstructural level in which similarity of parts only points to the homogeneity of a style or a technique, rather than to a complex unity in the aesthetic sense. Although personal, the painter's touch, described by constants of pressure, rhythm, and size of strokes, may have no obvious relation to other unique characteristics of the larger forms. There are styles in which large parts of a work are conceived and executed differently, without destroying the harmony of the whole. In African sculpture an exceedingly naturalistic, smoothly carved head rises from a rough, almost shapeless body. A normative aesthetic might regard this as imperfect work, but it would be hard to justify this view. In Western paintings of the fifteenth century, realistic figures and landscapes are set against a gold background, which in the Middle Ages had a spiritualistic sense. In Islamic art, as in certain African and Oceanic styles, forms of great clarity and simplicity in three dimensions—metal vessels and animals or the domes of buildings—have surfaces spun with rich mazy patterns; in Gothic and Baroque art, on the contrary, a complex surface treatment is associated with a correspondingly complicated silhouette of the whole. In Romanesque art the proportions of figures are not submitted to a single canon, as in Greek art, but two or three distinct systems of proportioning exist even within the same sculpture, varying with the size of the figure.

Such variation within a style is also known in literature, sometimes in great works, like Shakespeare's plays, where verse and prose of different texture occur together. French readers of Shakespeare, with the model of their own classical drama before them, were disturbed by the elements of comedy in Shakespeare's tragedies. We understand this contrast as a necessity of the content and the poet's conception of man—the different modes of expression pertain to contrasted types of humanity—but a purist classical taste condemned this as inartistic. In modern literature both kinds of style, the rigorous and the free, coexist and express different viewpoints. It is possible to see the opposed parts as contributing elements in a whole that owes its character to the interplay and balance of contrasted qualities. But the notion of style has lost in that case the crystalline uniformity and simple correspondence of part to whole with which we began. The integration may be of a looser, more complex kind, operating with unlike parts.

Another interesting exception to the homogeneous in style is the difference between the marginal and the dominant fields in certain arts. In early Byzantine works, rulers are represented in statuesque, rigid forms, while the smaller accompanying figures, by the same artist, retain the liveliness of an older episodic, naturalistic style. In Romanesque art this difference can be so marked that scholars have mistakenly supposed that certain Spanish works were done partly by a Christian and partly by a Moslem artist. In some instances the forms in the margin or in the background are more advanced in style than the central parts, anticipating a later stage of the art. In medieval work the unframed figures on the borders of illuminated manuscripts or on cornices, capitals, and pedestals is often freer and more naturalistic than the main figures. This is surprising, since we would expect to find the most advanced forms in the dominant content. But in medieval art the sculptor or painter is often bolder where he is less bound to an external requirement; he even seeks out and appropriates the regions of freedom. In a similar way an artist's drawings or sketches are more advanced than the finished paintings and suggest another side of his personality. The execution of the landscape backgrounds behind the religious figures in paintings of the fifteenth century is sometimes amazingly modern and in great contrast to the precise forms of the large figures. Such observations teach us the importance of considering in the description and explanation of a style the unhomogeneous, unstable aspect, the obscure tendencies toward new forms.

If in all periods artists strive to create unified works, the strict ideal of consistency is essentially modern. We often observe in civilized as well as primitive art the combination of works of different style into a single whole. Classical gems were frequently incorporated into medieval reliquaries. Few great medieval buildings are homogeneous, since they are the work of many generations of artists. This is widely recognized by historians, although theoreticians of culture have innocently pointed to the conglomerate cathedral of Chartres as a model of stylistic unity, in contrast to the heterogeneous character of stylelessness of the arts of modern society. In the past it was not felt necessary to restore a damaged work or to complete an unfinished one in the style of the original. Hence the strange juxtapositions of styles within some medieval objects. It should be said, however, that some styles, by virtue of their open, irregular forms, can tolerate the unfinished and heterogeneous better than others.

Just as the single work may possess parts that we would judge to belong to different styles, if we found them in separate contexts, so an individual may produce during the same short period works in what are regarded as two styles. An obvious example is the writing of bilingual authors or the work of the same man in different arts or even in different genres of the same art—monumental and easel painting, dramatic and lyric poetry. A large work by an artist who works mainly in the small, or a small work by a master of large forms, can deceive an expert in styles. Not only will the touch change, but also the expression and method of grouping. An artist is not present in the same degree in everything he does, although some traits may be constant. In the twentieth century, some artists have changed their styles so radically during a few years that it would be difficult, if not impossible, to identify these as works of the same hand, should their authorship be forgotten. In the case of Picasso, two styles—Cubism and a kind of classicizing naturalism— were practiced at the same time. One might discover common characters in small features of the two styles—in qualities of the brushstroke, the span of intensity, or in subtle constancies of the spacing and tones—but these are not the elements through which either style would ordinarily be characterized. Even then, as in a statistical account small and large samples of a population give different results, so in works of different scale of parts by one artist the scale may influence the frequency of the tiniest elements or the form of the small units. The modern experience of stylistic variability and of the unhomogeneous within an art style will perhaps lead to a more refined conception of style. It is evident, at any rate, that the conception of style as a visibly unified constant rests upon a particular norm of stability of style and shifts from the large to the small forms, as the whole becomes more complex.

What has been said here of the limits of uniformity of structure in the single work and in the works of an individual also applies to the style of a group. The group style, like a language, often contains elements that belong to different historical strata. While research looks for criteria permitting one to distinguish accurately the works of different groups and to correlate a style with other characteristics of a group, there are cultures with two or more collective styles of art at the same moment. This phenomenon is often associated with arts of different function or with different classes of artists. The arts practiced by women are of another style than those of the men; religious art differs from profane, and civic from domestic; and in higher cultures the stratification of social classes often entails a variety of styles, not only with respect to the rural and urban, but within the same urban community. This diversity is clear enough today in the coexistence of an official-academic, a mass-commercial, and a freer avant-garde art. But more striking still is the enormous range of styles within the latter—although a common denominator will undoubtedly be found by future historians.

While some critics judge this heterogeneity to be a sign of an unstable, unintegrated culture, it may be regarded as a necessary and valuable consequence of the individual's freedom of choice and of the world scope of modern culture, which permits a greater interaction of styles than was ever possible before. The present diversity continues and intensifies a diversity already noticed in the preceding stages of our culture, including the Middle Ages and the Renaissance, which are held up as models of close integration. The unity of style that is contrasted with the present diversity is one type of style formation, appropriate to particular aims and conditions; to achieve it today would be impossible without destroying the most cherished values of our culture.

If we pass to the relation of group styles of different visual arts in the same period, we observe that, while the Baroque is remarkably similar in architecture, sculpture, and painting, in other periods, e.g., the Carolingian, the early Romanesque, and the modern, these arts differ in essential respects. In England, the drawing and painting of the tenth and eleventh centuries—a time of great accomplishment, when England was a leader in European art—are characterized by an enthusiastic linear style of energetic, ecstatic movement, while the architecture of the same period is inert, massive, and closed and is organized on other principles. Such variety has been explained as a sign of immaturity; but one can point to similar contrasts between two arts in later times, for example, in Holland in the seventeenth cen-

tury where Rembrandt and his school were contemporary
with classicistic Renaissance buildings.

When we compare the styles of arts of the same period in
different media—literature, music, painting—the differences
are no less striking. But there are epochs with a far-reaching
unity, and these have engaged the attention of students more
than the examples of diversity. The concept of the Baroque
has been applied to architecture, sculpture, painting, music,
poetry, drama, gardening, script, and even philosophy and
science. The Baroque style has given its name to the entire
culture of the seventeenth century, although it does not exclude contrary tendencies within the same country, as well
as a great individuality of national arts. Such styles are the
most fascinating to historians and philosophers, who admire
in this great spectacle of unity the power of a guiding idea or
attitude to impose a common form upon the most varied contexts. The dominant style-giving force is identified by some
historians with a world outlook common to the whole society;
by others with a particular institution, like the church or the
absolute monarchy, which under certain conditions becomes
the source of a universal viewpoint and the organizer of
all cultural life. This unity is not necessarily organic; it
may be likened also, perhaps, to that of a machine with
limited freedom of motion; in a complex organism the parts
are unlike and the integration is more a matter of functional
interdependence than of the repetition of the same pattern in
all the organs.

Although so vast a unity of style is an impressive accomplishment and seems to point to a special consciousness of
style—the forms of art being felt as a necessary universal
language—there are moments of great achievement in a single
art with characteristics more or less isolated from those of
the other arts. We look in vain in England for a style of painting that corresponds to Elizabethan poetry and drama; just
as in Russia in the nineteenth century there was no true
parallel in painting to the great movement of literature. In
these instances we recognize that the various arts have
different roles in the culture and social life of a time and
express in their content as well as style different interests
and values. The dominant outlook of a time—if it can be
isolated—does not affect all the arts in the same degree, nor
are all the arts equally capable of expressing the same outlook. Special conditions within an art are often strong enough
to determine a deviant expression.

5

The organic conception of style has its counterpart in the search for biological analogies in the growth of forms. One view, patterned on the life-history of the organism, attributes to art a recurrent cycle of childhood, maturity, and old age, which coincides with the rise, maturity, and decline of the culture as a whole. Another view pictures the process as an unfinished evolution from the most primitive to the most advanced forms, in terms of a polarity evident at every step.

In the cyclical process each stage has its characteristic style or series of styles. In an enriched schema, for which the history of Western art is the model, the archaic, classic, baroque, impressionist, and archaistic are types of style that follow in an irreversible course. The classic phase is believed to produce the greatest works; the succeeding ones are a decline. The same series has been observed in the Greek and Roman world and somewhat less clearly in India and the Far East. In other cultures this succession of styles is less evident, although the archaic type is widespread and is sometimes followed by what might be considered a classic phase. It is only by stretching the meaning of the terms that the baroque and impressionist types of style are discovered as tendencies within the simpler developments of primitive arts.

(That the same names, "baroque," "classic," and "impressionist," should be applied both to a unique historical style and to a recurrent type or phase is confusing. We will distinguish the name of the unique style by a capital, e.g., "Baroque." But this will not do away with the awkwardness of speaking of the late phase of the Baroque style of the seventeenth century as "baroque." A similar difficulty exists also with the word "style," which is used for the common forms of a particular period and the common forms of a phase of development found in many periods.)

The cyclical schema of development does not apply smoothly even to the Western world from which it has been abstracted. The classic phase in the Renaissance is preceded by Gothic, Romanesque, and Carolingian styles, which cannot all be fitted into the same category of the archaic. It is possible, however, to break up the Western development into two cycles—the medieval and the modern—and to interpret the late Gothic of northern Europe, which is contemporary with the Italian Renaissance, as a style of the baroque type. But contemporary with the Baroque of the seventeenth century is a classic style which in the late eighteenth century replaces the Baroque.

It has been observed, too, that the late phase of Greco-Roman art, especially in architecture, is no decadent style marking a period of decline, but something new. The archaistic trend is only secondary beside the original achievement of late imperial and early Christian art. In a similar way, the complex art of the twentieth century, whether regarded as the end of an old culture or the beginning of a new, does not correspond to the categories of either a declining or an archaic art.

Because of these and other discrepancies, the long-term cyclical schema, which also measures the duration of a culture, is little used by historians of art. It is only a very rough approximation to the character of several isolated moments in Western art. Yet certain stages and steps of the cycle seem to be frequent enough to warrant further study as typical processes, apart from the theory of a closed cyclical form of development.

Some historians have therefore narrowed the range of the cycles from the long-term development to the history of one or two period styles. In Romanesque art, which belongs to the first stage of the longer Western cycle and shares many features with early Greek and Chinese arts, several phases have been noted within a relatively short period that resemble the archaic, the classic, and the baroque of the cyclical scheme; the same observation has been made about Gothic art. But in Carolingian art the order is different; the more baroque and impressionistic phases are the earlier ones, the classic and archaic come later. This may be due in part to the character of the older works that were copied then; but it shows how difficult it is to systematize the history of art through the cyclical model. In the continuous line of Western art, many new styles have been created without breaks or new beginnings occasioned by the exhaustion or death of a preceding style. In ancient Egypt, on the other hand, the latency of styles is hardly confirmed by the slow course of development; an established style persists here with only slight changes in basic structure for several thousand years, a span of time during which Greek and Western art run twice through the whole cycle of stylistic types.

If the exceptional course of Carolingian art is due to special conditions, perhaps the supposedly autonomous process of development also depends on extra-artistic circumstances. But the theorists of cyclical development have not explored the mechanisms and conditions of growth as the biologists have done. They recognize only a latency that conditions might accelerate or delay but not produce. To account for the individuality of the arts of each cycle, the evident difference between a Greek, a western European, and a Chinese style of the same stage, they generally resort to racial theory, each cycle being carried by a people with unique traits.

In contrast to the cyclical organic pattern of development, a more refined model has been constructed by Heinrich Wölfflin, excluding all value judgment and the vital analogy of birth, maturity, and decay. In a beautiful analysis of the art of the High Renaissance and the seventeenth century, he devised five pairs of polar terms, through which he defined the opposed styles of the two periods. These terms were applied to architecture, sculpture, painting, and the so-called "decorative arts." The linear was contrasted with the picturesque or painterly (*malerisch*), the parallel surface form with the diagonal depth form, the closed (or tectonic) with the open (or a-tectonic), the composite with the fused, the clear with the relatively unclear. The first terms of these pairs characterize the classic Renaissance stage, the second belong to the Baroque. Wölfflin believed that the passage from the first set of qualities to the others was not a peculiarity of the development in this one period, but a necessary process which occurred in most historical epochs. Adama van Scheltema applied these categories to the successive stages of northern European arts from the prehistoric period to the age of the migrations. Wölfflin's model has been used in studies of several other periods as well, and it has served the historians of literature and music and even of economic development. He recognized that the model did not apply uniformly to German and Italian art; and, to explain the deviations, he investigated peculiarities of the two national arts, which he thought were "constants"—the results of native dispositions that modified to some degree the innate normal tendencies of development. The German constant, more dynamic and unstable, favored the second set of qualities, and the Italian, more relaxed and bounded, favored the first. In this way, Wölfflin supposed he could explain the precociously *malerisch* and baroque character of German art in its classic Renaissance phase and the persistent classicism in the Italian Baroque.

The weaknesses of Wölfflin's system have been apparent to most students of art. Not only is it difficult to fit into his

scheme the important style called "Mannerism" which comes
between the High Renaissance and the Baroque; but the pre-
Classic art of the fifteenth century is for him an immature,
unintegrated style because of its inaptness for his terms.
Modern art, too, cannot be defined through either set of
terms, although some modern styles show features from both
sets—there are linear compositions which are open and
painterly ones which are closed. It is obvious that the linear
and painterly are genuine types of style, of which examples
occur, with more or less approximation to Wölfflin's model,
in other periods. But the particular unity of each set of terms
is not a necessary one (although it is possible to argue that
the Classic and Baroque of the Renaissance are "pure"
styles in which basic processes of art appear in an ideally
complete and legible way). We can imagine and discover in
history other combinations of five of these ten terms. Mannerism, which had been ignored as a phenomenon of deca-
dence, is now described as a type of art that appears in other
periods. Wölfflin cannot be right, then, in supposing that,
given the first type of art—the classic phase—the second will
follow. That depends perhaps on special circumstances which
have been effective in some epochs, but not in all. Wölfflin,
however, regards the development as internally determined;
outer conditions can only retard or facilitate the process, they
are not among its causes. He denied that his terms have any
other than artistic meaning; they describe two typical modes
of seeing and are independent of an expressive content; although artists many choose themes more or less in accord
with these forms, the latter do not arise as a means of expression. It is remarkable, therefore, that qualities associated
with these pure forms should be attributed also to the psychological dispositions of the Italian and German people.

How this process could have been repeated after the seventeenth century in Europe is a mystery, since that required—
as in the passage from Neo-Classicism to Romantic painting
—a reverse development from the Baroque to the Neo-
Classic.

In a later book Wölfflin recanted some of his views, admitting that these pure forms might correspond to a world outlook and that historical circumstances, religion, politics, etc.,
might influence the development. But he was unable to modify his schemas and interpretations accordingly. In spite of
these difficulties, one can only admire Wölfflin for his at-

tempt to rise above the singularities of style to a general construction that simplifies and organizes the field.

To meet the difficulties of Wölfflin's schema, Paul Frankl has conceived a model of development which combines the dual polar structure with a cyclical pattern. He postulates a recurrent movement between two poles of style—a style of Being and a style of Becoming; but within each of these styles are three stages: a preclassic, a classic, and a postclassic; and in the first and third stages he assumes alternative tendencies which correspond to those historical moments, like Mannerism, that would be anomalous in Wölfflin's scheme. What is most original in Frankl's construction—and we cannot begin to indicate its rich nuancing and complex articulation—is that he attempts to deduce this development and its phases (and the many types of style comprehended within his system) from the analysis of elementary forms and the limited number of possible combinations, which he has investigated with great care. His scheme is not designed to describe the actual historical development—a very irregular affair—but to provide a model or ideal plan of the inherent or normal tendencies of development, based on the nature of forms. Numerous factors, social and psychological, constrain or divert the innate tendencies and determine other courses; but the latter are unintelligible, according to Frankl, without reference to his model and his deduction of the formal possibilities.

Frankl's book—a work of over a thousand pages—appeared unfortunately at a moment (1938) when it could not receive the attention it deserved; and since that time it has been practically ignored in the literature, although it is surely the most serious attempt in recent years to create a systematic foundation for the study of art forms. No other writer has analyzed the types of style so thoroughly.

In spite of their insights and ingenuity in constructing models of development, the theoreticians have had relatively little influence on investigation of special problems, perhaps because they have provided no adequate bridge from the model to the unique historical style and its varied developments. The principles by which are explained the broad similarities in development are of a different order from those by which the singular facts are explained. The normal motion and the motion due to supposedly perturbing factors belong to different worlds; the first is inherent in the morphology of styles, the second has a psychological or social origin. It is as if mechanics had two different sets of laws, one for irregular and the other for regular motions; or one for the first and another for the second approximation, in dealing with the same phenomenon. Hence those who are most concerned with a unified approach to the study of art have split the history of style into two aspects which cannot be derived from each other or from some common principle.

Parallel to the theorists of cyclical development, other scholars have approached the development of styles as a continuous, long-term evolutionary process. Here, too, there are poles and stages and some hints of a universal, though not cyclical, process; but the poles are those of the earliest and latest stages and are deduced from a definition of the artist's goal or the nature of art or from a psychological theory.

The first students to investigate the history of primitive art conceived the latter as a development between two poles, the geometrical and the naturalistic. They were supported by observation of the broad growth of art in the historical cultures from geometric or simple, stylized forms to more natural ones; they were sustained also by the idea that the most naturalistic styles of all belonged to the highest type of culture, the most advanced in scientific knowledge, and the most capable of representing the world in accurate images. The process in art agreed with the analogous development in nature from the simple to the complex and was paralleled by the growth of the child's drawings in our own culture from schematic or geometrical forms to naturalistic ones. The origin of certain geometrical forms in primitive industrial techniques also favored this view.

It is challenging and amusing to consider in the light of these arguments the fact that the Paleolithic cave paintings, the oldest known art, are marvels of representation (whatever the elements of schematic form in those works, they are more naturalistic than the succeeding Neolithic and Bronze Age art) and that in the twentieth century naturalistic forms have given way to "abstraction" and so-called "subjective" styles. But, apart from these paradoxical exceptions, one could observe in historical arts—e.g., in the late classic and early Christian periods—how free naturalistic forms are progressively stylized and reduced to ornament. In the late nineteenth century, ornament was often designed by a method of stylization, a geometrizing of natural motives; and those who knew contemporary art were not slow to discern in the geometrical styles of existing primitives the traces of an older

more naturalistic model. Study shows that both processes occur in history; there is little reason to regard either one as
more typical or more primitive. The geometrical and the
naturalistic forms may arise independently in different contexts and coexist within the same culture. The experience of
the art of the last fifty years suggests further that the degree
of naturalism in art is not a sure indication of the technological or intellectual level of a culture. This does not mean
that style is independent of that level but that other concepts than those of the naturalistic and the geometrical must
be applied in considering such relationships. The essential
opposition is not of the natural and the geometric but of certain modes of composition of natural and geometric motives.
From this point of view, modern "abstract" art in its taste for
open, asymmetrical, random, tangled, and incomplete forms
is much closer to the compositional principles of realistic or
Impressionist painting and sculpture than to any primitive
art with geometrical elements. Although the character of the
themes, whether "abstract" or naturalistic, is important for
the concrete aspect of the work of art, historians do not
operate so much with categories of the naturalistic and
geometrical as with subtler structural concepts, which apply
also to architecture, where the problem of representation
seems irrelevant. It is with such concepts that Wölfflin and
Frankl have constructed their models.

Nevertheless, the representation of natural forms has been
a goal in the arts of many cultures. Whether we regard it
as a spontaneous common idea or one that has been diffused
from a single prehistorical center, the problem of how to
represent the human and animal figure has been attacked
independently by various cultures. Their solutions present not
only similar features in the devices of rendering but also a
remarkable parallelism in the successive stages of the solutions. It is fascinating to compare the changing representation
of the eyes or of pleated costume in succeeding styles of
Greek, Chinese, and medieval European sculpture. The development of such details from a highly schematic to a naturalistic type in the latter two can hardly be referred to a
direct influence of Greek models; for the similarities are not
only of geographically far separated styles but of distinct
series in time. To account for the Chinese and Romanesque
forms as copies of the older Greek, we would have to assume
that at each stage in the post-Greek styles the artists had
recourse to Greek works of the corresponding stage and in

the same order. Indeed, some of the cyclical schemas discussed above are, in essence, descriptions of the stages in the development of representation; and it may be asked whether the formal schemas, like Wölfflin's, are not veiled categories of representation, even though they are applied to architecture as well as to sculpture and painting; for the standards of representation in the latter may conceivably determine a general norm of plasticity and structure for all the visual arts.

This aspect of style—the representation of natural forms —has been studied by the classical archaeologist Emmanuel Löwy; his little book on *The Rendering of Nature in Early Greek Art*, published in 1900, is still suggestive for modern research and has a wider application than has been recognized. Löwy has analyzed the general principles of representation in early arts and explained their stages as progressive steps in a steady change from conceptual representation, based on the memory image, to perspective representation, according to direct perception of objects. Since the structure of the memory image is the same in all cultures, the representations based on this psychological process will exhibit common features: (1) The shape and movement of figures and their parts are limited to a few typical forms; (2) the single forms are schematized in regular linear patterns; (3) representation proceeds from the outline, whether the latter is an independent contour or the silhouette of a uniformly colored area; (4) where colors are used, they are without gradation of light and shadow; (5) the parts of a figure are presented to the observer in their broadest aspect; (6) in compositions the figures, with few exceptions, are shown with a minimum of overlapping of their main parts; the real succession of figures in depth is transformed in the image into a juxtaposition on the same plane; (7) the representation of the three-dimensional space in which an action takes place is more or less absent.

Whatever criticisms may be made of Löwy's notion of a memory image as the source of these peculiarities, his account of archaic representation as a universal type, with a characteristic structure, is exceedingly valuable; it has a general application to children's drawings, to the work of modern untrained adults, and to primitives. This analysis does not touch on the individuality of archaic styles, nor does it help us to understand why some cultures develop beyond them and others, like the Egyptian, retain the archaic features for many centuries. Limited by an evolutionary view and a naturalistic value norm, Löwy ignored the perfection and expressiveness of archaic works. Neglecting the specific content of the representations, this approach fails to recognize the role of the content and of emotional factors in the proportioning and accentuation of parts. But these limitations do not lessen the importance of Löwy's book in defining so clearly a widespread type of archaic representation and in tracing the stages of its development into a more naturalistic art.

I may mention here that the reverse process of the conversion of naturalistic to archaic forms, as we see it wherever works of an advanced naturalistic style are copied by primitives, colonials, provincials, and the untrained in the high cultures, can also be formulated through Löwy's principles.

We must mention, finally, as the most constructive and imaginative of the historians who have tried to embrace the whole of artistic development as a single continuous process, Alois Riegl, the author of *Stilfragen* and *Die spätrömische Kunstindustrie*.

Riegl was especially concerned with transitions that mark the beginning of a world-historical epoch (the Old Oriental to the Hellenic, the ancient to the medieval). He gave up not only the normative view that judges the later phases of a cycle as a decline but also the conception of closed cycles. In late Roman art, which was considered decadent in his time, he found a necessary creative link between two great stages of an open development. His account of the process is like Wölfflin's, however, though perhaps independent; he formulates as the poles of the long evolution two types of style, the "haptic" (tactile) and the "optic" (or painterly, impressionistic), which coincide broadly with the poles of Wölfflin's shorter cycles. The process of development from the haptic to the optic is observable in each epoch, but only as part of a longer process, of which the great stages are millennial and correspond to whole cultures. The history of art is, for Riegl, an endless necessary movement from representation based on vision of the object and its parts as proximate, tangible, discrete, and self-sufficient, to the representation of the whole perceptual field as a directly given, but more distant, continuum with merging parts, with an increasing role of the spatial voids, and with a more evident reference to the knowing subject as a constituting factor in perception. This artistic process is also described by Riegl in terms of a faculty psychology; will, feeling, and thought are the successive

dominants in shaping our relations to the world; it corresponds in philosophy to the change from a predominantly
objective to a subjective outlook.

Riegl does not study this process simply as a development
of naturalism from an archaic to an impressionistic stage.
Each phase has its special formal and expressive problems,
and Riegl has written remarkably penetrating pages on the
intimate structure of styles, the principles of composition,
and the relations of figure to ground. In his systematic account of ancient art and the art of the early Christian
period, he has observed common principles in architecture,
sculpture, painting, and ornament, sometimes with surprising
acuteness. He has also succeeded in showing unexpected relationships between different aspects of a style. In a work on
Dutch group portraiture of the sixteenth and seventeenth
centuries, a theme that belongs to art and social history, he
has carried through a most delicate analysis of the changing
relations between the objective and the subjective elements
in portraiture and in the correspondingly variable mode of
unifying a represented group which is progressively more attentive to the observer.

His motivation of the process and his explanation of its
shifts in time and space are vague and often fantastic. Each
great phase corresponds to a racial disposition. The history
of Western man from the time of the Old Oriental kingdoms
to the present day is divided into three great periods, characterized by the successive predominance of will, feeling, and
thought, in Oriental, Classical, and Western Man. Each race
plays a prescribed role and retires when its part is done, as if
participating in a symphony of world history. The apparent
deviations from the expected continuities are saved for the
system by a theory of purposive regression which prepares a
people for its advanced role. The obvious incidence of social
and religious factors in art is judged to be simply a parallel
manifestation of a corresponding process in these other fields
rather than a possible cause. The basic, immanent development from an objective to a subjective standpoint governs the
whole of history, so that all contemporary fields have a deep
unity with respect to a common determining process.

This brief summary of Riegl's ideas hardly does justice to
the positive features of his work, and especially to his conception of art as an active creative process in which new
forms arise from the artist's will to solve specifically artistic
problems. Even his racial theories and strange views about

the historical situation of an art represent a desire to grasp large relationships, although distorted by an inadequate psychology and social theory; this search for a broad view has become rare in the study of art since his time. And still rarer is its combination with the power of detailed research that Riegl possessed to a high degree.

To summarize the results of modern studies with respect to the cyclical and evolutionary theories:

(1) From the viewpoint of historians who have tried to reconstruct the precise order of development, without presuppositions about cycles, there is a continuity in the Near East and Europe from the Neolithic period to the present —perhaps best described as a tree with many branches—in which the most advanced forms of each culture are retained, to some extent, in the early forms of succeeding cultures.

(2) On the other hand, there are within that continuity at least two long developments—the ancient Greek and the Western European medieval-modern—which include the broad types of style described in various cyclical theories. But these two cycles are not unconnected; artists in the second cycle often copied surviving works of the first, and it is uncertain whether some of the guiding principles in Western art are not derived from the Greeks.

(3) Within these two cycles and in several other cultures (Asiatic and American) occur many examples of similar short developments, especially from an archaic linear type of representation to a more "pictorial" style.

(4) Wherever there is a progressive naturalistic art, i.e., one which becomes increasingly naturalistic, we find in the process stages corresponding broadly to the line of archaic, classic, baroque, and impressionist in Western art. Although these styles in the West are not adequately described in terms of their method of representation, they embody specific advances in range or method of representation from a first stage of schematized, so-called "conceptual," representation of isolated objects to a later stage of perspective representation in which continuities of space, movement, light and shadow, and atmosphere have become important.

(5) In describing the Western development, which is the model of cyclical theories, historians isolate different aspects of art for the definition of the stylistic types. In several theories the development of representation is the main source of the terms; in others formal traits, which can be

found also in architecture, script, and pottery shapes, are isolated; and, in some accounts, qualities of expression and content are the criteria. It is not always clear which formal traits are really independent of representation. It is possible that a way of seeing objects in nature—the perspective vision as distinguished from the archaic conceptual mode—also affects the design of a column or a pot. But the example of Islamic art, in which representation is secondary, suggests that the development of the period styles in architecture and ornament need not depend on a style of representation. As for expression there exist in the Baroque art of the seventeenth century intimate works of great tragic sensibility, like Rembrandt's, and monumental works of a profuse splendor; either of these traits can be paralleled in other periods in forms of non-baroque type. But a true counterpart of Rembrandt's light and shadow will not be found in Greek or Chinese painting, although both are said to have baroque phases.

6

We shall now consider the explanations of style proposed without reference to cycles and polar developments.

In accounting for the genesis of a style, early investigators gave great weight to the technique, materials, and practical functions of an art. Thus wood carving favors grooved or wedge-cut relief, the column of the tree trunk gives the statue its cylindrical shape, hard stone yields compact and angular forms, weaving begets stepped and symmetrical patterns, the potter's wheel introduces a perfect roundness, coiling is the source of spirals, etc. This was the approach of Semper and his followers in the last century. Boas, among others, identified style, or at least its formal aspect, with motor habits in the handling of tools. In modern art this viewpoint appears in the program of functionalist architecture and design. It is also behind the older explanation of the Gothic style of architecture as a rational system derived from the rib construction of vaults. Modern sculptors who adhere closely to the block, exploiting the texture and grain of the material and showing the marks of the tool, are supporters of this theory of style. It is related to the immense role of the technological in our own society; modern standards of efficient production have become a norm in art.

There is no doubt that these practical conditions account

for some peculiarities of style. They are important also in explaining similarities in primitive and folk arts which appear to be independent of diffusion or imitation of styles. But they are of less interest for highly developed arts. Wood may limit the sculptor's forms, but we know a great variety of styles in wood, some of which even conceal the substance. Riegl observed long ago that the same forms occurred within a culture in works of varied technique, materials, and use; it is this common style that the theory in question has failed to explain. The Gothic style is, broadly speaking, the same in buildings; sculptures of wood, ivory, and stone; panel paintings; stained glass; miniatures; metalwork, enamels, and textiles. It may be that in some instances a style created in one art under the influence of the technique, material, and function of particular objects has been generalized by application to all objects, techniques, and materials. Yet the material is not always prior to the style but may be chosen because of an ideal of expression and artistic quality or for symbolism. The hard substances of Old Egyptian art, the use of gold and other precious luminous substances in arts of power, the taste for steel, concrete, and glass in modern design, are not external to the artist's first goal but parts of the original conception. The compactness of the sculpture cut from a tree trunk is a quality that is already present in the artist's idea before he begins to carve. For simple compact forms appear in clay figures and in drawings and paintings where the matter does not limit the design. The compactness may be regarded as a necessary trait of an archaic or a "haptic" style in Löwy's or Riegl's sense.

Turning away from material factors, some historians find in the content of the work of art the source of its style. In the arts of representation, a style is often associated with a distinct body of subject matter, drawn from a single sphere of ideas or experience. Thus in Western art of the fourteenth century, when a new iconography of the life of Christ and of Mary was created in which themes of suffering were favored, we observe new patterns of line and color, which possess a more lyrical, pathetic aspect than did the preceding art. In our own time, a taste for the constructive and rational in industry has led to the use of mechanical motives and a style of forms characterized by coolness, precision, objectivity, and power.

The style in these examples is viewed by many writers as

the objective vehicle of the subject matter or of its governing idea. Style, then, is the means of communication, a language not only as a system of devices for conveying a precise message by representing or symbolizing objects and actions but also as a qualitative whole which is capable of suggesting the diffuse connotations as well and intensifying the associated or intrinsic affects. By an effort of imagination based on experience of his medium, the artist discovers the elements and formal relationships which will express the values of the content and look right artistically. Of all the attempts made in this direction, the most successful will be repeated and developed as a norm.

The relationship of content and style is more complex than appears in this theory. There are styles in which the correspondence of the expression and the values of the typical subjects are not at all obvious. If the difference between pagan and Christian art is explained broadly by the difference in religious content, there is nevertheless a long period of time—in fact, many centuries—during which Christian subjects are represented in the style of pagan art. As late as 800, the *Libri Carolini* speak of the difficulty of distinguishing images of Mary and Venus without the labels. This may be due to the fact that a general outlook of late paganism, more fundamental than the religious doctrines, was still shared by Christians or that the new religion, while important, had not yet transformed the basic attitudes and ways of thinking. Or it may be that the function of art within the religious life was too slight, for not all concepts of the religion find their way into art. But even later, when the Christian style had been established, there were developments in art toward a more naturalistic form and toward imitation of elements of ancient pagan style which were incompatible with the chief ideas of the religion.

A style that arises in connection with a particular content often becomes an accepted mode governing all representations of the period. The Gothic style is applied in religious and secular works alike; and, if it is true that no domestic or civil building in that style has the expressiveness of a cathedral interior, yet in painting and sculpture the religious and secular images are hardly different in form. On the other hand, in periods of a style less pervasive than the Gothic, different idioms or dialects of form are used for different fields of content; this was observed in the discussion of the concept of stylistic unity.

It is such observations that have led students to modify the simple equation of style and the expressive values of a subject matter, according to which the style is the vehicle of the main meanings of the work of art. Instead, the meaning of content has been extended, and attention has been fixed on broader attitudes or on general ways of thinking and feeling, which are believed to shape a style. The style is then viewed as a concrete embodiment or projection of emotional dispositions and habits of thought common to the whole culture. The content as a parallel product of the same viewpoint will therefore often exhibit qualities and structures like those of the style.

These world views or ways of thinking and feeling are usually abstracted by the historian from the philosophical systems and metaphysics of a period or from theology and literature and even from science. Themes like the relation of subject and object, spirit and matter, soul and body, man and nature or God, and conceptions of time and space, self and cosmos are typical fields from which are derived the definitions of the world view (or *Denkweise*) of a period or culture. The latter is then documented by illustrations from many fields, but some writers have attempted to derive it from the works of art themselves. One searches in a style for qualities and structures that can be matched with some aspect of thinking or a world view. Sometimes it is based on a priori deduction of possible world views, given the limited number of solutions of metaphysical problems; or a typology of the possible attitudes of the individual to the world and to his own existence is matched with a typology of styles. We have seen how Riegl apportioned the three faculties of will, feeling, and thought among three races and three major styles.

The attempts to derive style from thought are often too vague to yield more than suggestive *aperçus;* the method breeds analogical speculations which do not hold up under detailed critical study. The history of the analogy drawn between the Gothic cathedral and scholastic theology is an example. The common element in these two contemporary creations has been found in their rationalism and in their irrationality, their idealism and their naturalism, their encyclopedic completeness and their striving for infinity, and recently in their dialectical method. Yet one hesitates to reject such analogies in principle, since the cathedral belongs to the same religious sphere as does contemporary theology.

It is when these ways of thinking and feeling or world
views have been formulated as the outlook of a religion or
dominant institution or class of which the myths and values
are illustrated or symbolized in the work of art that the
general intellectual content seems a more promising field for
explanation of style. But the content of a work of art often
belongs to another region of experience than the one in which
both the period style and the dominant mode of thinking
have been formed; an example is the secular art of a period
in which religious ideas and rituals are primary, and, conversely, the religious art of a secularized culture. In such
cases we see how important for a style of art is the character of the dominants in culture, especially of institutions.
Not the content as such, but the content as part of a dominant set of beliefs, ideas, and interests, supported by institutions and the forms of everyday life, shapes the common
style.

Although the attempts to explain styles as an artistic
expression of a world view or mode of thought are often a
drastic reduction of the concreteness and richness of art,
they have been helpful in revealing unsuspected levels of
meaning in art. They have established the practice of interpreting the style itself as an inner content of the art,
especially in the nonrepresentational arts. They correspond
to the conviction of modern artists that the form elements
and structure are a deeply meaningful whole related to
metaphysical views.

7

The theory that the world view or mode of thinking
and feeling is the source of long-term constants in style
is often formulated as a theory of racial or national character. I have already referred to such concepts in the work
of Wölfflin and Riegl. They have been common in
European writing on art for over a hundred years and have
played a significant role in promoting national consciousness and race feeling; works of art are the chief concrete
evidences of the affective world of the ancestors. The persistent teaching that German art is by nature tense and
irrational, that its greatness depends on fidelity to the racial
character, has helped to produce an acceptance of these
traits as a destiny of the people.

The weakness of the racial concept of style is evident
from analysis of the history and geography of styles, with-

out reference to biology. The so-called "constant" is less constant than the racially (or nationally) minded historians have assumed. German art includes Classicism and the Biedermeier style, as well as the work of Grünewald and the modern Expressionists. During the periods of most pronounced Germanic character, the extension of the native style hardly coincides with the boundaries of the preponderant physical type or with the recent national boundaries. This discrepancy holds for the Italian art which is paired with the German as a polar opposite.

Nevertheless, there are striking recurrences in the art of a region or nation which have not been explained. It is astonishing to observe the resemblances between German migrations art and the styles of the Carolingian, Ottonian, and late Gothic periods, then of German rococo architecture, and finally of modern Expressionism. There are great gaps in time between these styles during which the forms can scarcely be described in the traditional German terms. To save the appearance of constancy, German writers have supposed that the intervening phases were dominated by alien influences or were periods of preparation for the ultimate release, or they conceived the deviant qualities as another aspect of German character: the Germans are both irrational and disciplined.

If we restrict ourselves to more modest historical correlations of styles with the dominant personality types of the cultures or groups that have created the styles, we meet several difficulties; some of these have been anticipated in the discussion of the general problem of unity of style.

(1) The variation of styles in a culture or group is often considerable within the same period.

(2) Until recently, the artists who create the style are generally of another mode of life than those for whom the arts are designed and whose viewpoint, interests, and quality of life are evident in the art. The best examples are the arts of great monarchies, aristocracies, and privileged institutions.

(3) What is constant in all the arts of a period (or of several periods) may be less essential for characterizing the style than the variable features; the persistent French quality in the series of styles between 1770 and 1870 is a nuance which is hardly as important for the definition of the period style as the traits that constitute the Rococo, Neo-Classic, Romantic, Realistic, and Impressionist syles.

To explain the changing period styles, historians and critics have felt the need of a theory that relates particular forms to tendencies of character and feeling. Such a theory, concerned with the elements of expression and structure, should tell us what affects and dispositions determine choices of forms. Historians have not waited for experimental psychology to support their physiognomic interpretations of style but, like the thoughtful artists, have resorted to intuitive judgments, relying on direct experience of art. Building up an unsystematic, empirical knowledge of forms, expressions, affects, and qualities, they have tried to control these judgments by constant comparison of works and by reference to contemporary sources of information about the content of the art, assuming that the attitudes which govern the latter must also be projected in the style. The interpretation of Classical style is not founded simply on firsthand experience of Greek buildings and sculptures; it rests also on knowledge of Greek language, literature, religion, mythology, philosophy, and history, which provide an independent picture of the Greek world. But this picture is, in turn, refined and enriched by experience of the visual arts, and our insight is sharpened by knowledge of the very different arts of the neighboring peoples and of the results of attempts to copy the Greek models at later times under other conditions. Today, after the work of nearly two centuries of scholars, a sensitive mind, with relatively little information about Greek culture, can respond directly to the "Greek mind" in those ancient buildings and sculptures.

In physiognomic interpretations of group styles, there is a common assumption that is still problematic: that the psychological explanations of unique features in a modern individual's art can be applied to a whole culture in which the same or similar features are characteristics of a group or period style.

If schizophrenics fill a sheet of paper with closely crowded elements in repeat patterns, can we explain similar tendencies in the art of a historic or primitive culture by a schizophrenic tendency or dominant schizoid personality type in that culture? We are inclined to doubt such interpretations for two reasons. First, we are not sure that this pattern is uniquely schizoid in modern individuals; it may represent a component of the psychotic personality which also exists in other temperaments as a tendency associated with particular emotional contents or problems. Secondly, this pattern, originating in a single artist of schizoid type, may crystallize as a common convention, accepted by other artists and the public because it satisfies a need and is most adequate to a special problem of decoration or representation, without entailing, however, a notable change in the broad habits and attitudes of the group. This convention may be adopted by artists of varied personality types, who will apply it in distinct ways, filling it with an individual content and expression.

A good instance of this relationship between the psychotic, the normal individual, and the group is the practice of reading object forms in relatively formless spots—as in hallucination and in psychological tests. Leonardo da Vinci proposed this method to artists as a means of invention. It was practiced in China, and later in Western art; today it has become a standard method for artists of different character. In the painter who first introduced the practice and exploited it most fully, it may correspond to a personal disposition; but for many others it is an established technique. What is personally significant is not the practice itself but the kinds of spots chosen and what is seen in them; attention to the latter discloses a great variety of individual reactions.

If art is regarded as a projective technique—and some artists today think of their work in these terms—will interpretation of the work give the same result as a projective test? The tests are so designed as to reduce the number of elements that depend on education, profession, and environment. But the work of art is very much conditioned by these factors. Hence, in discerning the personal expression in a work of art, one must distinguish between those aspects that are conventional and those that are clearly individual. In dealing with the style of a group, however, we consider only such superindividual aspects, abstracting them from the personal variants. How, then, can one apply to the interpretation of the style concepts from individual psychology?

It may be said, of course, that the established norms of a group style are genuine parts of an artist's outlook and response and can be approached as the elements of a modal personality. In the same way the habits and attitudes of scientists that are required by their profession may be an important part of their characters. But do such traits also constitute the typical ones of the culture or the society as a whole? Is an art style that has crystallized as a result of special problems necessarily an expression of the whole group? Or is it only in the special case where the art is open to the common outlook and everyday interests of the entire group that its content and style can be representative of the group?

A common tendency in the physiognomic approach to group style has been to interpret all the elements of representation as expressions. The blank background or negative features like the absence of a horizon and of consistent perspective in paintings are judged to be symptomatic of an attitude to space and time in actual life. The limited space in Greek art is interpreted as a fundamental trait of Greek personality. Yet this blankness of the background, we have seen, is common to many styles; it is found in prehistoric art, in Old Oriental art, in the Far East, in the Middle Ages, and in most primitive painting and relief. The fact that it occurs in modern children's drawings and in the drawings of untrained adults suggests that it belongs to a universal primitive level of representation. But it should be observed that this is also the method of illustration in the most advanced scientific work in the past and today.

This fact does not mean that representation is wholly without expressive personal features. A particular treatment of the "empty" background may become a powerful expressive factor. Careful study of so systematic a method of representation as geometrical perspective shows that within such a scientific system there are many possible choices; the position of the eye-level, the intensity of convergence, the distance of the viewer from the picture plane—all these are expressive choices within the conditions of the system. Moreover, the existence of the system itself presupposes a degree of interest in the environment which is already a cultural trait with a long history.

The fact that an art represents a restricted world does not allow us to infer, however, a corresponding restriction of interests and perceptions in everyday life. We would have to suppose, if this were true, that in Islam people were unconcerned with the human body, and that the present vogue of "abstract" art means a general indifference to the living.

An interesting evidence of the limitations of the assumed identities of the space or time structure of works of art and the space or time experience of individuals is the way in which painters of the thirteenth century represented the new cathedrals. These vast buildings with high vaults and endless vistas in depth are shown as shallow structures, not much larger than the human beings they enclose. The conventions of representation provided no means of re-creating the experience of architectural space, an experience that was surely a factor in the conception of the cathedral and was reported in contemporary descriptions. (It is possible to relate the architectural and pictorial spaces; but the attempt would take us beyond the problems of this paper.) The space of the cathedrals is intensely expressive, but it is a constructed, ideal space, appealing to the imagination, and not an attempt to transpose the space of everyday life. We will understand it better as a creation adequate to a religious conception than as one in which an everyday sentiment of space has been embodied in architecture. It is an ideological space, too, and, if it conveys the feelings of the most inspired religious personalities, it is not a model of an average, collective attitude to space in general, although the cathedral is used by everyone.

The concept of personality in art is most important for the theory that the great artist is the immediate source of the period style. This little-explored view, implicit in much historical research and criticism, regards the group style as an imitation of the style of an original artist. Study of a line of development often leads to the observation that some individual is responsible for the change in the period form. The personality of the great artist and the problems inherited from the preceding generation are the two factors studied. For the personality as a whole is sometimes substituted a weakness or a traumatic experience which activates the individual's will to create. Such a view is little adapted to the understanding of those cultures or historical epochs that left us no signed works or biographies of artists; but it is the favored view of many students of the art of the last four centuries in Europe. It may be questioned whether it is applicable to cultures in which the individual has less mobility and range of personal action and in which the artist is not a deviant type. The main difficulty, however, arises from the fact that similar stylistic trends often appear independently in different arts at the same time; that great contemporary artists in the same field—Leonardo, Michelangelo, Raphael—show a parallel tendency of style, although each artist has a personal form; and that the new outlook expressed by a single man of genius is anticipated or prepared in preceding works and thought. The great artists of the Gothic period and the Renaissance constitute families with a common heritage and trend. Decisive changes are most often associated with original works of outstanding quality; but the new direction of style and its acceptance are unintelligible without reference to the conditions of the moment and the common ground of the art.

These difficulties and complexities have not led scholars to abandon the psychological approach; long experience with art has established as a plausible principle the notion that an individual style is a personal expression; and continued research has found many confirmations of this, wherever it has been possible to control statements about the personality, built upon the work, by referring to actual information about the artist. Similarly, common traits in the art of a culture or nation can be matched with some features of social life, ideas, customs, general dispositions. But such correlations have been of single elements or aspects of a style with single traits of a people; it is rarely a question of wholes. In our own culture, styles have changed very rapidly, yet the current notions about group traits do not allow sufficiently for corresponding changes in the behavior patterns or provide such a formulation of the group personality that one can deduce from it how that personality will change under new conditions.

It seems that for explanation of the styles of the higher cultures, with their great variability and intense development, the concepts of group personality current today are too rigid. They underestimate the specialized functions of art which determine characteristics that are superpersonal. But we may ask whether some of the difficulties in applying characterological concepts to national or period styles are not also present in the interpretation of primitive arts. Would a psychological treatment of Sioux art, for example, give us the same picture of Sioux personality as that provided by analysis of Sioux family life, ceremony, and hunting?

8

We turn last to explanations of style by the forms of social life. The idea of a connection between these forms and styles is already suggested by the framework of the history of art. Its main divisions, accepted by all students, are also the boundaries of social units—cultures, empires, dynasties, cities, classes, churches, etc.—and periods which mark significant stages in social development. The great historical epochs of art, like antiquity, the Middle Ages, and the modern era, are the same as the epochs of economic history; they correspond to great systems, like feudalism and capitalism. Important economic and political shifts within these systems are often accompanied or followed by shifts in the centers of art and their styles. Religion and major world views are broadly coordinated with these eras in social history.

In many problems the importance of economic, political, and ideological conditions for the creation of group style (or of a world view that influences a style) is generally admitted. The distinctiveness of Greek art among the arts of the ancient world can hardly be separated from the forms of Greek society and the city-state. The importance of the burgher class, with its special position in society and its mode of life, for the medieval and early Renaissance art of Florence and for Dutch art of the seventeenth century, is a commonplace. In explaining Baroque art, the Counter-Reformation and the absolute monarchy are constantly cited as the sources of certain features of style. We have interesting studies on a multitude of problems concerning the relationship of particular styles and contents of art to institutions and historical situations. In these studies ideas, traits, and values arising from the conditions of economic, political, and civil life are matched with the new characteristics of an art. Yet, with all this experience, the general principles applied in explanation and the connection of types of art with types of social structure have not been investigated in a systematic way. By the many scholars who adduce piecemeal political or economic facts in order to account for single traits of style or subject matter, little has been done to construct an adequate comprehensive theory. In using such data, scholars will often deny that these "external" relationships can throw any light on the artistic phenomenon as such. They fear "materialism" as a reduction of the spiritual or ideal to sordid practical affairs.

Marxist writers are among the few who have tried to apply a general theory. It is based on Marx's undeveloped view that the higher forms of cultural life correspond to the economic structure of a society, the latter being defined in terms of the relations of classes in the process of production and the technological level. Between the economic relationships and the styles of art intervenes the process of ideological construction, a complex imaginative transposition of class roles and needs, which affects the special field—religion, mythology, or civil life—that provides the chief themes of art.

The great interest of the Marxist approach lies not only in the attempt to interpret the historically changing relations of art and economic life in the light of a general theory of society but also in the weight given to the differences and conflicts within the social group as motors of development, and to the effects of these on outlook, religion, morality, and philosophical ideas.

Only broadly sketched in Marx's works, the theory has rarely been applied systematically in a true spirit of investigation, such as we see in Marx's economic writings. Marxist writing on art has suffered from schematic and premature formulations and from crude judgments imposed by loyalty to a political line.

A theory of style adequate to the psychological and historical problems has still to be created. It waits for a deeper knowledge of the principles of form construction and expression and for a unified theory of the processes of social life in which the practical means of life as well as emotional behavior are comprised.

Style and Stylistics

RENÉ WELLEK AND AUSTIN WARREN*

STYLISTICS, OF COURSE, cannot be pursued successfully without a thorough grounding in general linguistics, since precisely one of its central concerns is the contrast of the language system of a literary work of art with the general usage of the time. Without knowledge of what is common speech, even unliterary speech, and what are the different social languages of a time, stylistics can scarcely transcend impressionism. The assumption that, especially for past periods, we know the distinction between common speech and artistic deviation is, regrettably, quite unfounded.

* Mr. Wellek is primarily responsible for this chapter. Ed.

From Theory of Literature, Third Edition, by René Wellek and Austin Warren. Copyright, 1942, 1947, 1949, © 1956 by Harcourt, Brace & World, Inc. Reprinted by permission of Harcourt, Brace & World, Inc., and Jonathan Cape Ltd.

Much closer study must be given to the diversely stratified speech of remote times before we shall possess the proper background for judgment of the diction of an author or of a literary movement.

In practice we simply apply instinctively the standards we derive from our present-day usage. But such standards may be largely misleading. On occasion, in the reading of older poetry, we need to shut out our modern linguistic consciousness. We must forget the modern meaning even in such lines as Tennyson's [*Edwin Morris*]:

> And this is well
> To have a dame indoors, who trims us up
> And keeps us tight.

But if we admit the necessity of historical reconstruction in such obvious cases, can we stipulate its possibility in all cases? Can we ever learn Anglo-Saxon or Middle English, not to speak of ancient Greek, well enough to forget our own current language? And if we could, are we necessarily better critics by constituting ourselves linguistic contemporaries of the author? Could not the retention of the modern association in verses like Marvell's [*To His Coy Mistress*]:

> My vegetable love would grow
> Vaster than empires and more slow

be defended as an enrichment of its meanings? Louis Teeter comments:

> The grotesque conception of an erotic cabbage outlasting the pyramids and overshadowing them seems the result of studied artistry. We may be sure, however, that Marvell himself had no such precise effect in mind. To the seventeenth century, *vegetable* meant *vegetative,* and the poet probably was using it in the sense of the life-giving principle. He could scarcely have had in mind the truckgarden connotation that it bears today.[1]

One may ask, with Teeter, whether it is desirable to get rid of the modern connotation and whether, at least, in extreme cases, it is possible. We are again at the question of historical "reconstructionism," its possibility and desirability.

[1] "Scholarship and the Art of Criticism," *ELH*, V (1938), p. 183.

There have been attempts, like that of Charles Bally, [2] to make stylistics a mere subdivision of linguistics; but stylistics, whether an independent science or not, has its own very definite problems. Some of these, it would seem, belong to all or practically all human speech. Stylistics, conceived in this wide sense, investigates all devices which aim at some specific expressive end and thus embraces far more than literature or even rhetoric. All devices for securing emphasis or explicitness can be classed under stylistics: metaphors, which permeate all languages, even of the most primitive type; all rhetorical figures; syntactical patterns. Nearly every linguistic utterance can be studied from the point of view of its expressive value. It seems impossible to ignore this problem, as the "behavioristic" school of linguistics in America very consciously does.

In traditional stylistics, these questions are usually answered in a haphazard and arbitrary fashion. Figures are dichotomized into intensifying or minimizing. The intensifying figures, such as repetition, accumulation, hyperbole, and climax, have been associated with the "sublime" style, described in some detail in the famous *On the Sublime,* ascribed to Longinus. In connection with Homer, and then with Shakespeare, Milton, and Dante, the "grand style" has been discussed by Matthew Arnold and Saintsbury, who elaborately confounded psychological problems with problems of literary evaluation. [3]

It seems impossible, however, to prove that specific figures and devices must, under all circumstances, have specific effects or "expressive values." In the Bible and in chronicles, the coordinate sentence constructions ("and . . . and . . . and") have a leisurely effect of narration; yet in a romantic poem, a series of *ands* may be steps in a stair of breathlessly excited questions. A hyperbole may be tragic or pathetic, but it may also be grotesque and comic. Besides, certain figures or syntactic features recur so frequently, and in so many different contexts, that they cannot have specific expressive meaning. One notices that Cicero uses *litotes* or

[2] Charles Bally, *Traité de la stylistique française*, Heidelberg, 1909.

[3] On "Grand Style," see Matthew Arnold's *On Translating Homer* and G. Saintsbury's "Shakespeare and the Grand Style," "Milton and the Grand Style," and "Dante and the Grand Style," *Collected Essays and Papers*, London, 1923, Vol. III.

a *praeteritio* [4] several times in a few pages; one counts so many hundred balances in the *Ramblers* of Johnson. Both practices suggest play with words, disregard of meaning.

But while the atomistic view of a one-to-one relation between a figure and a specific "expressive value" must be abandoned, the establishment of a specific relation between stylistic traits and effects is not impossible. One way is to show that certain figures recur again and again, combined with other recurrent figures, in passages with certain meaningtone: sublime, comic, graceful, or naïve. One can argue, as W.K. Wimsatt does, that mere repetition of a device does not make it meaningless; "Sentence-patterns recur, like declensions and conjugations; but they are still expressive forms." One need not be content, after the manner of classical antiquity, with classifying styles as high and low, Asiatic and Attic, and the like; one can think out complex schemes such as those propounded in Wilhelm Schneider's *Ausdruckswerte der deutschen Sprache* (1931). According to the relations of words to the object, styles are divisible into conceptual and sensuous, succinct and long-winded, or minimizing and exaggerating, decisive and vague, quiet and excited, low and high, simple and decorated; according to the relations among the words, into tense and lax, plastic and musical, smooth and rough, colorless and colorful; according to the relations of words to the total system of the language, into spoken and written, cliché and individual; and, according to the relation of the words to the author, into objective and subjective. Such classifications can be applied to practically all linguistic utterances; but obviously most of the evidence is drawn from works of literature and directed to an analysis of literary style. Thus conceived, stylistics seems to have found the right mean between the old disjointed study of figures based on the classifications of rhetoric and the more grandiose but less concrete speculation of period styles (the Gothic or Baroque).

Much of this work, unfortunately, has been inspired either by narrowly prescriptive purposes—which make stylistics the recommendation of a certain "middle" style of exposition, with its ideals of precision and clarity, and presently a pedagogic discipline—or by nationalistic exaltation of a specific language. The Germans are especially guilty of fanciful generalizations on the differences between the main Eu-

---

[4] *litotes*, affirming by denying the contrary, "He's not a bad sort"; *praeteritio*, "I will not now dwell on . . ." *Ed.*

ropean languages. Even prominent scholars like Wechssler, Vossler, and Deutschbein indulge in conjectures not really verifiable and rush to conclusions about national psychology. This is not to deny the existence of a problem: the "behavioristic" point of view that all languages are equal seems manifestly absurd if we compare a language without developed literature with one of the great European languages. The great European languages differ widely in syntactical patterns, "idioms," and other conventions, as any translator has discovered. For certain purposes, English or French or German seems less fit than one of its rivals. But the differences are undoubtedly due to social, historical, and literary influences which, though describable, have not yet been described fully enough to warrant reduction to basic national psychologies. A "comparative" stylistics seems a science of the distant future.

A purely literary and aesthetic use of stylistics limits it to the study of a work of art or a group of works which are to be described in terms of their aesthetic function and meaning. Only if this aesthetic interest is central will stylistics be a part of literary scholarship; and it will be an important part because only stylistic methods can define the specific characteristics of a literary work. There are two possible methods of approaching such a stylistic analysis: the first is to proceed by a systematic analysis of its linguistic system and to interpret its features, in terms of the aesthetic purpose of the work, as "total meaning." Style then appears as the individual linguistic system of a work, or a group of works. A second, not contradictory, approach is to study the sum of individual traits by which this system differs from comparable systems. The method here is that of contrast: we observe the deviations and distortions from normal usage, and try to discvoer their aesthetic purpose. In ordinary communicative speech, no attention is drawn to the sound of words, or to word order (which, in English at least, will normally pass from actor to action), or to sentence structure (which will be enumerative, coordinate). A first step in stylistic analysis will be to observe such deviations as the repetitions of sound, the inversion of word order, the construction of involved hierarchies of clauses, all of which must serve some aesthetic function such as emphasis or explicitness or their opposites—the aesthetically justified blurring of distinction or obscurity.

With some works and some authors, such a task will be

comparatively easy. The sound-schemes and similes drawn from the bestiaries in Lyly's *Euphues* are unmistakable.[5] Spenser, who according to Johnson wrote "no language," uses an easily analyzable set of archaisms, neologisms, and provincialisms.[6] Milton not only uses a Latinized vocabulary, in which English words have the sense of their archetypes, but also has his own peculiar sentence structures. The diction of Gerard Manley Hopkins is characterized by its Saxon and dialectal words, its studied avoidance of the Latin vocabulary, prompted by theory and backed by a movement of linguistic Teutonizers, and its peculiar word formations and compounds.[7] It is not difficult to analyze the style of such pronouncedly "mannered" authors as Carlyle, Meredith, Pater, or Henry James, or even of authors who, though of little artistic importance, cultivated their idiosyncrasies.

In many other cases, however, it will be far more difficult to isolate and define the stylistic characteristics of an author. A delicate ear and subtle observation are needed to discern a recurrent trait, especially in writers who, like many Elizabethan dramatists or eighteenth-century essayists, use a uniform style. One must be skeptical of such claims as J.M. Robertson's that certain words or "idioms" are the exclusive signatures of men like Peele, Greene, Marlowe, and Kyd.[8] In many of these investigations, stylistic analysis is indiscriminately combined with study of content-links, sources, and other matters such as recurrent allusions. When that is the case, stylistics serves only as a tool for a different purpose: the identification of an author, the establishment of authenticity, a detective job at most preparatory to literary study.

Difficult practical problems are raised by the existence of prevalent styles, by the power of a single author to excite imitation and vogue. Formerly, the idea of genre had a great

[5] See Morris W. Croll's Introduction to Harry Clemon's edition of Lyly's *Euphues,* London, 1916.

[6] See Henry C. Wyld, *Spenser's Diction and Style,* London, 1930; B.R. McElderry, Jr., "Archaism and Innovation in Spenser's Poetic Diction," *PMLA,* XLVII (1932), pp. 144-70; Herbert W. Sugden, *The Grammar of Spenser's Fairie Queene,* Philadelphia, 1936.

[7] See Austin Warren, "Instress of Inscape," *Gerard Manley Hopkins, By the Kenyon Critics,* Norfolk, Conn., 1945, pp. 72-88, and in *Rage for Order,* Chicago, 1948, pp. 52-65.

[8] J.M. Robertson, *The Shakespeare Canon,* four vols., London, 1922-32.

influence on stylistic tradition. In Chaucer, for example, there is a wide differentiation of styles between the individual stories of the *Canterbury Tales* and, more generally, between his works of different periods and literary types. In the eighteenth century, a Pindaric ode, a satire, a ballad had each its own required vocabulary and style. "Poetic diction" was confined to specific genres, while a homely vocabulary was permitted or even prescribed in low genres. Even Wordsworth, in spite of his condemnation of poetic diction, wrote very differently when he composed an ode, a topographical reflective poem like "Tintern Abbey," a Miltonic sonnet, or a "lyrical ballad." If we ignore such distinctions, we characterize but futilely the style of an author who has cultivated many genres or passed through a long personal evolution. It is probably best to speak of the "styles" of Goethe, since we cannot reconcile the enormous differences between the early *Sturm und Drang* style, that of the classical period, and the late, pompous, and involved manner of the *Elective Affinities*.

This method of stylistic analysis—of concentrating on the peculiarities of style, on traits differentiating it from the surrounding linguistic systems—has obvious dangers. We are likely to accumulate isolated observations, specimens of the marked traits, and to forget that a work of art is a whole. We are likely to overstress "originality," individuality, the merely idiosyncratic. Preferable is the attempt to describe a style completely and systematically, according to linguistic principles. In Russia, Viktor Vinogradov has written masterly studies of Pushkin's and Tolstoy's language. In Poland and in Czechoslovakia, systematic stylistics has attracted many able practitioners; and in Spain, Dámaso Alonso has begun the systematic analysis of Góngora's poetry, while Amado Alonso has sensitively analyzed the poetic style of Pablo Neruda. The danger of the method is the ideal of a "scientific" completeness. The analyst may forget that artistic effect and emphasis are not identical with the mere frequency of a device. Thus Miss Josephine Miles is misled by statistical evidence into stressing the Pre-Raphaelite element in Hopkins' diction.[9]

Stylistic analysis seems most profitable to literary study when it can establish some unifying principle, some general

[9] Josephine Miles, "The Sweet and Lovely Language," *Gerard Manley Hopkins, By the Kenyon Critics,* Norfolk, Conn., 1945, pp. 55-71.

aesthetic aim pervasive of a whole work. If we take, for example, an eighteenth-century descriptive poet such as James Thomson, we should be able to show how his stylistic traits interlock. The Miltonic blank verse puts certain denials and demands on the choice of vocabulary. The vocabulary requires periphrasis, and periphrasis implies a tension between word and thing: the object is not named but its qualities are enumerated. Stress on qualities and their enumeration implies description; and the particular type of nature description practiced in the eighteenth century implies a specific philosophy, the argument from design. In his book on Pope, and his essays on eighteenth-century poetic diction, Geoffrey Tillotson has accumulated many acute observations of this kind, e.g. on the peculiar ideology of poetic diction, its "physico-theological nomenclature," as he calls it; but he has failed to integrate them into a total analysis of the style.[10] Such a procedure, leading from metrical considerations to problems of content and even philosophy must not, of course, be misunderstood to mean a process ascribing priority, either logical or chronological, to any one of these elements. Ideally, we should be able to start at any given point and should arrive at the same results.

This type of demonstration shows how stylistic analysis can easily lead to problems of content. In an intuitive, unsystematic fashion, critics have long analyzed styles as expressive of particular philosophical attitudes. In his *Goethe,* Gundolf sensitively analyzed the language of the early poems, showing how the poet's dynamic speech reflects his turn towards a dynamic conception of nature. Herman Nohl has tried to show that stylistic traits can be associated with the three types of philosophy devised by Dilthey.

German scholars have also developed a more systematic approach, called *Motiv und Wort,* based on the assumption of a parallelism between linguistic traits and content-elements. Leo Spitzer early applied it by investigating the recurrence of such motifs as blood and wounds in the writings of Henri Barbusse, and Josef Körner has fully studied the motifs in Arthur Schnitzler's writings. Later, Spitzer has tried to establish the connection between recurrent stylistic traits and the philosophy of the author, e.g. he connects the

[10] Geoffrey Tillotson, *Essays in Criticism and Research,* Cambridge, 1942, p. 84.

repetitive style of Péguy with his Bergsonism and the style of Jules Romains with his Unanimism. Analysis of the word myths of Christian Morgenstern (the author of nonsense verse vaguely comparable to Lewis Carroll's) shows that he must have read Mauthner's nominalistic *Kritik der Sprache*, drawing from it the conclusion that over an impenetrably dark world language only swathes further veils.

Some of Leo Spitzer's papers go very far in inferring the psychological characteristics of an author from the traits of his style. Proust lends himself to such a procedure; in Charles Louis Phillipe, there is the recurrent construction *à cause de*, interpreted as a *pseudo-objektive Motivierung*, implying a belief in a melancholy, somewhat personal fatalism; in Rabelais, Spitzer analyzes word formations which, using a known root such as *Sorbonne*, combine it with dozens of fantastic suffixes for the creation of multitudinous repulsive nicknames (e.g. *Sorbonnagre*=*Sorbonne*+*onagre*, wild ass), in order to show that there is in Rabelais a tension between the real and the unreal, between comedy and horror, between Utopia and naturalism. The basic assumption is here, as Spitzer formulates it, that a

> mental excitement which deviates from the normal *habitus* of our mental life must have a coordinate linguistic deviation from normal usage.

Spitzer has himself later admitted that psychological stylistics applies

> only to writers who think in terms of the "individual genius," of an individual manner of writing, that is, to writers of the eighteenth and later centuries; in previous periods the writer (even a Dante) sought to express objective things in an objective style. Precisely the insight that "psychological stylistics" is not valid for earlier writers (Montaigne being a glaring exception) has reinforced in me another tendency which was present in my work from the beginning, that of applying to literary art a structural method that seeks to define their unity without recourse to the personality of the author.[11]

Indeed, however ingenious some of its suggestions may be,

[11] From *Comparative Literature*, X (1958), p. 371. See my article "Leo Spitzer (1887-1960)" in *Comparative Literature*, XII (1960), pp. 310-34. With full bibliography of Spitzer's numerous writings.

psychological stylistics seems open to two objections. Many relationships professing to be thus established are not based on conclusions really drawn from the linguistic material but rather start with a psychological and ideological analysis and seek for confirmation in the language. This would be unexceptionable if in practice the linguistic confirmation did not itself seem frequently strained or based on very slight evidence. Work of this type often assumes that true or great art must be based on experience, *Erlebnis,* a term which invokes a slightly revised version of the biographical fallacy. Furthermore, the assumption of a necessary relationship between certain stylistic devices and certain states of mind would appear fallacious. For example, in the discussion of the Baroque, most German scholars assume an inevitable correspondence between dense, obscure, twisted language and a turbulent, divided, and tormented soul. But an obscure, twisted style can certainly be cultivated by craftsmen and technicians. The whole relationship between psyche and word is looser and more oblique than is usually assumed.

Thus German psychological *Stilforschung* has to be treated with considerable caution. Frequently, it would appear to be only a disguised genetic psychology, and assuredly its assumptions are very different from those of Croce's aesthetics, usually considered its model. In Croce's system, which is completely monistic, no distinction can be made between state of mind and linguistic expression. Croce consistently denies the validity of all stylistic and rhetorical categories, the distinction between style and form, between form and content, and ultimately, between word and soul, expression and intuition. In Croce, this series of identifications leads to a theoretical paralysis: an initially genuine insight into the implications of the poetical process is pushed so far that no distinctions are possible. It now seems clear that process and work, form and content, expression and style, must be kept apart, provisionally and in precarious suspense, till the final unity: only thus are possible the whole translation and rationalization which constitute the process of criticism.

If we can describe the style of a work or of an author, there is no doubt that we can also describe the style of a group of works, of a genre: the Gothic novel, the Elizabethan drama, the Metaphysical poem; that we can also analyze stylistic types such as the Baroque style of seventeenth-century prose.[12] One can generalize even further and describe the style of a period or movement. In practice, this seems extraordinarily difficult to do with any empirical closeness. Books like E. Barat's *Le Style poétique et la révolution romantique* or Luise Thon's *Die Sprache des deutschen Impressionismus* trace many stylistic devices or traits of syntax and vocabulary in a whole school or movement. And much has been done to describe the style of Old Teutonic poetry. But these are mostly communal styles, fairly uniform in their nature, which can be treated almost like the works of a single author. The stylistic description of whole ages and whole literary movements like Classicism and Romanticism encounters almost unsurmountable difficulties, since we must find the common denominator between the most diverse writers, sometimes writers of many countries.

As art history has established a widely accepted series of styles, e.g. the classical, the Gothic, the Renaissance, and the Baroque, it seems attractive to try to transfer these terms into literature. But in so doing, we have come back to the question of the relation between the arts and literature, the parallelism of the arts, and the succession of the great periods of our civilization.

[12] See Morris W. Croll's excellent essay, "The Baroque Style in Prose," *Studies in English Philology: A Miscellany in Honor of F. Klaeber*, Minneapolis, 1929, pp. 427-56; also George Williamson, *The Senecan Amble*, Chicago, 1951.

II. THE TRADITION

On Prose Style, from the Rhetoric

ARISTOTLE

c. 1. (A) Style. It is not enough to know what to
say; we must also say it in the right way. Upon the
subject of delivery (which presents itself here) no systematic treatise has been composed, though this art has
much to do with oratory (as with poetry). The matter has, however, been touched upon by Thrasymachus
in his "Appeals to Pity." As to the place of style:
the right thing in speaking really is that we should
fight our case with no help beyond the bare facts; and
yet the arts of language cannot help having a small
but real importance, whatever it is we have to expound to others. Through the influence of the poets, the
language of oratorical prose at first took a poetical
color, as in the case of Gorgias. But the language of
prose is distinct from that of poetry; and, further, the
writers of tragic poetry itself have now given up those
words, not used in ordinary talk, which adorned the
early drama.[1]

Our next subject will be the style of expression.[2] For it
is not enough to know *what* we ought to say; we must also
say it *as* we ought; much help is thus afforded toward
producing the right impression of a speech. The first question to receive attention was naturally the one that comes
first naturally—how persuasion can be produced from the

[1] To enable the reader to follow Aristotle's analysis more easily
the chapter summaries from the Oxford translation have been prefixed to each chapter. *Ed.*

[2] *lexis:* to be translated "language," "speech," "diction,"
"style," "expression," "wording," etc., according to the shade of
meaning conveyed in each context.

From Book 3, translated by W. Rhys Roberts, The Oxford Aristotle, Oxford University
Press. By permission of the Clarendon Press, Oxford.

facts themselves. The second is how to set these facts out
in language. A third would be the proper method of delivery; this is a thing that affects the success of a speech
greatly; but hitherto the subject has been neglected. Indeed,
it was long before it found a way into the arts of tragic
drama and epic recitation: at first poets acted [3] their tragedies themselves. It is plain that delivery has just as much
to do with oratory as with poetry. (In connection with poetry,
it has been studied by Glaucon of Teos among others.) It
is, essentially, a matter of the right management of the
voice to express the various emotions—of speaking loudly,
softly, or between the two; of high, low, or intermediate
pitch; of the various rhythms that suit various subjects.
These are the three things—volume of sound, modulation
of pitch, and rhythm—that a speaker bears in mind. It is
those who *do* bear them in mind who usually win prizes in
the dramatic contests; and just as in drama the actors now
count for more than the poets, so it is in the contests of
public life, owing to the defects of our political institutions.
No systematic treatise upon the rules of delivery has yet been
composed; indeed, even the study of language [4] made no
progress till late in the day. Besides, delivery is—very properly—not regarded as an elevated subject of inquiry.[5] Still,
the whole business of rhetoric being concerned with appearances, we must pay attention to the subject of delivery,
unworthy though it is, because we cannot do without it.
The right thing in speaking really is that we should be
satisfied not to annoy our hearers, without trying to delight
them: we ought in fairness to fight our case with no help
beyond the bare facts: nothing, therefore, should matter except the proof of those facts. Still, as has been already said,
other things affect the result considerably, owing to the
defects of our hearers.[6] The arts of language cannot help
having a small but real importance, whatever it is we have to
expound to others: the way in which a thing is said does
affect its intelligibility. Not, however, so much importance
as people think. All such arts are fanciful and meant to

[3] Or, "delivered."

[4] From this and other indications it would seem that Aristotle regards delivery as a subordinate part of *lexis,* "expression."

[5] Or, "is thought to be vulgar, when viewed from a lofty standpoint," "on any noble view."

[6] The average member of a large audience is regarded as a
"sorry creature," carried away by his feelings and paying little
heed to reason.

charm the hearer. Nobody uses fine language when teaching geometry.

When the principles of delivery have been worked out, they will produce the same effect as on the stage. But only very slight attempts to deal with them have been made and by a few people, as by Thrasymachus in his "Appeals to Pity." Dramatic ability is a natural gift, and can hardly be systematically taught. The principles of good diction can be so taught, and therefore we have men of ability in this direction too, who win prizes in their turn, as well as those speakers who excel in delivery—speeches of the written or literary kind owe more of their effect to their diction than to their thought.

It was naturally the poets who first set the movement [7] going; for words represent things, and they had also the human voice at their disposal, which of all our organs can best represent other things. Thus the arts of recitation and acting were formed, and others as well. Now it was because poets seemed to win fame through their fine language when their thoughts were simple enough, that the language of oratorical prose at first took a poetical color, e.g. that of Gorgias. Even now most uneducated people think that poetical language makes the finest discourses. That is not true: the language of prose is distinct from that of poetry. This is shown by the state of things today, when even the language of tragedy has altered its character. Just as iambics were adopted, instead of tetrameters, because they are the most prose-like [8] of all meters, so tragedy has given up all those words, not used in ordinary talk, which decorated the early drama and are still used by the writers of hexameter poems. It is therefore ridiculous to imitate a poetical manner which the poets themselves have dropped; and it is now plain that we have not to treat in detail the whole question of style, but may confine ourselves to that part of it which concerns our present subject, rhetoric. The other—the poetical—part of it has been discussed in the treatise on the *Art of Poetry*.[9]

c. 2. Still, in the main, the same definition and methods apply alike to poetical and to prose style. Style, to be good, must be clear; it must also be appropriate,

[7] i.e., the movement toward the conscious cultivation of beautiful language.

[8] Or, "speech-like."

[9] See below. *Ed.*

avoiding both meanness and excess of dignity. How these qualities may be attained. Rare, compound, and invented words must be used sparingly in prose; in which, over and above the regular and proper terms for things, metaphorical terms only can be used with advantage, and even these need care. The language of oratorical prose should, in fact, be like that of ordinary conversation. Some discussion of metaphor.

We may, then, start from the observations there made, including the definition of style. Style to be good must be clear, as is proved by the fact that speech which fails to convey a plain meaning will fail to do just what speech has to do. It must also be appropriate, avoiding both meanness and undue elevation; poetical language is certainly free from meanness, but it is not appropriate to prose.[1] Clearness is secured by using the words (nouns and verbs alike) that are current and ordinary. Freedom from meanness, and positive adornment too, are secured by using the other words mentioned in the *Art of Poetry*. Such variation from what is usual makes the language appear more stately. People do not feel toward strangers as they do toward their own countrymen, and the same thing is true of their feeling for language. It is therefore well to give to everyday speech an unfamiliar air: people like what strikes them, and are struck by what is out of the way. In verse such effects are common, and there they are fitting: the persons and things there spoken of are comparatively remote from ordinary life. In prose passages they are far less often fitting because the subject-matter is less exalted. Even in poetry, it is not quite appropriate that fine language should be used by a slave or a very young man, or about very trivial subjects: even in poetry the style, to be appropriate, must sometimes be toned down, though at other times heightened. We can now see that a writer must disguise his art and give the impression of speaking naturally and not artificially. Naturalness is persuasive, artificiality is the contrary; for our hearers are prejudiced and think we have some design against them, as if we were mixing their wines for them. It is like the difference between the quality of Theodorus' voice and the voices of all other actors: his really seems to be that of

---

[1] This last clause explains the cautious addition just made to the definition as given in the *Poetics*. Poetry, it is pointed out, often heightens expression in a way which would seem pretentious and intolerable in prose; cp. the examples from Euripides and Dionysius the Brazen below. Still, in the main, the same definition and methods apply to both poetical and prose style.

the character who is speaking, theirs do not. We can hide our purpose successfully by taking the single words of our composition from the speech of ordinary life. This is done in poetry by Euripides, who was the first to show the way to his successors.

Language is composed of nouns and verbs. Nouns are of the various kinds considered in the treatise on Poetry. Strange words, compound words, and invented words must be used sparingly and on few occasions: on *what* occasions we shall state later. The reason for this restriction has been already indicated: they depart from what is suitable, in the direction of excess. In the language of prose, besides the regular and proper terms for things, metaphorical terms only can be used with advantage. This we gather from the fact that these two classes of terms, the proper or regular and the metaphorical —these and no others—are used by everybody in conversation. We can now see that a good writer can produce a style that is distinguished without being obtrusive, and is at the same time clear, thus satisfying our definition of good oratorical prose. Words of ambiguous meaning are chiefly useful to enable the sophist to mislead his hearers. Synonyms are useful to the poet, by which I mean words whose ordinary meaning is the same, e.g. *poreuesthai* (*advancing*) and *badizein* (*proceeding*); these two are ordinary words and have the same meaning.

In the *Art of Poetry*, as we have already said, will be found definitions of these kinds of words; a classification of Metaphors; and mention of the fact that metaphor is of great value both in poetry and in prose. Prose writers must, however, pay especially careful attention to metaphor, because their other resources are scantier than those of poets. Metaphor, moreover, gives style clearness, charm, and distinction as nothing else can: and it is not a thing whose use can be taught by one man to another. Metaphors, like epithets, must be fitting, which means that they must fairly correspond to the thing signified: failing this, their inappropriateness will be conspicuous: the want of harmony between two things is emphasized by their being placed side by side. It is like having to ask ourselves what dress will suit an old man; certainly not the crimson cloak that suits a young man. And if you wish to pay a compliment, you must take your metaphor from something better in the same line; if to disparage, from something worse. To illustrate my meaning: since opposites are in the same class, you do what I have suggested if you say that a man who begs "prays," and a man who prays "begs"; for praying and begging are both varieties of asking. So Iphicrates called Callias a "mendicant priest" instead of a "torch-bearer," and Callias replied that Iphicrates must be uninitiated or he would have called him not a "mendicant priest" but a "torch-bearer." Both are religious titles, but one is honorable and the other is not. Again, somebody calls actors "hangers-on of Dionysus," but they call themselves "artists": each of these terms is a metaphor, the one intended to throw dirt at the actor, the other to dignify him. And pirates now call themselves "purveyors." We can thus call a crime a mistake, or a mistake a crime. We can say that a thief "took" a thing, or that he "plundered" his victim. An expression like that of Euripides' Telephus,

> King of the oar, on Mysia's coast he landed,

is inappropriate; the word "king" goes beyond the dignity of the subject, and so the art is *not* concealed. A metaphor may be amiss because the very syllables of the words conveying it fail to indicate sweetness of vocal utterance. Thus Dionysius the Brazen in his elegies calls poetry "Calliope's screech." Poetry and screeching are both, to be sure, vocal utterances. But the metaphor is bad, because the sounds of "screeching," unlike those of poetry, are discordant and unmeaning. Further, in using metaphors to give names to nameless things, we must draw them not from remote but from kindred and similar things, so that the kinship is clearly perceived as soon as the words are said. Thus in the celebrated riddle

> I marked how a man glued bronze with fire to another man's body,

the process is nameless; but both it and gluing are a kind of application, and that is why the application of the cupping-glass is here called a "gluing." Good riddles do, in general, provide us with satisfactory metaphors: for metaphors imply riddles, and therefore a good riddle can furnish a good metaphor. Further, the materials of metaphors must be beautiful; and the beauty, like the ugliness, of all words may, as Licymnius says, lie in their sound or in their meaning. Further, there is a third consideration—one that upsets the fallacious argument of the sophist Bryson, that there is no such thing as foul language, because in whatever words you put a given thing your meaning is the same. This is untrue.

One term may describe a thing more truly than another, may be more like it, and set it more intimately before our eyes. Besides, two different words will represent a thing in two different lights; so on this ground also one term must be held fairer or fouler than another. For both of two terms will indicate what *is* fair, or what *is* foul, but not simply their fairness or their foulness, or if so, at any rate not in an equal degree. The materials of metaphor must be beautiful to the ear, to the understanding, to the eye or some other physical sense. It is better, for instance, to say "rosy-fingered morn," than "crimson-fingered" or, worse still, "red-fingered morn." The epithets that we apply, too, may have a bad and ugly aspect, as when Orestes is called a "mother-slayer"; or a better one, as when he is called his "father's avenger." Simonides, when the victor in the mule race offered him a small fee, refused to write him an ode, because, he said, it was so unpleasant to write odes to half-asses: but on receiving an adequate fee, he wrote

> Hail to you, daughters of storm-footed steeds,

though of course they were daughters of asses too. The same effect is attained by the use of diminutives, which make a bad thing less bad and a good thing less good. Take, for instance, the banter of Aristophanes in the *Babylonians* where he uses "goldlet" for "gold," "cloaklet" for "cloak," "scofflet" for "scoff," and "plaguelet." But alike in using epithets and in using diminutives we must be wary and must observe the mean.

c. 3. Four faults of prose style, with illustrative examples: (1) misuse of compound words; (2) employment of strange words; (3) long, unseasonable, or frequent epithets; (4) inappropriate metaphors.

Bad taste in language may take any of four forms:—

(1) The misuse of compound words. Lycophron, for instance, talks of the "*many-visaged* heaven" above the "*giant-crested* earth," and again the "*strait-pathed* shore"; and Gorgias of the "*pauper-poet* flatterer" and "oath-breaking and *over-oath-keeping*." Alcidamas uses such expressions as "the soul filling with rage and face becoming *flame-flushed*," and "he thought their enthusiasm would be *issue-fraught*" and "*issue-fraught* he made the persuasion of his words," and "*somber-hued* is the floor of the sea." The way all these

words are compounded makes them, we feel, fit for verse only. This, then, is one form in which bad taste is shown.

(2) Another is the employment of strange words. For instance, Lycophron talks of "the *prodigious* Xerxes" and "*spoliative* Sciron"; Alcidamas of "a *toy* for poetry" and "the *witlessness* of nature," and says "*whetted* with the *unmitigated* temper of his spirit."

(3) A third form is the use of long, unseasonable, or frequent epithets. It is appropriate enough for a poet to talk of "white milk," but in prose such epithets are sometimes lacking in appropriateness or, when spread too thickly, plainly reveal the author turning his prose into poetry. Of course we must use some epithets, since they lift our style above the usual level and give it an air of distinction. But we must aim at the due mean, or the result will be worse than if we took no trouble at all; we shall get something actually bad instead of something merely not good. That is why the epithets of Alcidamas seem so tasteless; he does not use them as the seasoning of the meat, but as the meat itself, so numerous and swollen and aggressive are they. For instance, he does not say "sweat," but "the *moist* sweat"; not "to the Isthmian games," but "to the *world-concourse* of the Isthmian games"; not "laws," but "the laws *that are monarchs of states*"; not "at a run," but "*his heart impelling him to speed of foot*"; not "a school of the Muses," but "*Nature's* school of the Muses had he inherited"; and so "*frowning* care of heart," and "achiever" not of "popularity" but of "*universal* popularity," and "*dispenser* of pleasure to his audience," and "he concealed it" not "with boughs" but "with boughs *of the forest trees*," and "he clothed" not "his body" but "*his body's nakedness*," and "his soul's desire was *counter-imitative*" (this is at one and the same time a compound and an epithet, so that it seems a poet's effort), and "so *extravagant* the excess of his wickedness." We thus see how the inappropriateness of such poetical language imports absurdity and tastelessness into speeches, as well as the obscurity that comes from all this verbosity—for when the sense is plain, you only obscure and spoil its clearness by piling up words.

The ordinary use of compound words is where there is no term for a thing and some compound can be easily formed, like "pastime" (*chronotribein*); but if this is much done, the prose character disappears entirely. We now see why the language of compounds is just the thing for writers of dithyrambs, who love sonorous noises; strange words for writers of epic poetry, which is a proud and stately affair; and metaphor for iambic verse, the meter which (as has been already said) is widely used today.

c. 4. The simile is a full-blown metaphor. Similes are useful in prose as well as in verse; but they must not be used often, since they are of the nature of poetry. Instances of simile, from Plato and the orators. Metaphors can easily be turned into similes, and similes into metaphors. The proportional [as defined in the *Poetics*, c. 21] metaphor must always apply reciprocally to either of its coordinate terms.

There remains the fourth region in which bad taste may be shown, metaphor. Metaphors like other things may be inappropriate. Some are so because they are ridiculous; they are indeed used by comic as well as tragic poets. Others are too grand and theatrical; and these, if they are far-fetched, may also be obscure. For instance, Gorgias talks of "events that are green and full of sap," and says "foul was the deed you sowed and evil the harvest you reaped." That is too much like poetry. Alcidamas, again, called philosophy "a fortress that threatens the power of law," and the *Odyssey* "a goodly looking-glass of human life," [1] and talked about "offering no such toy to poetry": all these expressions fail, for the reasons given, to carry the hearer with them. The address of Gorgias to the swallow, when she had let her droppings fall on him as she flew overhead, is in the best tragic manner. He said, "Nay, shame, O Philomela." Considering her as a bird, you could not call her act shameful; considering her as a girl, you could; and so it was a good gibe to address her as what she was once and not as what she is.

The Simile also is a metaphor; the difference is but slight. When the poet says of Achilles that he

Leaped on the foe as a lion,

this is a simile; when he says of him "the lion leaped," it is

---

[1] This metaphor apparently strikes Aristotle as "far-fetched" and incongruous, and as reflecting the surface only: it makes a peep-show of the great epic of human life. It would probably obscure his point to render "a fair *mirror* of the life of man," since "mirror" is now one of the most familiar and edge-worn of metaphors.

a metaphor—here, since both are courageous, he has transferred to Achilles the name of "lion." Similes are useful in prose as well as in verse; but not often, since they are of the nature of poetry. They are to be employed just as metaphors are employed, since they are really the same thing except for the difference mentioned.

The following are examples of similes. Androtion said of Idrieus that he was like a terrier let off the chain, that flies at you and bites you—Idrieus too was savage now that he was let out of *his* chains. Theodamas compared Archidamus to an Euxenus who could not do geometry—a proportional simile, implying that Euxenus is an Archidamus who *can* do geometry. In Plato's *Republic* those who strip the dead are compared to curs which bite the stones thrown at them but do not touch the thrower; and there is the simile about the Athenian people, who are compared to a ship's captain who is strong but a little deaf; and the one about poets' verses, which are likened to persons who lack beauty but possess youthful freshness—when the freshness has faded the charm perishes, and so with verses when broken up into prose. Pericles compared the Samians to children who take their pap but go on crying; and the Boeotians to holm-oaks, because they were ruining one another by civil wars just as one oak causes another oak's fall. Demosthenes said that the Athenian people were like seasick men on board ship. Again, Democrates compared the political orators to nurses who swallow the bit of food themselves and then smear the children's lips with the spittle. Antisthenes compared the lean Cephisodotus to frankincense, because it was his consumption that gave one pleasure. All these ideas may be expressed either as similes or as metaphors; those which succeed as metaphors will obviously do well also as similes, and similes, with the explanation omitted, will appear as metaphors. But the proportional metaphor [2] must always apply reciprocally to either of its coordinate terms. For instance, if a drinking-bowl is the shield of Dionysus, a shield may fittingly be called the drinking-bowl of Ares.

[Chapters 5, 6, and 7 are thought to be an earlier version of

[2] i.e. metaphor or *simile: metaphora* used as being the more general and inclusive term (cp. beginning of chapter).

the preceding chapters, as is clear from the following summaries. *Ed.*]

c. 5. The foundation of good style is correctness of language, which is discussed under five heads: (1) right use of connecting words; (2) use of special, and not vague, general terms; (3) avoidance of ambiguity; (4) observance of gender; (5) correct indication of grammatical number. A composition should be easy to read and therefore easy to deliver; it should avoid (1) uncertainties as to punctuation, (2) zeugma, (3) parenthesis.

c. 6. Impressiveness of style. Six heads: (1) the use of a description instead of a simple name; (2) metaphors and epithets; (3) plural for singular number; (4) repetition of the article; (5) connecting words; (6) description by means of negation.

c. 7. Appropriateness. An appropriate style will adapt itself to (1) the emotions of the hearers, (2) the character of the speaker, (3) the nature of the subject. Tact and judgment are needed in all varieties of oratory.

c. 8. Prose rhythm. The form of the language should not be metrical, nor, on the other hand, without any rhythm at all. Of the various possible rhythms, the heroic is too grand, the iambic too ordinary, and the trochaic too like a riotous dance. The best rhythm for prose is the paean, since from this alone no definite meter arises. The paean —∪∪∪ should be used for the beginning, and the paean ∪∪∪— for the end, of a sentence.

The form of a prose composition should be neither metrical nor destitute of rhythm. The metrical form destroys the hearer's trust by its artificial appearance, and at the same time it diverts his attention, making him watch for metrical recurrences, just as children catch up the herald's question, "Whom does the freedman choose as his advocate?" with the answer "Cleon!" On the other hand, unrhythmical language is too unlimited; we do not want the limitations of meter, but some limitation we must have, or the effect will be vague and unsatisfactory. Now it is number that limits all things; and it is the numerical limitation of the form of a composition that constitutes rhythm, of which meters are definite sections.

Prose, then, is to be rhythmical, but not metrical, or it

will become not prose but verse. It should not even have too
precise a prose rhythm, and therefore should only be rhythmical to a certain extent.

Of the various rhythms, the heroic has dignity, but lacks
the tones of the spoken language. The iambic is the very
language of ordinary people, so that in common talk iambic
lines occur oftener than any others: but in a speech we need
dignity and the power of taking the hearer out of his ordinary self. The trochee is too much akin to wild dancing: we
can see this in tetrameter verse, which is one of the trochaic
rhythms.

There remains the paean, which speakers began to use in
the time of Thrasymachus, though they had then no name
to give it. The paean is a third class of rhythm, closely akin
to both the two already mentioned; it has in it the ratio of
three to two, whereas the other two kinds have the ratio of
one to one, and two to one respectively. Between the two
last ratios comes the ratio of one-and-a-half to one, which is
that of the paean.

Now the other two kinds of rhythm must be rejected in
writing prose, partly for the reasons given, and partly because they are too metrical; and the paean must be adopted,
since from this alone of the rhythms mentioned no definite
meter arises, and therefore it is the least obtrusive of them.
At present the same form of paean is employed at the beginning as at the end of sentences, whereas the end should differ from the beginning. There are two opposite kinds of
paean, one of which is suitable to the beginning of a sentence, where it is indeed actually used; this is the kind that
begins with a long syllable and ends with three short ones.
[Here, as below, the Greek example is omitted. *Ed.*]

The other paean begins, conversely, with three short syllables and ends with a long one.

This kind of paean makes a real close: a short syllable can
give no effect of finality, and therefore makes the rhythm
appear truncated. A sentence should break off with the long
syllable: the fact that it is over should be indicated not by
the scribe, or by his period-mark in the margin, but by the
rhythm itself.

We have now seen that our language must be rhythmical
and not destitute of rhythm, and what rhythms, in what
particular shape, make it so.

c. 9. Periodic style. The language of prose must be

either (1) free-running, like that of Herodotus; or (2) compact (i.e. periodic). A period may be defined as a portion of speech that has in itself a beginning and an end, being at the same time not too big to be taken in at a glance. It may have one member (clause), or more than one. A period of more than one member may be either (*a*) simply divided, or (*b*) antithetical. Antithesis implies contrast of sense. *Parisosis* makes the two members of a period equal in length. *Paromoeosis* makes the first or last word of both members like each other. *Homoeoteleuton* denotes similarity in terminations only.

The language of prose must be either free-running, with its parts united by nothing except the connecting words, like the preludes in dithyrambs; or compact and antithetical, like the strophes of the old poets. The free-running style is the ancient one, e.g., "Herein is set forth the inquiry of Herodotus the Thurian." Everyone used this method formerly; not many do so now. By "free-running" style I mean the kind that has no natural stopping-places, and comes to a stop only because there is no more to say of that subject. This style is unsatisfying just because it goes on indefinitely—one always likes to sight a stopping-place in front of one: it is only at the goal that men in a race faint and collapse; while they see the end of the course before them, they can keep going. Such, then, is the free-running kind of style; the compact is that which is in periods. By a period I mean a portion of speech that has in itself a beginning and an end, being at the same time not too big to be taken in at a glance. Language of this kind is satisfying and easy to follow. It is satisfying, because it is just the reverse of indefinite; and moreover, the hearer always feels that he is grasping something and has reached some definite conclusion; whereas it is unsatisfactory to see nothing in front of you and get nowhere. It is easy to follow, because it can easily be remembered; and this because language when in periodic form can be numbered,[1] and number is the easiest of all things to remember. That is why verse, which is measured, is always more easily remembered than prose, which is not: the measures of verse can be numbered. The period must, further, not be completed until the sense is complete: it must not be capable of breaking off

[1] i.e., is recognized as consisting of a countable number of parts or divisions.

abruptly, as may happen with the following iambic lines of
Sophocles—

> Calydon's soil is this; of Pelops' land
> The smiling plains face us across the strait.

By a wrong division [2] of the words the hearer may take
the meaning to be the reverse of what it is: for instance, in
the passage quoted, one might imagine that Calydon is in
the Peloponnesus.

A Period may be either divided into several members [3]
or simple. The period of several members is a portion of
speech (1) complete in itself, (2) divided into parts, and (3)
easily delivered at a single breath—as a whole, that is; not by
fresh breath being taken at the division. A member is one of
the two parts of such a period. By a "simple" period, I
mean that which has only one member. The members, and
the whole periods, should be neither curt nor long. A member which is too short often makes the listener stumble; he
is still expecting the rhythm to go on to the limit his mind
has fixed for it; and if meanwhile he is pulled back by the
speaker's stopping, the shock is bound to make him, so to
speak, stumble. If, on the other hand, you go on too long,
you make him feel left behind, just as people who when
walking pass beyond the boundary before turning back leave
their companions behind. So too if a period is too long you
turn it into a speech, or something like a dithyrambic prelude.
The result is much like the preludes that Democritus of
Chios jeered at Melanippides for writing instead of antis-
trophic stanzas—

> He that sets traps for another man's feet
> > Is like to fall into them first;
> And long-winded preludes do harm to us all,
> > But the preluder catches it worst.

Which applies likewise to long-membered [4] orators. Periods
whose members are altogether too short are not periods at
all; and the result is to bring the hearer down with a crash.

The periodic style which is divided into members is of

---

[2] i.e., by coming to an abrupt stop at the end of the first line
and making no pause in its middle.

[3] *kolon: limb of a period, clause of a sentence.*

[4] i.e., long-winded framers of long-membered periods; possibly
with a play on "long-limbed," "lanky."

two kinds. It is either simply divided, as in "I have often wondered at the conveners of national gatherings and the founders of athletic contests"; or it is antithetical, where, in each of the two members, one of one pair of opposites is put along with one of another pair, or the same word is used to bracket two opposites, as "They aided both parties—not only those who stayed behind but those who accompanied them: for the latter they acquired new territory larger than that at home, and to the former they left territory at home that was large enough." Here the contrasted words are "staying behind" and "accompanying," "enough" and "larger." So in the example, "Both to those who want to get property and to those who desire to enjoy it," where "enjoyment" is contrasted with "getting." Again, "it often happens in such enterprises that the wise men fail and the fools succeed"; "they were awarded the prize of valor immediately, and won the command of the sea not long afterward"; "to sail through the mainland and march through the sea, by bridging the Hellespont and cutting through Athos"; "nature gave them their country and law took it away again"; "some of them perished in misery, others were saved in disgrace"; "Athenian citizens keep foreigners in their houses as servants, while the city of Athens allows her allies by thousands to live as the foreigner's slaves"; and "to possess in life or to bequeath at death." There is also what someone said about Peitholaus and Lycophron in a lawcourt, "These men used to sell you when they were at home, and now they have come to you here and bought you." All these passages have the structure described above. Such a form of speech is satisfying, because the significance of contrasted ideas is easily felt, especially when they are thus put side by side, and also because it has the effect of a logical argument; it is by putting two opposing conclusions side by side that you prove one of them false.

Such, then, is the nature of *antithesis. Parisosis* is making the two members of a period equal in length. *Paromoeosis* is making the extreme words of both members like each other. This must happen either at the beginning or at the end of each member. If at the beginning, the resemblance must always be between whole words; at the end, between final syllables or inflexions of the same word or the same word repeated. Thus, at the beginning [5]

---

[5] In the following examples, since it is a question of sound, the translations must be inadequate. *Ed.*

> A field he took from him, a fallow field.

and

> Yet might they by presents be won, and by pleadings be
> pacified.

At the end

> They didn't imagine that he *had borne* the child, but that
> he was the cause of its *having been borne*.

and

> In the midst of plenteous cares and exiguous hopes.

An example of inflexions of the same word is

> Is he worthy to have a copper statue, when he is not
> worth a copper?

Of the same word repeated,

> When he was alive you spoke evil of him, and now you
> write evil of him.

Of one syllable,

> Would it have been very shocking to you if you had seen
> a man idling?

It is possible for the same sentence to have all these features
together—*antithesis, parison,* and *homoeoteleuton.* (The possible beginnings of periods have been pretty fully enumerated in the *Theodectea.*) There are also spurious antitheses,
like that of Epicharmus—

> There one time I as their guest did stay,
> And they were my hosts on another day.

c. 10. Smart and popular sayings. Three chief features of these clever, pointed sayings are: (1) antithesis, (2) metaphor, and (3) actuality or vividness, (i.e.,
the power of "setting the scene before our eyes").

We may now consider the above points settled, and pass
on to say something about the way to devise lively and
taking sayings. Their actual invention can only come through
natural talent or long practice; but this treatise may indicate
the way it is done. We may deal with them by enumerating
the different kinds of them. We will begin by remarking that
we all naturally find it agreeable to get hold of new ideas

easily: words express ideas, and therefore those words are the most agreeable that enable us to get hold of new ideas. Now strange words simply puzzle us; ordinary words convey only what we know already; it is from metaphor that we can best get hold of something fresh. When the poet calls old age "a withered stalk," he conveys a new idea, a new fact, to us by means of the general notion of "lost bloom," which is common to both things. The similes of the poets do the same, and therefore, if they are good similes, give an effect of brilliance. The simile, as has been said before, is a metaphor, differing from it only in the way it is put; and just because it is longer it is less attractive. Besides, it does not say outright that "this" *is* "that," and therefore the hearer is less interested in the idea. We see, then, that both speech and reasoning are lively in proportion as they make us seize a new idea promptly. For this reason people are not much taken either by obvious arguments (using the word "obvious" to mean what is plain to everybody and needs no investigation), nor by those which puzzle us when we hear them stated, but only by those which convey their information to us as soon as we hear them, provided we had not the information already; or which the mind only just fails to keep up with. These two kinds do convey to us a sort of information: but the obvious and the obscure kinds convey nothing, either at once or later on. It is these qualities, then, that, so far as the meaning of what is said is concerned, make an argument acceptable. So far as the style is concerned, it is the antithetical form that appeals to us, e. g., "judging that the peace common to all the rest was a war upon their own private interests," where there is an antithesis between war and peace. It is also good to use metaphorical words; but the metaphors must not be far-fetched, or they will be difficult to grasp, nor obvious, or they will have no effect. The words, too, ought to set the scene before our eyes; for events ought to be seen in progress rather than in prospect. So we must aim at these three points: Antithesis, Metaphor, and Actuality.

Of the four kinds of Metaphor the most taking is the proportional kind. Thus Pericles, for instance, said that the vanishing from their country of the young men who had fallen in the war was "as if the spring were taken out of the year." Leptines, speaking of the Lacedaemonians, said that he would not have the Athenians let Greece "lose one of her two eyes." When Chares was pressing for leave to be examined upon his share in the Olynthiac war, Cephisodotus was

indignant, saying that he wanted his examination to take
place "while he had his fingers upon the people's throat." [1]
The same speaker once urged the Athenians to march to
Euboea, "with Miltiades' decree as their rations." Iphicrates,
indignant at the truce made by the Athenians with Epidaurus
and the neighboring seaboard, said that they had stripped
themselves of their traveling money for the journey of war.
Peitholaus called the state-galley "the people's big stick," and
Sestos "the corn-bin of the Peiraeus." Pericles bade his countrymen remove Aegina, "that eyesore of the Peiraeus." And
Moerocles said he was no more a rascal than was a certain
respectable citizen he named, "whose rascality was worth
over thirty per cent per annum to him, instead of a mere ten
like his own." There is also the iambic line of Anaxandrides
about the way his daughters put off marrying—

> My daughters' marriage-bonds are overdue.

Polyeuctus said of a paralytic man named Speusippus that he
could not keep quiet, "though fortune had fastened him in
the pillory of disease." Cephisodotus called warships "painted
millstones." Diogenes the Dog called taverns "the messrooms
of Attica." Aesion said that the Athenians had "emptied"
their town into Sicily: this is a graphic metaphor. "Till all
Hellas shouted aloud" may be regarded as a metaphor, and
a graphic one again. Cephisodotus bade the Athenians take
care not to hold too many "parades." Isocrates used the same
word of those who "parade" at the national festivals. Another
example occurs in the Funeral Speech: "It is fitting that
Greece should cut off her hair beside the tomb of those who
fell at Salamis, since her freedom and their valor are buried
in the same grave." Even if the speaker here had only said
that it was right to weep when valor was being buried in
their grave, it would have been a metaphor, and a graphic
one; but the coupling of "their valor" and "her freedom"
presents a kind of antithesis as well. "The course of my
words," said Iphicrates, "lies straight through the middle of
Chares' deeds": this is a proportional metaphor, and the
phrase "straight through the middle" makes it graphic.
The expression "to call in one danger to rescue us from
another" is a graphic metaphor. Lycoleon said, defending
Chabrias, "They did not respect even that bronze statue of

---

[1] i.e., while he was still in command of his mercenaries, and so
could coerce the people.

his that intercedes for him yonder." This was a metaphor for the moment, though it would not always apply; a vivid metaphor, however; Chabrias is in danger, and his statue intercedes for him—that lifeless yet living thing which records his services to his country.[2] "Practicing in every way littleness of mind" is metaphorical, for practicing a quality implies increasing it.[3] So is "God kindled our reason to be a lamp within our souls," for both reason and light reveal things. So is "we are not putting an end to our wars, but only postponing them," for both literal postponement and the making of such a peace as this apply to future action. So is such a saying as "This treaty is a far nobler trophy than those we set up on fields of battle; *they* celebrate small gains and single successes; *it* celebrates our triumph in the war as a whole; for both trophy and treaty are signs of victory. So is "A country pays a heavy reckoning in being condemned by the judgment of mankind," for a reckoning is damage deservedly incurred.

c. 11. The graphic power of "setting things before the eyes" implies the use of expressions that represent objects as in a state of activity: Homer often gives metaphorical life to lifeless things in this fashion. A touch of surprise also contributes to liveliness. People feel they have learned something; hence the pleasure given by apothegms, riddles, and puns. Similes, proverbs, and hyperboles also find a place here, being related to metaphors.

It has already been mentioned that liveliness is got by using the proportional type of metaphor and by being graphic (i.e., making your hearers *see* things). We have still to explain what we mean by their "seeing things," and what must be done to effect this. By "making them see things" I mean using expressions that represent things as in a state of activity. Thus, to say that a good man is "foursquare" is certainly a metaphor; both the good man and the square are perfect; but the metaphor does not suggest activity. On the other hand, in the expression "with his vigor in full bloom" there

---

[2] Or, "the great deeds of his country" (Chares' glory being regarded as the glory of Athens).

[3] "Practicing" being a *kind* of "increasing," the present metaphor is one "from species to genus."

is a notion of activity; and so in "But you must roam as free as a sacred victim"; and in

>Thereat up sprang the Hellenes to their feet,

where "up sprang" gives us activity as well as metaphor, for it at once suggests swiftness. So with Homer's common practice of giving metaphorical life to lifeless things: all such passages are distinguished by the effect of activity they convey. Thus,

>Downward anon to the valley rebounded the boulder *remorseless;*

and

>The bitter arrow *flew;*

and

>Flying on *eagerly;* [1]

and

>Stuck in the earth, still *panting* to feed on the flesh of the heroes; [2]

and

>And the point of the spear *in its fury* drove full through his breastbone.

In all these examples the things have the effect of being active because they are made into living beings; shameless behavior and fury and so on are all forms of activity. And the poet has attached these ideas to the things by means of proportional metaphors: as the stone is to Sisyphus, so is the shameless man to his victim. In his famous similes, too, he treats inanimate things in the same way:

>Curving and crested with white, host following host without ceasing. [3]

Here he represents everything as moving and living; and activity is movement.

Metaphors must be drawn, as has been said already, from things that are related to the original thing, and yet not obviously so related—just as in philosophy also an acute mind will perceive resemblances even in things far apart. Thus Archytas said that an arbitrator and an altar were the same, since the injured fly to both for refuge. Or you might say that an anchor and an overhead hook were the same,

---

[1] Here too an arrow is spoken of.
[2] *Iliad,* xi. 574. Spears are falling short of their mark.
[3] Ocean waves rolling to the shore.

since both are in a way the same, only the one secures things from below and the other from above. And to speak of states as "leveled" is to identify two widely different things, the equality of a physical surface and the equality of political powers.

Liveliness is especially conveyed by metaphor, and by the further power of surprising the hearer; because the hearer expected something different, his acquisition of the new idea impresses him all the more. His mind seems to say, "Yes, to be sure; I never thought of that." The liveliness of epigrammatic remarks is due to the meaning not being just what the words say: as in the saying of Stesichorus that "the cicadas will chirp to themselves on the ground." Well-constructed riddles are attractive for the same reason; a new idea is conveyed, and there is metaphorical expression. So with the "novelties" of Theodorus. In these the thought is startling, and, as Theodorus puts it, does not fit in with the ideas you already have. They are like the burlesque words that one finds in the comic writers. The effect is produced even by jokes depending upon changes of the letters of a word;[4] this too is a surprise. You find this in verse as well as in prose. The word which comes is not what the hearer imagined: thus

Onward he came, and his feet were shod with his—
    chilblains,

where one imagined the word would be "sandals." But the point should be clear the moment the words are uttered. Jokes made by altering the letters of a word consist in meaning, not just what you say, but something that gives a twist to the word used.

[A number of Greek puns are here omitted. *Ed.*]

Thou must not be a stranger stranger than
Thou should'st.

Do not the words "thou must not be," etc., amount to saying that the stranger must not always be strange? Here again is the use of one word in different senses. Of the same kind also is the much-praised verse of Anaxandrides:

Death is most fit before you do
Deeds that would make death fit for you.

[4] Plays upon words are meant.

This amounts to saying, "It is a fit thing to die when you are not fit to die," or "It is a fit thing to die when death is not fit for you," i.e., when death is not the fit return for what you are doing. The type of language employed is the same in all these examples; but the more briefly and antithetically such sayings can be expressed, the more taking they are, for antithesis impresses the new idea more firmly and brevity more quickly. They should always have either some personal application or some merit of expression, if they are to be true without being commonplace—two requirements not always satisfied simultaneously. Thus, "A man should die having done no wrong" is true but dull; "The right man should marry the right woman" is also true but dull. No, there must be both good qualities together, as in, "It is fitting to die when you are not fit for death." The more a saying has these qualities, the livelier it appears: if, for instance, its wording is metaphorical, metaphorical in the right way, antithetical, and balanced, and at the same time it gives an idea of activity.

Successful similes also, as has been said above, are in a sense metaphors, since they always involve two relations like the proportional metaphor. Thus: a shield, we say, is the "drinking-bowl of Ares," and a bow is the "chordless lyre." This way of putting a metaphor is not "simple," as it would be if we called the bow a lyre or the shield a drinking-bowl. There are "simple" similes also: we may say that a flute-player is like a monkey, or that a shortsighted man's eyes are like a lamp-flame with water dropping on it, since both eyes and flame keep winking.[5] A simile succeeds best when it is a converted metaphor, for it is possible to say that a shield *is like* the drinking-bowl of Ares, or that a ruin *is like* a house in rags, and to say that Niceratus *is like* a Philoctetes stung by Pratys—the simile made by Thrasymachus when he saw Niceratus, who had been beaten by Pratys in a recitation competition, still going about unkempt and unwashed. It is in these respects that poets fail worst when they fail, and succeed best when they succeed, i. e., when they give the resemblance pat, as in

> Those legs of his curl just like parsley leaves;

and

> Just like Philammon struggling with his punch-ball.

[5] Or, "that a shortsighted man is like a sputtering lamp, since both wink."

These are all similes; and that similes are metaphors has been stated often already.

Proverbs, again, are metaphors from one species to another. Suppose, for instance, a man to start some undertaking in hope of gain and then to lose by it later on; "Here we have once more the man of Carpathus and his hare," [6] says he. For both alike went through the said experience.

It has now been explained fairly completely how liveliness is secured and why it has the effect it has. Successful hyperboles are also metaphors, e. g., the one about the man with a black eye: "You would have thought he was a basket of mulberries"; here the "black eye" is compared to a mulberry. because of its color, the exaggeration lying in the quantity of mulberries suggested. The phrase "*like* so-and-so" may introduce a hyperbole under the form of a simile. Thus

> *Just like* Philammon struggling with his punch-ball

is equivalent to "*You would have thought he was* Philammon struggling with his punch-ball"; and

> Those legs of his curl *just like* parsley leaves

is equivalent to "His legs are so curly that *you would have thought* they were not legs but parsley leaves." Hyperboles are for young men to use; they show vehemence of character; and this is why angry people use them more than other people.

> Not though he gave me as much as the dust or the sands of the sea . . .
> But her, the daughter of Atreus' son, I never will marry,
> Nay, not though she were fairer than Aphrodite the Golden,
> Defter of hand than Athene . . .

(The Attic orators are particularly fond of this method of speech.) Consequently it does not suit an elderly speaker.

c. 12. Each kind of rhetoric has its own appropriate style. The style of written prose is not that of spoken oratory, nor are those of political and forensic speaking the same. The written style is the more finished: the spoken better admits of dramatic delivery—alike the

[6] Hares, introduced with good intention into the island, increased to a plague.

kind of oratory that reflects character and the kind
that stirs emotion. The style of oratory addressed to
public assemblies resembles scene-painting. In the one
and the other, high finish in detail is superfluous and
seems better away. The forensic style is more highly
finished. Ceremonial oratory is the most literary, for
it is meant to be read; and next to it forensic oratory.
To analyze style still further, and add that it must
be agreeable or magnificent, is useless; for why should
it have these traits any more than "restraint," "liberality," or any other moral excellence?

It should be observed that each kind of rhetoric has its
own appropriate style. The style of written prose is not that
of spoken oratory,[1] nor are those of political and forensic
speaking the same. Both written and spoken have to be
known. To know the latter is to know how to speak good
Greek. To know the former means that you are not obliged,
as otherwise you are, to hold your tongue when you wish to
communicate something to the general public.

The written style is the more finished: the spoken better
admits of dramatic delivery—alike the kind of oratory that
reflects character and the kind that reflects emotion. Hence
actors look out for plays written in the latter style, and poets
for actors competent to act in such plays. Yet poets whose
plays are meant to be read *are* read and circulated:[2]
Chaeremon, for instance, who is as finished as a professional
speech-writer; and Licymnius among the dithyrambic poets.
Compared with those of others, the speeches of professional
writers sound thin in actual contests. Those of the orators,
on the other hand, are good to hear spoken, but look ama-
teurish enough when they pass into the hands of a reader.
This is just because they are so well suited for an actual
tussle, and therefore contain many dramatic touches, which,
being robbed of all dramatic rendering, fail to do their own
proper work, and consequently look silly. Thus strings of unconnected words, and constant repetitions of words and
phrases, are very properly condemned in written speeches,
but not in spoken speeches—speakers use them freely, for
they have a dramatic effect. In this repetition there must be
variety of tone, paving the way, as it were, to dramatic ef-

[1] More strictly, the oratory of debate—of the actual "struggles"
of the lawcourts and the assembly; the "combative," "contro-
versial" style.

[2] Are carried about as "pocket-companions."

fect, e.g., "This is the villain among you who deceived you, who cheated you, who meant to betray you completely." This is the sort of thing that Philemon the actor used to do in the *Old Men's Madness* of Anaxandrides, whenever he spoke the words "Rhadamanthus and Palamedes," and also in the prologue to the *Saints* whenever he pronounced the pronoun "I." If one does not deliver such things cleverly, it becomes a case of "the man who swallowed a poker." [3] So too with strings of unconnected words, e.g., "I came to him; I met him; I besought him." Such passages must be *acted*, not delivered with the same quality and pitch of voice, as though they had only one idea in them. They have the further peculiarity of suggesting that a number of separate statements have been made in the time usually occupied by one. Just as the use of conjunctions makes many statements into a single one, so the omission of conjunctions acts in the reverse way and makes a single one into many. It thus makes everything more important: e.g., "I came to him; I talked to him; I entreated him"—what a lot of facts! the hearer thinks—"he paid no attention to anything I said." This is the effect which Homer seeks when he writes,

> Nireus likewise from Syme three well-fashioned ships did
> bring,
> Nireus, the son of Algaia and Charopus, bright-faced
> king,
> Nireus, the comeliest man of all that to Ilium's strand.

If many things are said about a man, his name must be mentioned many times; and therefore people think that, if his name is mentioned many times, many things have been said about him. So that Homer, by means of this illusion, has made a great deal of Nireus, though he has mentioned him only in this one passage, and has preserved his memory, though he nowhere says a word about him afterward.

Now the style of oratory addressed to public assemblies is really just like scene-painting. The bigger the throng, the more distant is the point of view: so that, in the one and the other, high finish in detail is superfluous and seems better away. The forensic style is more highly finished; still more so is the style of language addressed to a single judge, with whom there is very little room for rhetorical artifices, since he can take the whole thing in better, and judge of what is to

[3] Lit., "the man who carries the beam."

the point and what is not; the struggle is less intense and so the judgment is undisturbed. This is why the same speakers do not distinguish themselves in all these branches at once; high finish is wanted least where dramatic delivery is wanted most, and here the speaker must have a good voice, and above all, a strong one. It is ceremonial oratory that is most literary, for it is meant to be read; and next to it forensic oratory.

To analyze style still further, and add that it must be agreeable or magnificent, is useless; for why should it have these traits any more than "restraint," "liberality," or any other moral excellence? Obviously agreeableness will be produced by the qualities already mentioned, if our definition of excellence of style has been correct. For what other reason should style be "clear," and "not mean" but "appropriate"? If it is prolix, it is not clear; nor yet if it is curt. Plainly the middle way suits best. Again, style will be made agreeable by the elements mentioned, namely by a good blending of ordinary and unusual words, by the rhythm, and by the persuasiveness that springs from appropriateness.

This concludes our discussion of style, both in its general aspects and in its special applications to the various branches of rhetoric.

Appendix, from the Poetics

ARISTOTLE

WHATEVER ITS STRUCTURE, a Noun must always be either (1) the ordinary word for the thing, or (2) a strange word, or (3) a metaphor, or (4) an ornamental word, or (5) a coined word, or (6) a word lengthened out, or (7) curtailed, or (8) altered in form. By the ordinary word I mean that in general use in a country; and by a strange word, one in use elsewhere. So that the same word may obviously be at once strange and ordinary, though not in reference to the same people; *sigunon,* for instance, is an ordinary word in Cyprus, and a strange word with us. Metaphor consists in giving the thing a name that belongs to something else; the transference being either from genus to species, or from species to genus, or from species to species, or on grounds of analogy. That

Translated by Ingram Bywater, Oxford University Press, 1909. By permission of the Clarendon Press, Oxford.

from genus to species is exemplified in "Here stands my ship"; for lying at anchor is the "standing" of a particular kind of thing. That from species to genus in "Truly ten thousand good deeds has Ulysses wrought," where "ten thousand," which is a particular large number, is put in place of the generic "a large number." That from species to species in "Drawing the life with the bronze," and in "Severing with the enduring bronze"; where the poet uses "draw" in the sense of "sever" and "sever" in that of "draw," both words meaning to "take away" something. That from analogy is possible whenever there are four terms so related that the second (B) is to the first (A), as the fourth (D) to the third (C); for one may then metaphorically put D in lieu of B, and B in lieu of D. Now and then, too, they qualify the metaphor by adding on to it that to which the word it supplants is relative. Thus a cup (B) is in relation to Dionysus (A) what a shield (D) is to Ares (C). The cup accordingly will be metaphorically described as the "shield *of Dionysus*" (D + A), and the shield as the "cup *of Ares*" (B + C). Or to take another instance: As old age (D) is to life (C), so is evening (B) to day (A). One will accordingly describe evening (B) as the "old age *of the day*" (D +A)—or by the Empedoclean equivalent; and old age (D) as the "evening" or "sunset *of life*" (B + C). It may be that some of the terms thus related have no special name of their own, but for all that they will be metaphorically described in just the same way. Thus to cast forth seed-corn is called "sowing"; but to cast forth its flame, as said of the sun, has no special name. This nameless act (B), however, stands in just the same relation to its object, sunlight (A), as sowing (D) to the seed-corn (C). Hence the expression in the poet, "sowing around a god-created *flame*" *(D+A)*. There is also another form of qualified metaphor. Having given the thing the alien name, one may by a negative addition deny of it one of the attributes naturally associated with its new name. An instance of this would be to call the shield not the "cup of *Ares*," as in the former case, but a "cup *that holds no wine*." . . .

*   *   *   *   *

The perfection of Diction is for it to be at once clear and not mean. The clearest indeed is that made up of the ordinary words for things, but it is mean, as is shown by the poetry of Cleophon and Sthenelus. On the other hand the Diction

becomes distinguished and non-prosaic by the use of unfamiliar terms, i.e. strange words, metaphors, lengthened
forms, and everything that deviates from the ordinary modes
of speech.—But a whole statement in such terms will be
either a riddle or a barbarism; a riddle, if made up of
metaphors, a barbarism if made up of strange words. The
very nature indeed of a riddle is this, to describe a fact
in an impossible combination of words (which cannot be
done with the real names for things, but can be with their
metaphorical substitutes); e.g., "I saw a man glue brass on
another with fire," and the like. The corresponding use of
strange words results in a barbarism.—A certain admixture,
accordingly, of unfamiliar terms is necessary. These, the
strange word, the metaphor, the ornamental equivalent, etc.,
will save the language from seeming mean and prosaic,
while the ordinary words in it will secure the requisite clearness. What helps most, however, to render the Diction at
once clear and non-prosaic is the use of the lengthened,
curtailed, and altered forms of words. Their deviation
from the ordinary words will, by making the language unlike
that in general use, give it a non-prosaic appearance; and their
having much in common with the words in general use will
give it the quality of clearness . . .

A too apparent use of these licences has certainly a ludicrous effect, but they are not alone in that; the rule of
moderation applies to all the constituents of the poetic vocabulary; even with metaphors, strange words, and the rest,
the effect will be the same, if one uses them improperly and
with a view to provoking laughter. The proper use of them
is a very different thing. To realize the difference one should
take an epic verse and see how it reads when the normal
words are introduced. The same should be done too with the
strange word, the metaphor, and the rest; for one has only to
put the ordinary words in their place to see the truth of
what we are saying. The same iambic, for instance, is found
in Aeschylus and Euripides, and as it stands in the former it
is a poor line; whereas Euripides, by the change of a single
word, the substitution of a strange for what is by usage the
ordinary word, has made it seem a fine one. Aeschylus having
said in his *Philoctetes*:

The cancer that eats the flesh of my foot,

Euripides has merely altered the "eats" here into "feasts on."
. . . It is a great thing, indeed, to make a proper use of these

poetical forms, as also of compounds and strange words. But the greatest thing by far is to be a master of metaphor. It is the one thing that cannot be learned from others; and it is also a sign of genius, since a good metaphor implies an intuitive perception of the similarity in dissimilars.

Of the kinds of words we have enumerated it may be observed that compounds are most in place in the dithyramb, strange words in heroic, and metaphors in iambic poetry. Heroic poetry, indeed, may avail itself of them all. But in iambic verse, which models itself as far as possible on the spoken language, only those kinds of words are in place which are allowable also in an oration, i.e., the ordinary word, the metaphor, and the ornamental equivalent.

The Kinds of Style

CICERO

WE MUST NOW turn to the task of portraying the perfect orator and the highest eloquence. The very word "eloquent" shows that he excels because of this one quality, that is, in the use of language, and that the other qualities are overshadowed by this. For the all-inclusive word is not "discoverer," or "arranger," or "actor," but in Greek he is called *rhetor* from the word "to speak," and in Latin he is said to be "eloquent." For everyone claims for himself some part of the other qualities that go to make up an orator, but the supreme power in speaking, that is eloquence, is granted to him alone.

Certain philosophers, to be sure, had an ornate style—for example Theophrastus received his name from his divinely beautiful language, and Aristotle challenged even Isocrates, and the Muses were said to speak with the voice of Xenophon, and Plato was, in dignity and grace, easily the first of all writers or speakers—yet their style lacks the vigor and sting necessary for oratorical efforts in public life. They converse with scholars, whose minds they prefer to soothe rather than arouse; they converse in this way about unex-

Sections 61 through 101 of Orator, from Brutus, Orator, translated by H. M. Hubbell, Loeb Classical Library, Harvard University Press, 1952. Reprinted by permission of the publishers and The Loeb Classical Library.

citing and non-controversial subjects, for the purpose of instructing rather than captivating; and some think they exceed due bounds in aiming to give some little pleasure by their style. It is therefore easy to distinguish the eloquence which we are treating in this work from the style of the philosophers. The latter is gentle and academic; it has no equipment of words or phrases that catch the popular fancy; it is not arranged in rhythmical periods, but is loose in structure; there is no anger in it, no hatred, no ferocity, no pathos, no shrewdness; it might be called a chaste, pure, and modest virgin. Consequently it is called conversation rather than oratory. While all speaking is oratory, yet it is the speech of the orator alone which is marked by this special name.

More care must be taken to distinguish the oratorical style from the similar style of the Sophists mentioned above, who desire to use all the ornaments which the orator uses in forensic practice. But there is this difference, that, whereas their object is not to arouse the audience but to soothe it, not so much to persuade as to delight, they do it more openly than we and more frequently; they are on the lookout for ideas that are neatly put rather than reasonable; they frequently wander from the subject, they introduce mythology, they use far-fetched metaphors and arrange them as painters do color combinations; they make their clauses balanced and of equal length, frequently ending with similar sounds. History is nearly related to this style. It involves a narrative in an ornate style, with here and there a description of a country or a battle. It has also occasional harangues and speeches of exhortation. But the aim is a smooth and flowing style, not the terse and vigorous language of the orator. The eloquence which we are seeking must be distinguished from this no less than from the poetic style. For the poets have given rise to the inquiry as to the difference between them and the orators. It once seemed to be a matter of rhythm and verse, but now rhythm has become common in oratory. For everything which can be measured by the ear, even if it does not make a complete verse—that is certainly a fault in prose —is called rhythm, in Greek *rhuthmos*. For that reason some, I know, have held that the language of Plato and Democritus, which, though not in verse, has a vigorous movement and uses striking stylistic ornaments, has more right to be considered poetry than has comedy, which differs from ordinary conversation only by being in some sort of verse. However, this is not the chief mark of a poet, although he deserves more credit for seeking the virtues of the orator, limited as he is by the form of the verse. As for my own opinion, although some poets use grand and figurative language, I recognize that they have a greater freedom in the formation and arrangement of words than we orators have, and also that, with the approval of some critics, they pay more attention to sound than to sense. And indeed if they have one point in common—that is discernment in selection of subject matter and choice of words—we cannot for that reason pass over their dissimilarity in other things. But there is no doubt a difference between poetry and oratory, and if there is any dispute about it, the investigation is not necessary for our present purpose. Distinguishing the orator, then, in point of style from the philosopher, the sophist, the historian, and the poet, we must set forth what he is to be.

The man of eloquence whom we seek, following the suggestion of Antonius, will be one who is able to speak in court or in deliberative bodies so as to prove, to please, and to sway or persuade. To prove is the first necessity, to please is charm, to sway is victory; for it is the one thing of all that avails most in winning verdicts. For these three functions of the orator there are three styles, the plain style for proof, the middle style for pleasure, the vigorous style for persuasion; and in this last is summed up the entire virtue of the orator. Now the man who controls and combines these three varied styles needs rare judgment and great endowment; for he will decide what is needed at any point, and will be able to speak in any way which the case requires. For after all the foundation of eloquence, as of everything else, is wisdom. In an oration, as in life, nothing is harder than to determine what is appropriate. The Greeks call it *prepon:* let us call it "decorum" or "propriety." Much brilliant work has been done in laying down rules about this; the subject is in fact worth mastering. From ignorance of this mistakes are made not only in life but very frequently in writing, both in poetry and in prose. Moreover the orator must have an eye to propriety not only in thought but in language. For the same style and the same thoughts must not be used in portraying every condition in life, or every rank, position, or age, and in fact a similar distinction must be made in respect of place, time, and audience. The universal rule, in oratory as in life, is to consider propriety. This depends on the subject under discussion, and on the character of both the speaker and the audience. The philosophers are accustomed to consider this extensive subject under the head of duties—not when they discuss absolute perfection, for that is one and unchanging; the literary critics consider it in connection with poetry, orators in dealing with every kind of speech, and with every part thereof. How inappropriate it would be to employ general topics and the grand style when discussing cases of stillicide [1] before a single referee, or to use mean and meager language when referring to the majesty of the Roman people. This would be wrong in every respect; but others err in regard to character—either their own or that of the jury, or of their opponents; and not merely in the statement of facts, but often in the use of words. Although a word has no force apart from the thing, yet the same thing is often either approved or rejected according as it is expressed in one way or another. Moreover, in all cases the question must be "How far?" For although the limits of propriety differ for each subject, yet in general too much is more offensive than too little. Apelles said that those painters also make this error, who do not know when they have done enough. This is an important topic, Brutus, as you well know, and requires another large volume; but for our present discussion the following will be enough: Since we say, "This is appropriate"—a word we use in connection with everything we do or say, great or small— since, I repeat, we say, "This is appropriate," and "That is not appropriate," and it appears how important propriety is everywhere (and that it depends upon something else and is wholly another question whether you should say "appropriate" or "right"—for by "right" we indicate the perfect line of duty which everyone must follow everywhere, but "propriety" is what is fitting and agreeable to an occasion or person; it is important often in actions as well as in words, in the expression of the face, in gesture and in gait, and impropriety has the opposite effect); the poet avoids impropriety as the greatest fault which he can commit; he errs also if he puts the speech of a good man in the mouth of a villain, or that of a wise man in the mouth of a fool; so also the painter in portraying the sacrifice of Iphigenia, after representing Calchas as sad, Ulysses as still more so, Menelaus as in grief, felt that Agamemnon's head must be veiled, because the supreme sorrow could not be portrayed by his brush; even the actor seeks for propriety; what, then, think you, should the orator do? Since this is so important, let the

[1] The legal technicalities about water dripping from a roof on adjoining property.

orator consider what to do in the speech and its different divisions: it is certainly obvious that totally different styles must be used, not only in the different parts of the speech, but also that whole speeches must be now in one style, now in another.

It follows that we must seek the type and pattern of each kind—a great and arduous task, as we have often said; but we should have considered what to do when we were embarking; now we must certainly spread our sails to the wind, no matter where it may carry us. First, then, we must delineate the one whom some deem to be the only true "Attic" orator. He is restrained and plain, he follows the ordinary usage, really differing more than is supposed from those who are not eloquent at all. Consequently the audience, even if they are no speakers themselves, are sure they can speak in that fashion. For that plainness of style seems easy to imitate at first thought, but when attempted nothing is more difficult. For although it is not full-blooded, it should nevertheless have some of the sap of life, so that, though it lacks great strength, it may still be, so to speak, in sound health. First, then, let us release him from, let us say, the bonds of rhythm. Yes, the orator uses certain rhythms, as you know, and these we shall discuss shortly; they have to be employed with a definite plan, but in a different style of speech; in this style they are to be wholly eschewed. It should be loose but not rambling; so that it may seem to move freely but not to wander without restraint. He should also avoid, so to speak, cementing his words together too smoothly, for the hiatus and clash of vowels has something agreeable about it and shows a not unpleasant carelessness on the part of a man who is paying more attention to thought than to words. But his very freedom from periodic structure and cementing his words together will make it necessary for him to look to the other requisites. For the short and concise clauses must not be handled carelessly—there is such a thing even as a careful negligence. Just as some women are said to be handsomer when unadorned—this very lack of ornament becomes them—so this plain style gives pleasure even when unembellished: there is something in both cases which lends greater charm, but without showing itself. Also all noticeable ornament, pearls as it were, will be excluded; not even curling-irons will be used; all cosmetics, artificial white and red, will be rejected; only elegance and neatness will remain. The language will be pure Latin, plain and clear;

propriety will always be the chief aim. Only one quality will
be lacking, which Theophrastus mentions fourth among the
qualities of style—the charm and richness of figurative ornament. He will employ an abundance of apposite maxims dug
out from every conceivable hiding place; this will be the
dominant feature in this orator. He will be modest in his use
of what may be called the orator's stock-in-trade. For we
do have after a fashion a stock-in-trade, in the stylistic embellishments, partly in thought and partly in words. The
embellishment given by words is twofold, from single words
and from words as they are connected together. In the case
of "proper" and ordinary words, that individual word wins
approval which has the best sound, or best expresses the idea;
in the case of variations from the common idiom we approve
the metaphor, or a borrowing from the source, or a new
formation or the archaic and obsolete (yet even obsolete and
archaic words are to be classed as "proper" except that we
rarely use them). Words when connected together embellish a
style if they produce a certain symmetry which disappears
when the words are changed, though the thought remains the
same; for the figures of thought which remain even if the
words are changed are, to be sure, numerous, but relatively
few are noticeable. Consequently the orator of the plain style,
provided he is elegant and finished, will not be bold in coining
words, and in metaphor will be modest, sparing in the use of
archaisms, and somewhat subdued in using the other embellishments of language and of thought. Metaphor he may
possibly employ more frequently because it is of the commonest occurrence in the language of townsman and rustic
alike. The rustics, for example, say that the vines are "be-
jeweled," [2] the fields "thirsty," the crops "happy," the grain
"luxuriant." Any of these metaphors is bold enough, but there
is a similarity to the source from which the word is borrowed,
or if a thing has no proper term the borrowing seems to be
done in order to make the meaning clear, and not for en-
tertainment. The restrained speaker may use this figure a little
more freely than others, but not so boldly as if he were
speaking in the grandest style. Consequently impropriety—
the nature of which should be plain from what has been said
about propriety—appears here too, when a metaphor is
far-fetched, and one is used in the plain style which would be
appropriate in another. This unaffected orator whom certain
people call "Attic," and rightly so, except that he is not

[2] The buds are compared with jewels.

the only "Attic"—this orator will also use the symmetry that enlivens a group of words with the embellishments that the Greeks call *schemata*, figures of speech, as it were. (They apply the same word also to figures of thought.) He will, however, be somewhat sparing in using these. For as in the appointments of a banquet he will avoid extravagant display, and desire to appear thrifty, but also in good taste, and will choose what he is going to use. There are, as a matter of fact, a good many ornaments suited to the frugality of this very orator I am describing. For this shrewd orator must avoid all the figures that I described above, such as clauses of equal length, with similar endings, or identical cadences, and the studied charm produced by the change of a letter, lest the elaborate symmetry and a certain grasping after a pleasant effect be too obvious. Likewise if repetition of words requires some emphasis and a raising of the voice, it will be foreign to this plain style of oratory. Other figures of speech he will be able to use freely, provided only he breaks up and divides the periodic structure and uses the commonest words and the mildest of metaphors. He may also brighten his style with such figures of thought as will not be exceedingly glaring. He will not represent the State as speaking or call the dead from the lower world, nor will he crowd a long series of iterations into a single period. This requires stronger lungs, and is not to be expected of him whom we are describing or demanded from him. For he will be rather subdued in voice as in style. But many of these figures of thought will be appropriate to this plain style, although he will use them somewhat harshly: such is the man we are portraying. His delivery is not that of tragedy nor of the stage; he will employ only slight movements of the body, but will trust a great deal to his expression. This must not be what people call pulling a wry face, but must reveal in a well-bred manner the feeling with which each thought is uttered.

A speech of this kind should also be sprinkled with the salt of pleasantry, which plays an uncommonly great part in speaking. There are two kinds, humor and wit. He will use both; the former in a graceful and charming narrative, the latter in hurling the shafts of ridicule. Of this latter there are several kinds, but now we are discussing another subject. We here merely suggest that the orator should use ridicule with a care not to let it be too frequent lest it become buffoonery; nor ridicule of a smutty nature, lest it be that of low farce; nor pert, lest it be impudent; nor aimed at misfortune, lest it be brutal; nor at crime, lest laughter take the place of loathing; nor should the wit be inappropriate to his own character, to that of the jury, or to the occasion; for all these points come under the head of impropriety. He will also avoid far-fetched jests, and those not made up at the moment but brought from home; for these are generally frigid. He will spare friends and dignitaries, will avoid rankling insult; he will merely prod his opponents, nor will he do it constantly, nor to all of them nor in every manner. With these exceptions he will use wit and humor in a way in which none of these modern "Attics" do, as far as I know, though this is certainly an outstanding mark of Attic style. For my part, I judge this to be the pattern of the plain orator—plain but great and truly Attic; since whatever is witty and wholesome in speech is peculiar to the Athenian orators. Not all of them, however, are humorous. Lysias is adequate and so is Hyperides; Demades is said to have excelled them all: Demosthenes is considered inferior. Yet it seems to me that none is cleverer than he; still he is not witty so much as humorous; the former requires a bolder talent, the latter a greater art.

The second style is fuller and somewhat more robust than the simple style just described, but plainer than the grandest style, which we shall presently discuss. In this style there is perhaps a minimum of vigor, and a maximum of charm. For it is richer than the unadorned style, but plainer than the ornate and opulent style. All the ornaments are appropriate to this type of oration, and it possesses charm to a high degree. There have been many conspicuous examples of this style in Greece, but in my judgment Demetrius of Phalerum led them all. His oratory not only proceeds in calm and peaceful flow, but is lighted up by what might be called the stars of "transferred" words (or metaphor) and borrowed words. By "transferred" I now mean, as often before, words transferred by resemblance from another thing in order to produce a pleasing effect, or because of lack of a "proper" word; by "borrowed" I mean the cases in which there is substituted for a "proper" word another with the same meaning drawn from some other suitable sphere. It is, to be sure, a "transfer" when Ennius says,

I am bereft of citadel and town,

but a "transfer" of quite a different kind than when he says,

Dread Africa trembled with terrible tumult.

The latter is called "hypallage" by the rhetoricians, because words are exchanged for words, as it were; the grammarians call it "metonymy" because nouns are transferred. Aristotle, however, classifies them all under metaphor and includes also the misuse of terms, which they call "catachresis," for example, when we say a "minute" mind instead of "small"; and we misuse related words on occasion either because this gives pleasure or because it is appropriate. When there is a continuous stream of metaphors, a wholly different style of speech is produced; consequently the Greeks call it "allegory." They are right as to the name, but from the point of view of classification Aristotle does better in calling them all metaphors. The Phalerian uses these very frequently, and they are attractive to a degree; and although he has many metaphors, yet the cases of metonymy are more numerous than in any other orator. To the same oratorical style—I am discussing the mean and tempered style—belong all figures of language, and many of thought. This speaker will likewise develop his arguments with breadth and erudition, and use commonplaces without undue emphasis. But why speak at length? It is commonly the philosophic schools which produce such orators, and unless he be brought face to face with the more robust speaker, the orator whom I am describing will find approval on his own merits. It is, as a matter of fact, a brilliant and florid, highly colored and polished style in which all the charms of language and thought are intertwined. The sophists are the source from which all this has flowed into the forum, but scorned by the simple and rejected by the grand, it found a resting-place in this middle class of which I am speaking.

The orator of the third style is magnificent, opulent, stately, and ornate; he undoubtedly has the greatest power. This is the man whose brilliance and fluency have caused admiring nations to let eloquence attain the highest power in the state; I mean the kind of eloquence which rushes along with the roar of a mighty stream, which all look up to and admire, and which they despair of attaining. This eloquence has power to sway men's minds and move them in every possible way. Now it storms the feelings, now it creeps in; it implants new ideas and uproots the old. But there is a great difference between this and the other styles. One who has studied the plain and pointed style so as to be able to speak adroitly and neatly, and has not conceived of anything higher, if he has attained perfection in this style, is a great orator, if not the greatest. He is far from standing on slippery ground, and, when once he gets a foothold, he will never fall. The orator of the middle style, whom I call moderate and tempered, once he has drawn up his forces, will not dread the doubtful and uncertain pitfalls of speaking. Even if not completely successful, as often happens, he will not run a great risk; he has not far to fall. But this orator of ours whom we consider the chief—grand, impetuous and fiery, if he has natural ability for this alone, or trains himself solely in this, or devotes his energies to this only, and does not temper his abundance with the other two styles, he is much to be despised. For the plain orator is esteemed wise because he speaks clearly and adroitly; the one who employs the middle style is charming; but the copious speaker, if he has nothing else, seems to be scarcely sane. For a man who can say nothing calmly and mildly, who pays no attention to arrangement, precision, clarity, or pleasantry—especially when some cases have to be handled entirely in this latter style, and others, largely so—if without first preparing the ears of his audience he begins trying to work them up to a fiery passion, he seems to be a raving madman among the sane, like a drunken reveler in the midst of sober men.

We have him now, Brutus, the man whom we are seeking, but in imagination, not in actual possession. If I had once laid my hands on him, not even he with his mighty eloquence would have persuaded me to let him go. But we have certainly discovered that eloquent orator whom Antonius never saw. Who is he, then? I will describe him briefly, and then expand the description at greater length. He in fact is eloquent who can discuss commonplace matters simply, lofty subjects impressively, and topics ranging between in a tempered style. You will say, "There never was such a man." I grant it; for I am arguing for my ideal, not what I have actually seen, and I return to that Platonic Idea of which I had spoken; though we do not see it, still it is possible to grasp it with the mind. For it is not an eloquent person whom I seek, nor anything subject to death and decay, but that absolute quality, the possession of which makes a man eloquent. And this is nothing but abstract eloquence, which we can behold only with the mind's eye. He, then, will be an eloquent speaker—to repeat my former definition—who can discuss trivial matters in a plain style, matters of moderate significance in the tempered style, and weighty affairs in the grand manner.

On the Sublime

LONGINUS

1

THE LITTLE TREATISE of Caecilius "On the Sublime," when we examined it together, my dear Postumius Terentianus, as you will recall, was observed by us to be too abject for its theme of sublimity, and, as it quite failed to deal with the crucial points, to be of no great utility to the reader. And yet utility should be a writer's chief aim, as two things are required of everyone who composes a technical treatise: first, to show what the subject he treats of is, and second in order, but prior in importance, to show how and by what procedures it could be acquired by us. Yet Caecilius tries at great length to show what the sublime is, as though we did not know, but for some reason has omitted, as unnecessary, a discussion of how we might succeed in advancing our own natural capacities to some degree of sublimity. Perhaps, however, he is not so much deserving of censure for his omissions, as of praise for having conceived his plan and worked at it with zeal.

But as you have insisted that I too should set down, for your sake, some notes on sublimity, it is time to consider whether I be judged, in my speculations, to have produced anything of use for men in public life. You will yourself, my friend, help me to pass the frankest judgment on the details; you are fitted by nature for that task and it is your office to do so. The query "what is it we have in common with the gods?" was well answered by the person who replied "the conferring of benefits and the telling of the truth."

In addressing myself to you, my dear friend, cultivated and instructed as you are, I am, I may say, released from any further need to premise at greater length that sublimity is a certain superiority and preeminence in discourse, and

Translated by Benedict Einarson. Copyright 1945 by Packard and Company. Reprinted by permission of Benedict Einarson.

that it is from no other source than this that the greatest
poets and writers of prose have won the first place and
embraced eternity in their fame. For what is of transcendent
genius produces in the hearers not persuasion but transport;
and in all manners, what is wondrous, with its shattering of
the hearer's composure, ever prevails over what is persuasive
and pleasant, inasmuch as for the most part it rests with us
to be persuaded or not, but that which is wondrous and of
great genius, since it exercises domination and brings irresistible force to bear, gains an authority which places it
far above every hearer. And we observe that an author's skill
in invention and in the ordering and disposition of his subjects is seen not from a single passage or from two, but
scarcely appears even from the whole fabric of his discourse;
while sublimity brought forth at the right moment scatters
the subjects like a bolt of lightning, and immediately reveals the whole capacity of a speaker at a glance. These
and other similar observations, my dear Terentianus, you
could, with your experience, expound yourself.

2

I must, to begin with, discuss the problem of whether
there is any art of sublimity or of depth,[1] since certain
authors hold that men who reduce these matters to the
precepts of an art are wholly mistaken. These authors object that things of great genius are born and not acquired
through instruction, and that the only art of acquiring them
is to be born with the natural gift; and add that the products of nature are degraded and made quite pitiable when
their robust build is reduced to puny skin and bones in arts
of rhetoric. But I say that this view will be refuted if one
reflects that nature, as it is for the most part its own master
in matters concerned with the passions and with elevation,
is not on that account wholly without rule or procedure;
that while it is the first and primary element of production
in all things, yet a proper procedure can determine and provide us, in every case, with the due measure and the proper
moment, and further, the least erroneous course of training
and mode of application; and that greatness, when left to itself with no help from knowledge, is rather precarious—un-
supported and unballasted—left only to its impetus and un-
instructed boldness; for as greatness often needs the spur,

---

[1] It is disputed among scholars whether "depth" here is opposed
to sublimity or is synonymous with it.

so too it needs the rein. For the view Demosthenes expresses about human life in general, that the greatest good is good fortune, and second, yet not inferior, good judgment—which, if absent, makes good fortune of no avail—this we could apply to discourse; nature taking the place of good fortune, and art that of good judgment; but the most important point is that the very fact that in discourse certain things rest in the power of nature alone must be learned by us from art, and from nothing else; if then, as I said, that person who finds fault with the studious should reflect on this, he would no longer, I fancy, consider the investigation of the present subject superfluous and useless . . .

[two leaves of the ms. are missing here]

3

. . . and check the furnace' far-flung glow.
For should I see but one that holds to hearth
I'll swing on high one torrent tentacle
Fire his roof and burn it to a coal:
But yet have I not bellowed my bold song.[2]

This has ceased to be tragic: it is tragic parody—the "tentacles" and "vomiting forth to heaven" and the making of a flute-player out of Boreas, and the rest; the expression has rather been muddied and the imagery confused, than the effect been made terrible and intense; and if you examine the several expressions in the clear light of day, you will find them gradually recede from the dreadful to the contemptible. And if unseasonable turgidity is inexcusable in tragedy, a subject naturally stately and receptive of mouth-filling language, much less, I think, would it be admissible in speeches to be delivered in real life. It is in virtue of this that the expressions of Gorgias of Leontini excite derision, as when he calls Xerxes "the Persians' Zeus" and vultures "living graves," and the same fate befalls certain passages of Callisthenes, which are not lofty or sublime, but merely high-flown, and still more certain passages of Clitarchus: this author is full of padding, and to quote Sophocles, blows

On little pipes, but uses not the mouthpiece.

[2] Aeschylus, *Orithyia*. "Vomiting forth to heaven" and the description of Boreas as a flute-player no doubt occurred in the portion of the fragment lost in the lacuna.

Again, the writing of Amphicrates and Hegesias and Matris
are of this description: in many passages they are in their
own estimation inspired; but they are not really possessed;
they are merely fooling. In general it appears that turgidity
is extremely difficult to guard against. For all who aim at
grandeur, in avoiding the censure of feebleness and of dry-
ness, are by nature unaccountably swept down in the direction of turgidity, obeying the dictum that "to fail in the
attainment of great things is still a noble failure." But both
in human bodies and in discourses swellings and turgidities
that are inflated and unreal are an evil, and are like as not
to bring about in us the opposite condition: no man, it is
said, is so dry as he that has the dropsy.

While the turgid intends to rise higher than the sublime,
the sophomoric is in downright opposition to grandeur, for
it is utterly abject and small-souled and in reality the
meanest of faults. What then is the sophomoric? But the
answer is evident: it is a kind of thought characteristic of
the schools of rhetoric, which, through over-refinement, ends
in frigidity. Men fall into this vice through aiming at what
goes beyond the essential, at elaborate artifice, and especially
at charm, and drift away into trumpery and affectation.

By the side of these there is in passionate writing a third
kind of vice, which Theodorus used to call "the intrusive
thyrsus." [3] It is passion unseasonable and hollow, either
present where passion has no place or else used immoderately
where what is wanted is passion in moderation. For often,
as though from some kind of inebriation, men are swept off
toward passions which have ceased to belong to the subject in
hand, but are private to themselves and characteristic of
the schools, and then carry on in unbecoming fashion before an audience left unaffected. Unbecoming it is, and little
wonder, when the speaker is beside himself, his audience
not. But we have reserved a different place for the treatment
of matters pertaining to passion.

4

Of the other matter we mentioned, frigidity, Timaeus is
full, an able author in other respects, and on occasion not

---

[3] In the Greek *parenthyrson*, that is "that wherein the thyrsus
is wrongly included." The thyrsus was a wand wreathed in ivy and
vine leaves with a pine-cone at the top. It was used in Bacchic rites
and revels.

incapable of an impetus toward grandeur; a man of learning and ingenious; yet, while much given to exposing the faults of others, he is unaware of his own, and is often led astray by his infatuation for always stirring up some strange and original thought into extreme puerility. I shall quote from him only one or two passages, as Caecilius has anticipated the greater number. In praising Alexander the Great, Timaeus says that Alexander

> occupied the whole of Asia in fewer years than it took Isocrates to compose the Panegyric in favor of the Persian War.

This comparison of the great Macedonian with the rhetorician is astonishing. Evidently, my dear Timaeus, the Spartans were far inferior in valor to Isocrates, since it took them thirty years to win Messene, while Isocrates took only ten to compose his Panegyric. What is Timaeus' comment on the Athenians captured in Sicily? This:

> Since they had committed sacrilege against Hermes and mutilated his statues, they were brought to condign punishment mainly through the work of one man, Hermocrates the son of Hermon, a lineal descendant of the outraged god.

I begin to wonder dear Terentianus, why he does not write about Dionysius the tyrant to the following effect:

> Since he had committed sacrilege against Zeus and Heracles, it was Dion [4] and Heraclides that deposed him.

But why speak of Timaeus, when those heroes of old, Xenophon and Plato, trained though they were in the palaestra of Socrates, yet forget themselves at times for such small triumphs as these? Xenophon writes in his *Constitution of Sparta*:

> From these young men you could no more hear speech than from men of stone; you could no more attract their glances than from men of bronze; and you would think them more modest than the very maidens [5] in their eyes.

It was worthy of Amphicrates, but not of Xenophon, to call

---

[4] The name "Dion" is derived from Zeus (genitive *Dios*).

[5] In Greek "maiden" and "pupil of the eye" are expressed by the same word, *korē*.

the pupils of our eyes modest virgins. But good heavens! To believe that the eyes of the whole lot of them were modest, when it is generally recognized that nowhere is the shamelessness of certain people so made manifest as in their eyes! Homer refers to a forward man in the words:

Heavy with wine, with the eyes of a dog.

Yet Timaeus, as though laying hands on some purloined property of his own, has not left Xenophon in possession of even this piece of frigidity. Thus Timaeus says in telling of Agathocles' abduction of his cousin, who had been affianced to another, at the ceremony of unveiling:

Who could have perpetrated such a deed, save one who had trollops, not maidens, in his eyes?

Yet what does Plato, so divine in other respects, do? When he means "tablets" he says:

This they shall commit to writing, depositing in the temples memories of cypress wood.

And again:

As regards walls, Megillus, I should concur with Sparta, and let the walls lie sleeping in the earth, nor bid them rise.

And Herodotus' phrase is not far removed from these, when he calls beautiful women "pangs in the eyes." Yet this is to some extent palliated, since it is the barbarians who use these words in Herodotus, and they are tipsy; but it is not seemly, even from the mouths of such as these, through pettiness of soul to behave with indecorum in the face of all time.

5

Yet all such derogations to dignity arise in discourse from a single cause: zeal for novelty in the thoughts, in which above all else our contemporaries run wild. For the sources of the good are, one might say, the very sources from which the bad is commonly produced. Thus it is that beauties of style and sublimities and furthermore its graces are conducive to successful writing, and yet these very things are also principles and foundations, as of good writing, so of the opposite. Of this kind further are variations and the use of hyperboles and of plurals; we shall show in what follows the risk they appear to involve. For this reason it is necessary for us at this point to discuss and set down as our basis a way in which we can escape the vices intermingled with the sublime.

6

We can do so, my dear friend, if first we can obtain some clear understanding and criterion of what is truly sublime. Yet the matter is by no means easy: the judgment of literature is the last result supervening upon much experience; still, speaking merely as one who makes a recommendation, it may not be impossible to identify the sublime from the following considerations.

7

We must realize, my dear friend, that just as in our everyday life there is nothing great which it is also great to despise —thus wealth, position, reputation, absolute power, and all else that brings with it magnificent trappings, would not in the judgment of the wise man be surpassing goods, since the contempt of them is itself no mean good: thus it is not so much the possessors of such things who are admired as rather those persons who could possess them if they wished, and through greatness of soul look down on them—so too we must consider, in the case of elevated passages in verse and in prose, whether any of them present that sort of appearance of grandeur in which there is much idle adventitious accretion, but on being opened up and looked at closely, are found to be merely inflated and pretentious, and more nobly disregarded than admired. For in some natural fashion our soul is elevated by the truly sublime, and assuming a lofty stature, is filled with delight and proud elation, as if she herself had brought forth what she has merely heard. When then a passage is repeatedly heard by a man of judgment and experience in literature, and does not dispose his soul to a corresponding grandeur of thought nor leave behind in his mind more reflection on the thing said than was found in the words, but if you carefully consider to what it leads, diminishes in effect, such a passage would not be truly sublime, preserving its character, as it does, no further than the ear. For truly great is that whereon follows much reflection, and from the effect of which it is hard, or rather impossible, to rally, and the memory of which is strong and difficult to erase. And in general you must consider those sublimities fine and genuine which are pleasing at

all times and to all men. For when persons coming from
different pursuits, lives, interests, ages and walks of literature have all alike on the same matters the same view, then
this consensus of discordant elements assumes the character
of a "judgment," and the weight of conviction it brings
to bear on the admired passage becomes powerful and indis-
putable.

8

There are five "springheads" (as one might call them) most
productive of lofty language, competence in speaking, without which nothing at all is of any avail, being presupposed
as a foundation (as it were) common to all five. First and
most important is lofty enterprise in the thought, as we
have set forth in our work on Xenophon; second is strong
and inspired passion. These first two are sources of sublimity for the most part native to the man; the remaining
three also come through art. They are: a certain quality in
the construction of figures—of these there are two kinds:
figures of thought and figures of speech—; furthermore noble
expression, the parts of which are the choice of words, and
a diction which makes use of tropes and is elaborate, while
the fifth cause of sublimity, which binds together and en-
closes all that precedes, is majestic and elevated combination
or composition.

Let us examine the matters included in each of these, but
first note that Caecilius has omitted some, as, to take an
instance, passion. If he did so from considering that elevation and passion are one and the same, and held the
view that they are always coexistent and naturally of a piece,
he is in error; for certain passions are found dissociated from
elevation, and abject—as lamentations, pain, and fear—while
conversely, there are many instances of elevation where passion is quite absent, such as, to take one passage out of
countless others, the bold expressions of Homer, where he
speaks of the Aloadae:

> They strove to heap
> Ossa upon Olympus, and on Ossa
> The woods of Pelion, and climb to heaven.

and the yet grander expression that follows:

> And this they would have done.

Again, in the orators the encomia and the solemn and

epideictic passages are most certainly stately and sublime, but for the most part are devoid of passion; and it is for this reason that those orators who are full of passion are the least successful in encomia, while, on the other hand, those who excel at praise are the least impassioned. Again, if Caecilius held that the passionate never contributes to sublimity at all, and for this reason did not feel it deserved mention, he is much deceived: for I would confidently lay it down that nothing is so grand as noble passion—when in place—which, as in the stress of madness and inspiration, breathes forth its language as one possessed by a god, and, as it were, utters it with all the divine afflatus of a prophet.

9

Yet since the first of our sources, greatness of genius, has a greater portion in sublimity than the rest, we must here too, even though this is a gift rather than a thing acquired, nevertheless so far as possible train our souls for grandeur, and make them ever pregnant (as it were) of some touch of noble ardor. How, you ask, are we to do this? I have elsewhere written something to the following effect: sublimity is the ring of greatness in the soul. Thus even when not put into words, the thought is admired by itself for the very greatness of soul in it, as the silence of Ajax in the Visit to the Dead is grand and more sublime than any speech. First then we must lay down the source of sublimity as our prerequisite: that the true orator must have no abject and ignoble spirit. For it is quite impossible for men whose thoughts and acts throughout their lives are mean and slavish to bring forth aught that is admirable and worthy of all time; while it is only to be expected that men whose thoughts are weighty should have grandeur in their speech as well.

[six leaves of the ms. are missing here]

Of a quite different sort is the expression Hesiod (if we are to assume the *Shield* authentic) uses of Mist:

> And from her nostrils flowed the rheum.

For Hesiod here makes his figure not awful, but detestable, But how does Homer magnify things supernal?

> As far as sees a watcher on a height
> In the dim distance, scanning the wine-dark deep,

> So far the arching coursers of the gods
> Leap at a bound.

He measures their course by a measure fit for the universe.
Who then, because of this surpassing magnitude, would not
exclaim that if the divine steeds should but leap twice, they
would find no space left them in the world? Of transcendent
genius too are the images in the Battle of the Gods:

> And above them
> Great Heaven and Olympus clarioned;
> Below, grim Aïdoneus was affrighted,
> Lept from his throne and screamed, lest presently
> The Lord of Earthquakes rive the ground asunder
> And so reveal to mortals and immortals
> The mouldering habitations of the dead,
> So fell the very gods shrink back in horror.

Do you not behold, my friend, how, as the earth is broke
open from its depths and very Tartarus laid bare, while the
whole universe is overturned and rent asunder, all things
at once, Heaven and Hades, things mortal and things immortal, are involved in the heat and peril of that struggle?

But while all this is fraught with terror, yet, unless one
interpret it as allegory, it is quite impious and inappropriate.
For Homer appears to me, in presenting the gods to us as
subject to wounds, discord, vengeance, tears, bondage, and a
confused jumble of disasters, to have (so far as it lay with
him) made gods of the men of the Trojan age, and men of
the gods. Yet for our human misfortunes there is a haven
of refuge, death; the gods he has made eternal not in divinity,
but in woe. Much superior to the Battle of the Gods are
those passages which present the divine as something incon-
taminate and truly great, with no admixture of mortality,
as for example—the topic has been worked out by many
predecessors—the passage about Poseidon:

> And the great mountains trembled and the woods
> And peaks and Trojan town and ships of Greece
> Under the immortal feet of the passing god.
> Over the waves he drove, and the sea-beasts, sporting,
> Rose round him from their haunts, and knew their lord;
> For joy the sea made way; the coursers flew.

Thus too the lawgiver of the Jews, no ordinary person, since
he had the capacity worthily to receive the divine power

and show it forth, writes at the very beginning of his Legis-
lation: "And God said . . ." What was it God said? "Let
there be light, and there was light," "let there be land, and
there was land."

Perhaps, my friend, I should not be thought tedious if I
quote still one further passage from Homer and about things
human, for the sake of learning how he accustoms us to
enter upon heroic greatness with him. A sudden mist and
bewildering darkness has fallen and is holding back the
Greek onslaught: Ajax, in this strait, says:

> Oh Father Zeus, deliver us from darkness;
> Make the sky clear; grant vision to our eyes;
> So it be in the light, even slay us.

This feeling is most truly appropriate to Ajax, for he does
not pray for life—such a request would be too abject for
the dignity of that hero—but since in the obscurity he was
reduced to inaction and found himself unable to turn his
bravery to any noble use, he chafes that he must be idle in
battle, and begs for the speedy return of light, feeling that
he will on all accounts find a shroud worthy of his valor,
though Zeus be with the foe.

But here Homer blows like a brisk and favorable gale upon
his battles, and what he says of another applies to himself:

> He rages like bold Ares or the fire
> That rages on the wooded mountain tops;
> Foam gathers to his lips.

In the *Odyssey* however—for we must, for many reasons,
consider it too—he shows that a fondness for tales is peculiar to a great nature in its old age, when decline has set in.
For among the many considerations which make it evident
that he composed this subject later, not least is his inclusion
throughout the *Odyssey*, as subordinate incidents taken from
the Trojan war, of many left-overs of the disasters in the
Iliad, and indeed, his going on to allot to the heroes the
pity and lamentations which are their right, treating these
as matters known long in advance. For the *Odyssey* is nothing other than the epilogue of the *Iliad*:

> There lies the valiant Ajax, there Achilles,
> There lies Patroclus, god-like counsellor;
> There my dear son.

For the same reason, I believe, since he wrote the *Iliad*

at the height of his inspiration, he made the whole work
dramatic and gave it the spirit of actual contention, while
the Odyssey is for the most part narrative, and the narrative
character is peculiar to old age. One might then compare
Homer in the *Odyssey* to a setting sun, whose greatness, but
not intensity, remains. For here he no longer preserves a
pitch of vigor equal to that of his poem about Troy, nor
are the elevations everywhere level, with no depressions, nor
is there a similar pouring forth of passions in quick succession, nor yet the same rapid shifting from one point to another, the same sense of political reality, the same abundance
of imagery taken from actual things: but as when the Ocean
withdraws itself and leaves bare its own confines, so here
ebbings of grandeur are now seen, and he drifts from his
course into fabulous and incredible tales of wonders. In saying this I have not forgotten the storms in the *Odyssey*
and the part about the Cyclops and certain other passages:
but I am describing an old age, yet the old age of Homer.
Still, in all these passages, as you take them one after the
other, the fabulous quality prevails over that of belonging
to the world of action.

I have thus digressed, as I said, in order to show that what
is of great genius very readily falls into nonsense in its
decline, as in the passage about the bag of the winds, and the
men tended as swine by Circe, men whom Zoilus called
"pigs in tears," and Zeus fed like a nestling by the doves and
the man in the shipwreck remaining without food for ten
days and the implausible points in the Slaying of the Suitors.
For what are we to call such passages but "dreams of Zeus"
indeed? A second reason for appending this discussion on
the *Odyssey* is to acquaint you with the fact that passion, in
great writers of prose and poetry, in its decline subsides
into the portrayal of character. Of this description are the
passages about the household of Odysseus, told by the poet
with truth to ordinary life and with portrayal of character
—which are as it were a sort of comedy of manners.

10

Let us now examine whether we might find yet another
thing capable of making our language sublime. Now since
there are certain elements which naturally are found in association with all subjects of discourse and which coexist with
them, we find that the selection of the most telling of the
elements thus contained and the ability to form subsequent

combinations of them with one another and make as it were a single body out of them, would necessarily be a cause of sublimity; for the first procedure wins over the hearer by the choice of the ideas to be expressed, and the last does so by the compact fitting together of what has been chosen. Thus, for example, Sappho always takes the emotions in the madness of love from the phenomena accompanying it and from the reality itself. Where does she show her excellence? When she shows her skill in choosing the most preeminent of these and those of the most surpassing force and in combining them together:

> Peer of the gods he seems to me
> The man who sits facing thee
> And close to him thy sweet
> Utterance hears
>
> And thy delightful laughter; this it is
> That sets the heart in my breast astir;
> For once I see thee but a little, no more
> Does my voice come;
>
> But my tongue fails; and all at once
> A delicate fire spreads through my skin;
> My eyes see blank; my ears
> Reverberate;
>
> The sweat pours down me, and a quivering
> Seizes on all of me; and paler than grass
> Am I; I feel close to death,
> Agallis.
>
> . . .[6]

Do you not marvel how at the same moment she seeks in vain her soul and her body, her hearing and her tongue, her sight and her color, all of which have ceased to be her own, and in contrary fashion, is at once chilled and burned, irrational and sensible—for either she fears or is all but dead—so that there may be seen in her not one passion, but a concourse of passions? All things happen to lovers in this way; but the choosing of the extremes and combination of them together is what has made the preeminence here. In

[6] The last line or lines are corrupt, and have been omitted in the translation. A guess at the meaning would be: "But all must be endured, since this is so."

the same way Homer, in his description of storms, chooses
the most grievous of the accompanying circumstances; while
the author of the Arimaspea thinks that what follows is terrible:

> Another marvel there did I behold:
> Men dwelling on the seas, far off from land.
> Unhappy folk! And grievous is their toil:
> Eyes on the stars, and souls upon the deep.
> Haply in prayer they oft raise hands to heaven
> As wretchedly their inward parts are tossed.

It is, I think, obvious to everyone, that the passage has more
charm than terror. What does Homer do? I will quote one
passage out of many:

> He fell on them as when a wave falls on a swift ship—
> Violent, made great by the wind, with the storm-clouds
>   above it—
> And the whole ship is buried in spray, and the dread blast
>   of the wind
> Roars in the sail, and the sailors quake in their hearts
> In terror: for they scud on at but a space out-from-under
>   death.

Aratus too attempted to use this same metaphor: [7]

> A thin plank holds off death.

But Aratus has made it small and elegant, instead of terrible;
and furthermore, he has circumscribed the danger by saying
that the plank "holds off death:" it *holds* it *off* then. But
Homer does not circumscribe the danger to a single occasion,
but paints a picture of men continually being all but brought
to death again and again at every new wave. Further he has
taken prepositions, which are not naturally compounded with
one another, and compelled them to unite contrary to their
nature—"*out-from-under* death"—and thus tormented the
verse in the semblance of the torment of terror arising in it;
and by this contortion and compression of the verse he has
with superlative skill caught the likeness of the terror and all
but modelled in speech the peculiar quality of the danger:
"scud onward *out-from-under* death." Archilochus does not

---

[7] The metaphor referred to is that of calling a wave or water
death. Another possible translation is "Aratus tried to borrow this
same thing."

do otherwise in his description of the shipwreck, and Demosthenes in his account of the arrival of the news, in the passage beginning with the words "it was evening . . ." Their choice alighted on the best parts, merit being the only qualification (one might say) in their eyes, and left behind what was of less value; next they combined these parts together, inserting in between nothing padded or undignified or savoring of the schools. For such things injure the structure in its entirety, introducing into grandeurs interstices (as it were) and thin spots, the grandeurs else serving for their own proper placement, bedded as they are in the sound masonry of their own mutual relation.

11

At the side of the excellences mentioned above is the excellence called amplification. This is found when the subjects treated and the circumstances of delivery admit, at recurrent intervals, many new starts and places of rest and at each new step fresh grandeurs are continually introduced upon the old. Now whether this is done in the development of commonplace [8] or in the rousing of indignation or in the enforcing of facts or arguments, or in the effective arrangement of deeds or passions—there are untold forms of amplification—the orator must nevertheless realize that none of them can be by itself perfect and complete without sublimity, except to be sure in appeals to pity or in disparagements, while if you remove sublimity from any other of the forms of amplification, you will be removing the soul as it were from the body: for their character of belonging to the world of action is straightway deprived of its vigor and made inoperative, once it is not strengthened by sublimities.

We must now briefly distinguish for the sake of clarity wherein the present precepts differ from what went before—from the delimitation of the most preeminent of the ideas to be expressed and their combination into a unity—and wherein sublimity differs in general from amplification.

[8] Hermogenes. *Preliminary Exercises*, 6: The so-called "commonplace" contains an amplification of an admitted thing, it being assumed that the proofs have been already presented. We no longer inquire whether this man is a temple robber, or that man a hero, but taking this for granted, proceed to our amplification. The name "commonplace" is given to it, because it can be used against any temple robber, and in behalf of any hero.

12

The definition given by writers of arts of rhetoric is in my opinion unsatisfactory. "Amplification," they say, "is discourse which lends greatness to the matters treated." This definition can apply equally well to sublimity and passion and tropes, since these too all lend a certain grandeur to discourse. In my view, these differ the one from the other in that sublimity is found in elevation, while amplification is found in quantity as well; wherefore the former can occur many times in a single thought, while the latter can only occur in association with a certain quantity and fulness. And amplification, to speak roughly, is a "filling out," taken from all the particulars and topics contained in the subject, which adds forcefulness to the subject it develops by dwelling on it.

[two leaves of the ms. are missing]

Demosthenes, since he is more given to passion, has in virtue of that a great deal of incandescence and of anger bursting forth into flame, while the other,[9] composed and self-possessed in stateliness and a grand solemnity, is not on that account frigid, but has not the same urgency.

It is in just these respects, my dear Terentianus, as I think —if I, as a Greek, may be allowed an opinion—that Cicero differs from Demosthenes in his grandeurs. Demosthenes has a sublimity which for the most part is abrupt and sheer, while Cicero is expansive; and our Greek author might, because with his violence—and furthermore with his rapidity, strength and vehemence—he as it were both burns and scatters, be compared to a bolt of lightning, while Cicero, like an ample conflagration, spreads and dilates in all directions, as the quality of burning in him is always extensive and persistent, and is transmitted at different times in different ways, and fanned to flame at successive stages.

But you Romans could better judge these matters. The place for Demosthenic sublimity and surpassing vigor is in appeals to indignation and in intense passion, and where, to sum all up, it is required to shatter the hearer's composure; while the place for expansiveness is where there is need of showering him with a profusion of words: it is suitable for the most part for the development of commonplace, for perorations, digressions, and all eloquent and epideictic pas-

[9] Plato, *Ed.*

sages; for history and natural philosophy and a good many other things as well.

13

That Plato (to return), though he glides onward noiselessly with an expansive current such as we have described, does not for that reason fail to rise to grandeur, you know from his manner as you found it in the *Republic*. He says:

> For those men unacquainted with wisdom and virtue, who spend their lives ever in feasting and the like, are borne downwards, it appears, and wander in this lower region throughout their lives, never having raised their glance upward toward reality nor having been carried upwards thither, nor have they tasted of abiding and unadulterated pleasure, but like the beasts of the field they look ever downwards, and bent toward the earth and over tables, they roam their pasture, feeding and copulating, and in competing for a greater portion of this they kick and butt one another with horns and hooves of steel and slay one another because of this hunger in them that is never filled.

This author reveals to us—if we consent to take notice—that there is another path in addition to those mentioned, leading to the sublime. What is this path, and how do we describe it? It is the imitation and emulation of the great writers of prose and poetry of old. And my friend, let us hold fast to this endeavor. For many are inspired by a spirit not their own, as the Pythian priestess, it is said, approaches a tripod, where there is a crevasse in the earth, and breathes from thence a holy vapor, whence she becomes big with superhuman power and straightway prophesies through afflatus from on high: thus from the surpassing genius of the ancients, as from sacred outlets (one might say), channels run to the souls of those who emulate them, whereby even those not greatly susceptible to divine frenzy become inspired, and participate in the grandeur of others. Was Herodotus the only one to be "most Homeric?" Nay, Stesichorus was so before him and Archilochus, and most of all these Plato, who has diverted to himself countless rivulets fed from the great Homeric stream. Perhaps we should have needed to demonstrate this, if Ammonius had not collected the details and put them in writing. This is not plagiarism, but like taking the impression of a fair form in sculpture or some other kind of art. And I think Plato would never have

come to such fulness of powers in the doctrines of philosophy
nor have ventured, as so often he does, into the subjects and
expressions of poetry, if he had not with all his force con-
tended for the chief prize with Homer, as a young contestant
with one of great and standing repute—it may be with too
much heat and seeking, one might say, to transfix him on
his spear, yet this show of mettle brought him no little profit,
for as Hesiod says

This strife brings blessing to mankind.

And indeed this contest and the crown it brings is a noble
one, and well worth the winning, wherein even defeat at the
hands of older men is no disgrace.

14

It is excellent then for us too, when we are laboring on
some theme requiring lofty language and greatness of mind,
to feign in our souls how Homer (for instance) would have
expressed it, how Plato or Demosthenes would have elevated
it, or in history, Thucydides. For those men, as we think of
them in terms of emulation and see them, one might say,
stand out before our eyes, will somehow lead our souls upward toward those high standards we imagine; still more
would this be so, if we should add the following touch to
the pictures in our fancy: "how would Homer, if present, or
Demosthenes have listened to these words of mine? And what
impression would these words have left on them? For the
contest is indeed a great one, when you set up for your own
compositions such a court and such an audience, and in
make-believe submit your writings to scrutiny before wit-
nesses and judges of such stature. And a yet greater incentive
than this is to add the question: "How, when I have written
this or that, will eternity coming after listen to it?" If, for
instance, a man should fear that his words, like a payment
due at a certain date, would be defaulted if they went beyond the limit set by his own life and age, then of necessity
whatever is conceived by the soul of such a man must be
premature and blind, and as it were, abortive, inasmuch as
it is not brought to maturity in the full term of the days
of posterity.

15

Images too, my dear young man, are most productive of
stateliness and lofty language; they moreover cause tenseness

in the hearer. Some call images "idolopoeia" or the fashioning of pictures. Every notion which in any way on its occurrence produces speech is given the common name of *"phantasia"* or image; but the name by this time has come primarily to be applied to instances where, in the stress of inspiration and passion, you think you actually see that of which you are speaking, and make your hearers behold it. That the intention of imagery is not the same in oratory and in the poets, could not escape your notice, nor yet that the aim of imagery in poetry is to astound or strike, while its aim in oratory is vividness, while both alike, nevertheless, seek after the . . .[10] and agitated. Let me quote:

> Ah mother, I implore, set not on me
> The maids with eyes of blood and serpents' hair:
> Here! Here they are! They vault up at my side!

Again:

> Ah, it will kill me! Whither shall I flee?

Here the poet himself beheld the Furies, and what he had seen in his imagination he all but compelled his audience to see also. Now Euripides is much given to raising these two passions, madness and love, to tragic pitch, and in this succeeds better perhaps than in anything else; yet he is not without boldness in attacking other kinds of imagery. And though not in the least grand by nature, he has yet through his own agency compelled his nature in many points to become tragic, and in each instance of grandeur, to use Homer's words about a lion:

> Now one flank, now the other, with his tail
> He whips, and is his own goad to the fray.

Thus, in entrusting the reins to Phaëthon, the Sun says:

> And in thy course avoid the Afric sky,
> For, reft of moist admixture, it will not
> Buoy up thy wheels, but let them slip below

and then:

> Direct thy chariot toward the Pleiades.
> So much the lad heard; then he seized the reins
> And smote the winged team upon the flanks,

[10] A word, possibly "passionate," has dropped out.

Letting it go; the mares flew high in heaven.
Behind, his father mounting Sirius
Rode on to warn his son: Make for that point!
This way! This way the chariot turn!

Would you not say that the soul of the writer mounts on
the chariot with the driver, and sharing the danger, shares
the winged character of the steeds as well? Never, had it not
in its course kept pace with those events in heaven, could it
have conceived images like these. Similar is the passage concerning Cassandra:

Ye Trojan horsemen . . .

Although Aeschylus ventures on images of a most heroic
character, as when he speaks of the Seven Heroes who set
out against Thebes—

Seven heroes, captains resolute,
Bull-slaughtering into a black-bound shield,
Dipping their hands into the taurine gore
Bound them with oaths to Ares and Enyo
And Terror that loves blood—

who without a word of lamentation jointly took an oath
which devoted them to death (he sometimes however brings
forth ideas in the rough, as it were like undressed wool not
yet worked soft), Euripides nevertheless is undaunted, and
spurred on by rivalry, forces himself to encounter even such
bold and hazardous expressions as these. And in Aeschylus
the palace of Lycurgus, at the epiphany of Dionysus, is suddenly carried away by divine possession—

The halls are frenzied, the roof inspired—

while Euripides expresses the same thing differently, adding
a touch of charm:

And the whole mountain was inspired with them.

Sophocles too, in the case of the dying Oedipus, who conducts
his own funeral, to the accompaniment of signs from heaven,
has used imagery with superlative skill, and again, in presenting Achilles, when the Greeks sailed away from Troy,
appearing over his tomb to the army as it puts out to sea, a
spectacle which perhaps no one has painted more vividly than
Simonides—but it is impossible to quote all the passages.

For all that, the passages in the poets, as I said, exceed
in the direction of their fabulous character, an excess pass-

ing quite beyond credibility, while what is best in oratorical imagery is always its character of veracity and of belonging to the world of action. When the style of a speech is poetical and fabulous, and falls into all manner of impossibility, such departures are extravagant and outlandish; as when the eloquent orators of our day—like the tragedians—get to the point where they behold the Furies, and are, excellent souls, unable to comprehend that when Orestes says:

> Unhand me! Of my Furies thou art one
> And hold'st me fast, to hurl me down to Hell

he sees these images because he is mad. What is it then that oratorical imagery can do? It can contribute much of the spirit of contention and much passion to one's speeches, but not the least of its capacities is, in combination with developments of a factual character, not merely to persuade the hearer, but to subjugate him. Demosthenes says:

> Indeed, if some one at this very moment should hear a shouting in front of the court houses, and it should be reported that the prison doors had been thrown open, and the prisoners were escaping, no man, old or young, is so indifferent as not to lend his aid to the extent of his power; and if a speaker should rise before you and point out the person guilty of releasing the prisoners, that person, without so much as an opportunity to speak, would be put to death on the spot.

Ay, and thus Hyperides too, when he stood trial for passing a decree that the slaves should, after the defeat, be made free, said:

> It was not the orator who moved that decree, it was the battle at Chaeronea.

For while using a factual development, the orator at the same time has used images, and thus transcends the limits of mere persuasion in the idea he chooses to express. On all such occasions we naturally lend our ears to whatever is best; hence we are diverted from what has the character of proof to that which, in virtue of the imagery in it, can give us a shock, and in the brilliance of which the factual point lies hidden. It is not strange that we should be so affected: for when two things are joined together, the better and stronger of the two always absorbs the effectiveness of its partner into itself.

So much then for that sublimity which lies in the thought,

and is produced by greatness of soul, by imitation, or by imagery.

16

Here, in due order, is the place for the discussion of figures; these, as I said, if handled with the proper art, are no negligible part of grandeur. Since however it would be most laborious—or rather we should never see the end of it—if we went into every detail at present, we shall, to make our point convincing, discuss only a few of the figures bringing about grandeur of language. We proceed: Demosthenes is presenting a proof in defence of the policy for which he was responsible.[11] What was the natural way to put it? It was:

> You have not erred, men of Athens, in taking up arms for the freedom of Greece; you have examples of this from your own history: the men who fought at Marathon were not mistaken, nor yet the men who fought off Salamis and at Plataea.

But being suddenly inspired as by a god, and smitten as it were by a divine frenzy, he uttered this oath, made in the name of the champions of Greece:

> It cannot be that you were mistaken, I swear it in the name of those who were our champions at Marathon.

Here, solely through his use of a figure in the form of an oath —a figure which here I call an apostrophe—we see that he has made those ancestors divine, suggesting the idea that it is proper to swear by men who died in such a cause as one would swear by gods, and instils into the judges the spirit of the men who fought at Marathon, and has shifted the nature of demonstration, transferring it to superlative sublimity and passion and to the weight of conviction that resides in oaths unheard of before and of transcendent genius, at the same time that he distils into the souls of his audience a word of antidote and healing, that, elated by the praise, it might occur to them to be no less proud of their battle with Philip than of the trophies of Marathon and Salamis: and doing all this through his use of a figure, he snatched his audience away with him in a flash.

Yet it is said that the germ of this oath is found in Eupolis:

---

[11] Demosthenes' policy led to Philip's defeat of the Athenians at Chaeronea (338 B. C.).

Nay by the fight I fought at Marathon
They'll never vex me with impunity.

But it is not swearing by something in any fashion that is great, but swearing at a certain place, in a certain way, on certain occasions, and for a certain end. In Eupolis there is an oath and no more; and it is addressed to the Athenians while they were still fortunate and needed no consolation. Again, the poet did not make the *men* immortal in his oath —that he might beget in the hearers a due regard for their valor—but he has strayed from the champions to that inanimate thing, the battle. But the oath as handled by Demosthenes is directed to men in defeat, and makes Chaeronea no longer appear to the Athenians a losing battle, and is at the same time, as I said, a proof that no mistaken policy has been followed—an example, a use of oaths to carry conviction, an encomium, an exhortation. And since the orator was open to this objection: "you speak of your policy as culminating in defeat, and yet make bold to swear by victories?" he goes on, for this reason, to be absolute and exceedingly careful about his very words, showing us that even in bacchic transport one must keep a clear head. He says:

those who *risked all for us* at Marathon, and those who *fought in the sea-battles* at Salamis and Artemisium and *faced the enemy on land* at Plataea.

Nowhere does he speak of "winning a victory," but everywhere has contrived to suppress and spirit away the name of the outcome, since the outcome here was successful and different from what happened at Chaeronea. For this reason, keeping ahead of his hearers, he quickly goes on to add:

to all these men the state gave public obsequies, Aeschines, and not merely to those who were successful.

17

While we are on this subject I must not omit one of the points I have reached in my speculations, my dear friend— I will be very brief—namely, that in a way, figures are the natural allies of sublimity, and in return for that alliance are most marvelously supported by it. In what way and how this is so I proceed to indicate.

The use of figures is peculiarly liable to the suspicion of being a cloak for dishonesty; and such use arouses in the hearer the misgiving that he is being waylaid, plotted against,

and tricked with sophistry, especially when the speech is addressed to a judge in possession of authority, above all
tyrants, kings, and holders of high office; for such a man
immediately feels that he is being affronted and, like a silly
child, is being befooled with little figures by an artful orator,
and taking the sophistry as an indication of contempt for
himself, he is sometimes quite infuriated, and even if he
controls his anger, is most unfavorably disposed toward what
power of conviction the speech may contain. For this reason
a figure is reputed best when it is not even detected as a
figure. Sublimity then and passion are a preventive against the
suspicion arising from the use of figures and a most excellent
help for it, and the art of the deception is as it were taken
over by the beauties and sublimities, and thereafter sinks out
of sight and escapes all suspicion. Proof enough of this is
the expression quoted before: "I swear it in the name of those
who were our champions at Marathon." What has the orator
used here to conceal his figure? Clearly, its very radiance.
For just as pale lights, when surrounded by the sunlight,
become invisible in it, so are the tricks of rhetoric obscured
by being on all sides engulfed in grandeur. And perhaps
we find in painting an effect not very remote from this: for
when darkness and light are represented in pigments on the
same surface beside one another, the light nevertheless
reaches our eyes first, and not only stands out more distinctly
but appears to be much nearer. So then in discourses the passions and sublimities, lying closer to our souls, both because
of some natural affinity with them and because of their brilliance, appear in advance of the figures and cast a shadow
over their artfulness and keep them under cover so to speak.

18

And what shall we say about questions and inquiries? Do
they not, by the very fact of their having the form of
figures, lend greater vigor to what is said, making it more
alive with action and impressive?

> Or tell me, do you wish to go about and inquire of
> one another: "any news?" What newer and more un-
> heard of thing could there be than a Macedonian sub-
> duing Greece? "Is Philip dead?" "No, no; but he is
> ill." What difference is it to you? If this one dies, you
> will speedily make yourselves another Philip.

Again, Demosthenes says:

Let us sail against Macedonia. "Where shall we land?" someone asks. The war itself will find what is rotten in Philip's position.

If this had been put simply, it would have amounted to very little; as it is, the inspired character and abrupt alternation of question and answer and this replying to oneself as to someone else, have made the passage, through this use of a figure, not only more sublime but more convincing. For passionate passages then carry us away more readily, when they appear to be not the work of the speaker himself, but the offspring of the occasion; and a question addressed to oneself and the answer imitate this character of passion as being called forth by the occasion. For very much as persons when questioned by others are provoked on the spot and answer with the spirit of contention, taking their reply from the truth itself, so the figure of interrogation and response leads the hearer off into thinking that every point on which careful consideration has been spent has been called forth and spoken on the spur of the moment, and thus deceives him.

[two leaves of the ms. are missing here]

19

. . . the language falls out unconnectedly, and is as it were poured forth, all but getting ahead of the speaker himself. Xenophon says:

> And putting shield against shield they pressed against each other, fought, slew, were slain.

Again, there are the words of Eurylochus:

> We went through the thickets as thou badst, Odysseus;
> We saw in the glens the well-built palaces.

For expressions thus severed from one another and none the less precipitated upon one another, convey by implication the excitement which both obstructs a thing and at the same time hustles it on. Such are the notions Homer presents through his use of asyndeton.[12]

20

Further, a concourse of figures usually stirs the reader to a very high degree, when two or three figures, mixed to-

---

[12] A figure consisting in the omission of conjunctions.

gether in a kind of partnership, each contributes its share of
force, of conviction, of beauty, as in the passages directed
against Midias, where the instances of asyndeton are inter-
woven together with instances of anaphora[13] and with a vivid
delineation:

> For the assailant can do many things, some of which
> the victim could not so much as convey to another—
> with his posture, his look, his tone.

Then lest the speech as it goes on should come to a halt by
resting on the same points (for calmness is stationary, while
passion is disordered, being a rapid movement and turmoil of
the soul), he at once leaps to other instances of asyndeton
and to the use of anaphora:

> . . . with his posture, his look, his tone, when he strikes
> as one committing wanton outrage, when he strikes as
> an enemy, when he strikes with his fist, when he strikes
> you as a slave.

In these expressions the orator does exactly what the assailant
did: he strikes the minds of the jury with repeated impetus.
Then starting from here, like a thunderstorm, he makes another onset:

> . . . when he strikes with his fist, when he strikes you
> in the face: this puts men beside themselves, men un-
> accustomed to contumely and insult: no one reporting
> these things to you could convey their outrage.

Thus he everywhere preserves the native character of anaphora and asyndeton by his unbroken variation: to such a degree in him is order disordered, and conversely, does disorder
include a certain order.

21

Suppose you add the connectives, in the manner of the
Isocratean school:

> Neither must we fail to discuss how the assailant
> might do many things, in the first place with his pos-
> ture, next with his look, and finally with the mere tone
> of his voice.

You will realize as you thus go on rewriting the passage,
that this character in the passion of rapid urgency and in-

---

[13] Successive phrases or clauses beginning with the same word.
Ed.

creasing asperity, once you have levelled everything out to smoothness by the insertion of connectives, leaves no sting in its effect on us, and immediately flickers out. For just as one who should connect and conjoin the bodies of runners, takes away their swift motion, so the passion is impeded by the connectives and other additions, and chafes at them; for such a procedure destroys the freedom of running and the character of being hurled forth as from a catapult.

22

We must put the use of hyperbaton in the same class. Hyperbaton is an ordering of words or thoughts shifted from the normal sequence, and is the truest mark, as it were, of passion as we find it in actual contest. For just as persons really angry or frightened or indignant—whether from jealousy or some other cause (the passions are many, indeed innumerable—no one could tell how many there are)—keep slipping aside, and having set out to say one thing, often jump to something else, inserting remarks in between with no rhyme or reason, and then wheel back to their original remarks, and are abruptly jerked about in all manners hither and thither by their tension and excitement, as by a changing wind, and shift their words, their ideas, and the normal concatenation in every fashion into a thousand deviations; so imitation in the best writers of prose, through the use of hyperbaton, coincides with the works of nature. For art is then perfect and complete when it appears to be nature; and again, nature is successful when it contains undetected art. Thus Dionysius the Phocaean says in Herodotus:

> It hangs by a hair, men of Ionia, whether we shall be free men or slaves, and runaways at that. If you consent to bear hardships now, for the moment you will need to labor, but you will be able to overcome the enemy.

In this passage the orderly sequence would have been:

> Men of Ionia, now is the time for you to bear hardships: for our fortunes hang by a hair.

But the speaker put "men of Ionia" out of its proper order: he plunges immediately into his discourse with a mention of his fear, so that in face of the imminent terror he has not even called his hearers by their name; and in the next place he has reversed the order of the thoughts. For before saying that they must labor (this being the drift of his recommendation) he first tells the cause which makes labor necessary, saying "it hangs by a hair . . . ," so that he appears not to be making a studied speech, but to be saying what the circumstances force on him.

To a still greater extent Thucydides is given to taking even things by nature firmly united and inseparable, and through his use of hyperbaton, to separating them from one another. Demosthenes is not arbitrary to the same degree, but yet is of all men most addicted to this sort of figure, and through hyperbaton he reveals by implication a great abundance of agonistic quality, ay, and gives the impression of speaking on the spur of the moment and in addition involves his hearers together with himself in the hazard attending his long hyperbata; often suspending the meaning he started out to express, and in the meanwhile, as into an alien and unlikely order, rolling in one thing upon another, in the center and on the outskirts, casting the reader into a fear that the discourse will fall utterly flat, and compelling him, in anxiety, to share the speaker's danger, and then, unexpectedly, after a great interval, presenting the long awaited continuation just when it is needed, somewhere at the end, by this very daredeviltry and these hairbreadth escapes that go with his use of hyperbaton, he strikes the hearer and disturbs his composure much more than Thucydides. The examples are so numerous we shall forbear to quote them.

[Five short chapters dealing with grammatical figures, which do not have in English the effect they have in Greek, are here omitted.]

28

Again, no one would doubt that periphrasis is productive of sublimity. For just as in music the principal notes are made more pleasant by the so-called "accessory notes" or accompaniment, so periphrasis frequently mingles its tones with those of the expression periphrased, and their concord, in its amplitude, is ornamental, most of all when the periphrasis contains nothing diffuse or unmusical, but is pleasantly blended. Plato at the opening of his funeral oration is proof enough of this:

> So far as acts can go, these men have from us their due; and having it, they proceed on the fated journey, all with an official escort given by the state, each with an escort made up of his kinsmen.

Here he has called death "the fated journey," and the customary funeral rites "A public escort by their native land." Has he by this means but in a slight degree lent stateliness to the thought? Has he not rather taken the bare speech and put it into music, suffusing it with the melodiousness of the periphrasis as with some harmony? And Xenophon:

> You regard toil and hardship as the guide to happiness; you have stored in your souls the fairest harvest of all, and that most befitting warriors; for you take greater delight in praise than in aught else.

Here, instead of "you consent to bear hardship" he has by saying "you consider hardship the guide to happiness" and by similarly expanding the other parts included together with the praise a certain grand thought. There is too that inimitable passage in Herodotus:

> On those Scythians who had plundered the temple the goddess inflicted a feminine infirmity.

29

Yet this thing, periphrasis, is more liable to disaster than the rest, if one does not use it in the proper amount; for it at once makes an impression of feebleness and smells most fulsomely of the inane. Thus Plato—ever given to figures and now and then using them at the wrong moment—is ridiculed when he says in the *Laws*:

> We must not suffer Wealth, argentine or aureate, to be allotted its temple and abode within our city and be a habitant thereof.

It is said that if he had forbidden the possession of sheep, he would have spoken of "ovine and bovine wealth."

Let our excursion into ancient literature for the purpose of showing the use of figures for sublimity end here, my dear Terentianus: they all make what is said more passionate and agitated; and passion partakes of sublimity to the same extent that the depiction of character partakes of charm.

30

Now however that the thought in discourse, and the expression—that is, the greater part of either—has been presented, let us go on to consider anything belonging to the sphere of expression that may yet remain. Now that the

selection of magnificent proper[14] words has a most wondrous
effect in leading the hearers on and casting a spell over
them, and that in all orators and writers of prose this
practice is followed to a supreme degree, as it, through its
own agency, gives to their discourses at the same time
grandeur, a fine patina of antiquity, weight, strength and
authority, and furthermore brings out on the discourse as
on the surface of the fairest statues a brilliant lustre [15] and
as it were places a vocal soul in the subjects dealt with,
perhaps it would be superfluous to develop in detail before
persons that know it well already. For fine words are indeed a light peculiar to the thought. Yet their stateliness is
not in all respects serviceable, since the arraying of trivial
subjects in grand and august words would appear to be the
same as putting a great tragic mask on an infant.

[four leaves of the ms. are missing here]

31

Theopompus says:

Philip could excel at stomaching the political diet imposed on him.

We see that a low word often reveals much more than an
ornamental one; it is recognized from our daily life, and the
familiar is that much nearer to carrying conviction. Thus
"stomaching a political diet" has here been applied with
most vivid effect to a man who undergoes ugly and dirty
things with fortitude and pleasure for the sake of profit. So
too with the passages in Herodotus:

Cleomenes (he says) went mad and cut his own flesh
to small pieces with a dagger, until by the process of
mincing himself completely, he destroyed himself.

Again:

Pythes kept up fighting on board his vessel, until his
whole body was butchered to bits.

These passages graze the limits of vulgar and uncultivated
speech, but are not uncultivated in their expressiveness.

---

[14] That is, not used as in a trope, where the natural and
"proper" word is replaced by another word.
[15] Ancient statues were covered with a coating of specially treated
wax and oil in order to keep their colors from fading.

32

On quantity in metaphors too Caecilius appears to agree with those who lay it down that two or at the furthest three should be grouped in the same passage. Demosthenes is our limit in these matters as well: the right moment for their use is when passions rush on like a torrent and carry along with them, irresistible, the need to use a multitude of metaphors.

> Men (he says) vile and subservient, every one of whom has mutilated his native land, who have in their cups made a gift of their liberty to Philip, and now do the same to Alexander, who use their bellies and most shameful lusts as their measures for felicity, and have quite overthrown the freedom and the serving of no master, which were the limits and measures of prosperity for the Greeks of old.

Here the multitude of tropes is eclipsed and hidden by the anger of the orator against the traitors. In this connection, Aristotle and Theophrastus say that the following statements serve to soften bold metaphors: "as it were," "so to speak," "if one may put it so," and "if we may venture the expression;" for (they say) this abatement heals what is overbold. Now I accept their views; nevertheless, I say as I said for figures, that for the abundance and boldness of metaphors the antidotes peculiarly indicated are seasonable and intense passions, and noble and forthright sublimity, because with the swirling onrush of their course they carry all else with them and propel it onwards, or rather, demand venturesome language as their due, and give the hearer, sharing as he does the furor of the speaker, no leisure to tarry and find fault with their number.

Again, in the development of commonplace and in descriptions there is nothing that presents things so expressively as continuous and successive tropes. It is by means of these that the anatomy of the human frame is pictured in majestic fashion in Xenophon and yet more divinely in Plato. Plato calls the head of man a "citadel," and says that the neck has been "built as an isthmus" between the head and the breast, and that the vertebrae, as "pivots," are laid down as a solid base, and that pleasure is for mankind a "bait of evil," and the tongue the "tool for the assaying" of savor; that the heart is a "knot of the blood vessels and fountain of the coursing blood," placed "in the quarters of

the royal guards," while the various routes taken by the
passages he calls "alleys." And he says:

> For the leaping of the heart in the expectation of
> things terrible and when anger is aroused, for then it
> is suffused with fire, they devised a relief, and im-
> planted the lung—soft, bloodless, and containing cavi-
> ties within itself—as a sort of cushion, that whenever
> anger should seethe in the heart, the latter in its leap-
> ing should strike on yielding substance and thus escape
> harm.

And he called the dwelling place of the desires the "women's
quarters" and that of anger, the "men's"; and the spleen he
called the "mop" of the inner parts, saying that "in consequence it is filled with the matter cleansed away and becomes swollen and infected." He says that thereafter the
lesser gods made for everything a "shade" of flesh, setting
it up as a "screen" against things coming from the outside,
like coverings of "felt." He calls the blood the "pasture of
the flesh." And he says

> In order to provide nutriment, they made channels
> throughout the body, digging them as one might dig ir-
> rigation ditches in an orchard, so that as if from the
> flow of an incoming current, the body might be
> watered.

and that the "streams in the blood vessels" might "flow
through the body as through a narrow conduit." And when
death is at hand, he says that "the cables of the soul, as of
a ship, are unfastened" and that "the soul is set free." These
turns and others like them occur in countless numbers one
after the other; what has been adduced is enough to show
that tropes are grand by nature, that metaphors cause sublimity, and that it is passionate and eloquent passages which
most delight in them.

That however the use of tropes, as everything else that is
fine in discourse, ever tempts one to excess, is by now evident, even without my saying so. Indeed it is for these not
least that Plato is derided, since often he is carried away,
as if by a bacchic frenzy in language, into unmitigated and
harsh metaphors and high-flown allegory.

> It is not easy to conceive (he says) that a state must
> be tempered as the mixture in a mixing bowl, where
> the mad wine seethes when it has been poured in, but
> chastened by another, sober god, and assuming a fair
> partnership, makes a good and moderate drink.

Here it is remarked that to call water "a sober god," and mixture "chastening" is the work of a poet by no means sober himself. Although it is shortcomings of this description that Caecilius attacks, yet in his writings on Lysias he has even made bold to pronounce Lysias as altogether far superior to Plato. In so doing he has been moved by two uncritical passions: he loves Lysias with a love passing the love of self, and for all that he hates Plato much more than he loves Lysias. But Caecilius can be dismissed; he is moved by contentiousness, and even the positions he argues from are not the matters of common consent he fancied them to be. He alleges his orator free from error and above reproach, and Plato as faulty in many ways; but the truth, we find, is nothing even approximately of the kind.

33

Suppose we take some writer really free from error and irreproachable. Does not this very question deserve to be raised in its general form: which is better in poetry and prose, grandeur accompanied by a few failings, or that which at its best rises to a moderate height, while everywhere it is sound and free from fault? Nay further, whether in literature it is the more numerous excellences or the greater ones that should rightly carry off the prize? These questions are germane to the subject of sublimity and most certainly require decision.

Now I am aware that natures of surpassing greatness are the least free from admixture of error; exactitude in everything runs the risk of pettiness, while in grandeur, as in exceedingly great estates, we must expect, here and there, that something will pass unregarded; perhaps it is even necessary that abject and middling natures, because they never indulge in risks or aim at the heights, should continue to remain, for the most part, without fault, and in comparative security, while grandeurs are made insecure by their very greatness. Nor yet am I ignorant of this second point, that all human things are naturally better known by their worse side, and that the memory of errors remains uneffaced, while that of the good quickly ebbs away. Though I have myself quoted not a few errors of Homer and of the greatest authors besides him, and do not in the least acquiesce in their failings, yet, calling these not so much intentional errors as oversights brought forth accidentally and without design by a greatness of genius that did not pause to con-

sider, I nonetheless believe that the greater excellences, even
though they should not everywhere continue at the same
level, should always have our suffrage for the highest prize,
if for no other reason than the greatness of soul in them
alone. Consider: Apollonius is a correct poet in his
Argonauts, and Theocritus most successful (barring a few
externals) in bucolics: would you rather then be Apollonius
than Homer? Or be Eratosthenes in the *Erigone* (the little
poem is faultless throughout) than Archilochus (who rushes
on with a multitude of badly arranged matters) and that out-
burst, difficult to subject to law, of more than human inspiration? Is Eratosthenes the greater poet? In choral poetry
would you choose to be Bacchylides rather than Pindar, and
in tragedy Ion of Chios than Sophocles? You will admit that
the first are faultless, and everywhere, in point of elegance,
beautifully written, while Pindar and Sophocles at times in
their rapid course set as it were all things ablaze, yet often
are strangely quenched, and fail most lamentably. Or would
no man of sense esteem all of Ion's work put together as
worth the one play *Oedipus?*

34

If success were to be judged by the false criterion of taking a count, then Hyperides would be altogether superior to
Demosthenes. For Hyperides has a voice of wider range and
has a greater number of excellences, and is in all matters,
one might say, just one degree below supremacy, like the
athletes skilled at the pentathlon, so that he everywhere loses
the first prize to the other contestants, while he is first
among the untrained. Now Hyperides, in addition to repro-
ducing all the good points in Demosthenes (with the exception of the combination of words), has embraced over
and above that, the excellences and attractions of Lysias.
For he can patter on with a naive simplicity, where such
a tone is needed, and does not pass from one point to another with his voice keyed to the same pitch of intensity,
as Demosthenes does; he has combined with sweetness,
the pleasant grace that comes from portrayal of character—
a seasoning laid on in an unassuming manner—; there are
in him any number of sallies of wit, a gift of raillery that
has to the highest degree the character of belonging to the
world of actual affairs, a patrician air, an expertness in irony
as of a wrestler who can take and break all holds, jests not
tasteless nor ill-bred (according to the Athenian standard

of the day) but brought home with pertinence, a deft derisiveness, much comic "sting," aimed by banter that never misses the mark—it is impossible to convey his delightfulness in all these matters; again, he is most gifted in arousing pity, and further in telling of mythological matters (expanding out to do so), and in finding his way through a long exposition with superb skill in following the windings, in well-modulated tones: thus he has rendered the tale of Leto in poetic fashion, and his funeral oration with an epideictic quality never perhaps excelled. But Demosthenes has no touches of characterization, no power of expansion, least of all is he well modulated or epideictic; he is for the most part quite devoid of every single quality we mentioned before; when he forces himself to be amusing and witty, he excites not so much laughter as derision, and when he attempts an approach to delightfulness, he but recedes from it the more. Had he attempted the little speech about Phryne or Athenogenes he would have shown Hyperides to even greater advantage.

Yet, I take it, since the fine things in Hyperides, though numerous, are nevertheless without grandeur, and coming from one "sober at heart" are without effect, and permit the hearer to remain unmoved—no one, after all, is afraid when he reads Hyperides—while Demosthenes "strikes up his song" with that which bears the character of greatest genius and comes to the topmost degree of supremacy: excellences with no short-comings, intensity of lofty speech, passions that are alive, abundance beyond mere necessity, keenness of mind, rapidity (where it has its full effect), that vehemence and force unapproachable by all others,—since, I say, he has made these his own, as dread gifts from heaven (it would be impious to call them human), he for this reason, with the fine qualities he does possess, ever surpasses all other men, winning the victory even for those qualities he does not possess, and as it were out-thunders and out-flashes all orators of all time; and you could sooner look at hurtling thunderbolts with open eyes than face without flinching the quick succession of his passions.

35

In Plato's case, however, there is, as I said, yet another difference; for Lysias, although far inferior not only in the greatness of his excellences, but also in their number, yet exceeds Plato more in faults than he falls short of him in excellences.

What was it then that those godlike men saw, who aimed at what was greatest in writing, and scorned accuracy in every detail? They saw many things, and especially this, that Nature has not in her arbitrament judged us to be abject or man to be an ignoble animal, but bringing us into life and the whole of the universe as into some great festal assembly, to be spectators of the whole of her and most emulous contestants, has from the start implanted in our souls an irresistible love of whatever is great and stands to us as the more divine to the less. Wherefore not even the whole of the universe suffices for man's contemplation or scope of thought, but human speculations frequently exceed its compass; and if a man should look about him and survey life, as it lies around him, in its fulness of grandeur and beauty which everywhere transcends mere necessity, he would soon know for what purpose we are born. Hence indeed it is that moved by some natural impulse we do not marvel at small streams, clear and useful though they be, but at the Nile, the Danube, or the Rhine, and much more at the Ocean; nor yet are we stirred more by this flamelet that we kindle, when it keeps its light clear, than by the fires in heaven, dimmed though they often are, or consider it more wondrous than the craters of Aetna, whose outpourings carry from the depths rocks and whole precipices, and at times pour forth rivers of that earth-born and unadulterated fire. Nay, to all such things the remarks we should apply are these: that while men can easily procure the useful and necessary, what they admire is always the extraordinary.

36

When therefore we come to greatness of genius in literature, where the greatness does not (as before) overstep the limits of serviceability and use, we must conclude, with no need of further proof, that men so great, though far from faultless, yet are all superior to what is merely mortal; that other things reveal their users men, while sublimity raises them near to the greatness of soul of God; and that freedom from error merely escapes censure, while greatness goes further and awakens admiration. What need is there to add to what has been said, and go on to mention that each of these authors often redeems all his failures by a single sublimity and faultless passage, and what is the most important point, that if one should pick out all the failures in Homer, in Demosthenes, in Plato, and in all the other greatest writers, and collect them all together, they would be seen to be a very small part, rather not even the veriest fraction of what those heroes have produced that is entirely successful? Therefore all time, all life,—and envy cannot convict these of lunacy—has placed the prize of victory in their hands and to the present moment has kept it in their possession and to all appearances will keep it there.

So long as water flows, and tall trees bloom.

Yet in reply to the man who writes that the faulty colossus is not superior to the Spear-Bearer of Polyclitus, we may say, among other things, that in art the greatest exactitude is admired, but in the works of nature, grandeur, and man is by nature endowed with discourse; and that in statues we look for resemblance to man, but in discourse for that which (as I said) transcends the merely human. Nevertheless—and here our precept brings us back to the beginning of our notes—since faultlessness is for the most part a product of art, while that which is superlative (only here it is not sustained at an even level) is a product of greatness of genius, we should everywhere have recourse to art as an aid to nature; for perhaps the perfect state is that where each of these is in possession of the other.

So far we have had to go to settle the questions raised; yet let everyone take his pleasure where he finds it.

37

[Two leaves are missing in the ms.]

38

Wherefore one must know just how far to go in every instance: for sometimes passing too far destroys the superlative character of the hyperbole, and from overstretching leads to slackness and at times even turns about and produces the contrary effect. Thus Isocrates somehow behaves like a child from his ambition to amplify everything he says. The theme of his Panegyric is that Athens surpasses Sparta in benefits conferred on the Greeks. At the very opening of his speech he writes as follows:

Next, language has such power that it is possible to make great things abject, and to impart greatness to things mean; and express antiquity in a fresh way, and speak of recent happenings in an antique vein.

"Are you then" (someone will exclaim) "Isocrates, going to reverse in this fashion the merits of the Athenians and Spartans as well?" He has very nearly, in this encomium on language he has so prominently displayed, delivered to his hearers a prooemium which urges them to disbelief in himself. Perhaps then the best hyperboles—and this we said of figures as well—are those which are not even detected to be what they are. This happens when in the stress of overpowering passion they are expressed in a factual context of a certain gravity, as Thucydides does in the case of the army destroyed in Sicily:

> For the Syracusans (he says) climbed down and set to slaughtering mainly the men in the river, and the water was immediately polluted; but the men kept drinking it none the less, muddy as it was and fouled with blood, and the majority still fought to get at it.

That men fought to drink blood and mud is made credible by the transcendency of passion and the factual context. Similar is Herodotus' remark about the men of Thermopylae:

> Here (he says), as they defended themselves with knives— when they still had them—and their hands and their teeth, they were buried under by the barbarians.

"What!" you will exclaim, "Fighting with their teeth against armed men!" "Buried under missiles!" Yet the thing gains credence; for the fact does not give the impression of being included for the sake of the hyperbole, but the hyperbole appears to arise legitimately from the fact. For, as I do not cease to say, the solution and as it were panacea for any bold venture in diction is deeds and passions bordering on frenzy; thus it is that comic passages, though they pass belief, are yet credible because of their ridiculousness:—

> The farm he got had a lot less land
> Than the space of a Spartan letter—

for laughter too is passion—in pleasure. Again, hyperboles, as they exceed in the direction of greatness, so too exceed in that of smallness, since enhancement is common to both; and disparagement is in a way an amplification of the abject.

39

The fifth of the elements contributing to sublimity which we set forth at the beginning, still remains, my excellent friend: the character of the composition or combination of words—taken by itself—which pervades discourse. As we have given this subject sufficient treatment in two treatises —at least so far as we could attain to the understanding of the theory—we would add only this much, of necessity, to the present theme, that harmony is not only for men a natural instrument of persuasion and pleasure, but also, when accompanied by the spirit of a free man, a wondrous instrument of passion. Does not the flute instil certain passions in its hearers and render them beside themselves and full of a wild ecstasy, and when it gives the measure of some rhythm does it not compel the hearer to beat the time and make himself into a counterpart of the music, quite "stranger to the Muse" though he be? Nay, and do not the notes of the lyre, meaningless though they are in isolation, when they are varied in modulation and struck in concordant blending with one another, often (as you know) cast a wondrous spell? Yet these are mere counterfeit presentments and spurious imitations of persuasion, and not, as I said, true operations of the nature of man. And are we then not to think that composition, which is a certain harmony in discourses, things which are native to man and lay hold on his very soul, not merely on his hearing, a harmony which stirs up a variegated host of words, notions, things, of beauty, of melody—all things innate in us and of our blood—and which by commingling and setting in varied motion the notes which are its own, introduces the passion in the speaker into the souls of those who stand near him, making whosoever hears take part therein, and fits grandeurs together by its masonry and architecture of words—are we then not to think that by this very means it both casts a spell on us and at the same time puts us too into a disposition receptive to stateliness and dignity and sublimity and all else that this harmony includes within itself, in all manners gaining the ascendency over our minds? Yet even though it is madness to subject to verification a matter where men are to this point agreed—experience is proof enough—yet the thought Demosthenes mentions in commenting on his decree is felt to be sublime, and in truth is wondrous:—

This decree made the danger which then hung over
our city pass by like to a cloud—

but its peal of sound is no less due to the harmony in the
wording than to the thought alone. For the whole of it is
spoken in dactylic rhythms (and dactyls are most noble and
creative of grandeur, wherefore the finest rhythm known
of all that are put together by man is the heroic verse).

[A short passage in which the rhythm of the original
Greek sentence is discussed is here omitted.]

40

Especially productive of grandeur in language is the
following. As the conjunction of the limbs with one another (none of which severed from the rest has in isolation
any importance) fills out, when all are taken together, a
complete structure, so grandeurs when dispersed, with their
own dispersion dissipate sublimity as well, but when made
into an integrated whole by participating in harmony and
further being girt round by its bond, become, through this
very concentration and encompassment, vocal and resonant;
and we may say that in periods the grandeurs are the sum of
small contributions from a multitude.

Further, that many writers of prose and many poets, not
sublime by nature, perhaps even devoid of grandeur, have
none the less, though for the most part using commonplace and trivial words that introduce into their language
nothing beyond the ordinary, through the mere combination
and fitting together of these, assumed stateliness and amplitude and the appearance of not being abject, among others
Philistus, Aristophanes in certain passages and Euripides in
most, this we have sufficiently made clear. Thus Heracles
says, after he has slain his children:

Now I am filled with woe: no room for more.

The language is exceedingly commonplace, but it has become sublime in a fashion corresponding to the shaping of
figures: if you fit it together in any different way, you will
see that Euripides is poet of the combination rather than of
the sense. He says of Dirce dragged by the bull:

And when he came on aught,
Ranging about, he took and dragged it all,
Woman, rock, oak, in constant alternation.

The idea too is noble, but has become yet loftier through the circumstance that the harmony is not made too rapid, and does not bound off as if rolling away, but the words are buttressed against one another, and have "times" to rest on, as they stand firmly planted in a manner conductive to stable and stationary grandeur.

41

Nothing is so productive of meanness in sublime passages as a broken and agitated rhythm, such as pyrrhics (◡◡), trochees (|—◡|) and dichorees (—◡—◡), which go quite astray and end up in making the rhythm that of a dance; for everything that is overloaded with rhythms straightway appears affected and precious and most devoid of passion, since its character becomes obvious through the uniformity of the rhythms; and what is yet worse, just as ditties divert the attention of the hearer from the thing expressed and force it to attend to themselves, so too language saturated with rhythms strikes up in the hearers not the passion in the words, but that in the rhythm, so that sometimes the hearers, knowing in advance the cadences required, spontaneously beat time for the speaker, and, as happens in a chorus, anticipate the conductor. Similarly devoid of grandeur is language which bears too much the character of being put together, and is severed into small sections of but a few syllables each, bound together at the harsh breaks and commissures between them as with a row of bolts.

42

Again, an excessive telescoping in the expression also tends to diminish sublimity; for when the sublime is brought into too small a compass, its grandeur is cramped and maimed. What is meant at present is not language which is properly condensed and concentrated, but such as is small outright and reduced to little pieces; for telescoping mutilates the sense, brevity makes it direct. It is evident that on the other hand too great expansion is frigid, for such are all cases where resort is had to unseasonable length.

43

Also very effective in disfiguring sublimities is the meanness of the words used. Thus in Herodotus so far as the ideas go the storm is splendidly expressed, but there are included in the passage certain words which are unworthy of the matter. On the one hand there is his phrase "the sea had boiled (*zesāses*)" since *zesāses*, because of its cacophony, greatly lowers the sublimity; on the other hand there are the phrases "the wind got tired" and "an unpleasant end was the lot of the men clinging to the wreck." For "tire" is without dignity, a common word, and "unpleasant" scarcely fits a disaster of such magnitude.

Similarly Theopompus, though he elaborated his account of the descent of the Persian king into Egypt with surpassing genius, spoiled it all by a few little words:

> What city or what tribe in Asia did not send embassies to the Great King? What produce of the earth or what noble or precious work of art was not brought him as a gift? Were there not many costly coverlets and cloaks, some of the purple dye, some embroidered, some white, many wagons with canopies of gold, furnished with all the necessary provisions, many long robes too and precious couches? Moreover there was silver and gold plate, cunningly wrought, goblets and mixing bowls, some of which you would have observed to be studded with gems, and others of careful and rich workmanship. And further there were innumerable thousands of arms, some Greek, and others barbarian, beasts of burden in surpassing multitude, and other animals fattened for slaughter, many bushels of dainties, many pouches and sacks of papyrus and of all other useful things; and so much preserved meat of all sorts that the piles of it reached such a height that persons approaching from a distance thought they were bluffs and hills crowded upon each other.

From the direction of the sublime he runs to that of the abject, although amplification should be performed in the reverse order; instead, because he has mixed up the "pouches" and "dainties" and "sacks" in his admirable account of all the preparations, he gives the impression of some sort of butcher shop. For just as if some one on the actual scene of those preparations had come into the midst of the golden and bejewelled mixing-bowls and the silver plate and the canopies and goblets of massy gold, carrying pouches and sacks, and set them down there, the act would have produced on the eye the impression of being inappropriate, so too, the unseasonable inclusion of such words results in blemishes and as it were ugly spots in the style. He was free to pass over these things generally, and as he speaks of "bluffs" thrust together, so too to speak of wagons and camels and a multitude of beasts of burden "laden with all the supplies of luxurious living and the pleasures of the table" or word it as "heaps of all manner of grain and of all those products which are most esteemed as provisions for good living and a choice cuisine;" or if he insisted at all costs on setting these matters down with so little embellishment, he could have said "all the delicacies of servers and chefs." For among sublimities we must not descend to the vile and degraded, unless hard pressed by some necessity, but it is appropriate that we should use words of equal worth with the subjects treated, and imitate that Nature which fashioned man, and did not place our nameless parts on our faces, nor yet those colatories that serve our bulk in its entirety, but contrived, so far as possible, to conceal them, and as Xenophon says, "turned the channels appropriated to these purposes as far away as could be done," in no wise marring the beauty of the animal as a whole.

But we are under no pressure to enumerate things productive of smallness in detail: for since we have shown above all that makes what we say noble and sublime, it is evident that the opposites will for the most part make it abject and indecorous.

44

It remains for us to clear up a remaining point: for your instruction, dear Terentianus, we shall not hesitate to add a clarification of the question raised by a certain philosopher the other day. He said:

> I am amazed, and many others too, how it is that in our time there have been natures surpassingly persuasive and statesmanlike, keen and apt and excelling above all in the production of the graces of literature, while natures of great sublimity and transcendent grandeur, except rarely, are no longer brought forth. So great a universal dearth of literature obtains in our lifetime. Must we then accord credence to the common saying, that democracy is a good nurse of what is great, since men of eminence in literature reached their prime when she did, and when she died, died too, and this is true of democracy alone? For, as men say, freedom has power to nurture the pride and spirit of high-souled men, and give them hope, and at the same time permits them to run the full course of their eagerness

for contending with one another and for competing
for the highest prize. Yet more: because of the re-
wards made available in democratic governments, the
talents of orators are whetted and as it were rubbed
bright, and as is to be expected, shine forth with a
freedom answering to the freedom in the conduct of
affairs. But (the philosopher said) we men of today
would seem to have learned from childhood a slavery
we deserve and to have been all but swaddled from our
tenderest years in its habits and pursuits, and never
to have drunk of that spring which is most fair, whose
fruitful waters bring forth literature, I mean freedom
(he said); and for this reason we turn out to be of
great genius in nothing but in sycophancy. It is on
this account that all other attainments are found in
slaves as well as freemen, but no slave becomes an
orator, for should he make the attempt, at once there
wells up in him in all its bitterness that character of
guardedness in speech, of being held captive under sur-
veillance, that comes from a long habituation to repeated blows; for as Homer says,

> The day of slavery despoils a man
> Of half his virtue.

Just as then (he pursued) the boxes—if we can believe
the tale—in which the Pygmies, who are called
"dwarves," are reared, not only check the growth of the
persons confined within, but furthermore, because of
the cords passed over their bodies, . . .[16] so one might
call all slavery, deserved though it be, the box and
common prison-house of the soul.

Here I took up and said:

It is an easy thing, my dear fellow, and a characteristic of mankind, to decry those circumstances, whatever they be, in which one finds oneself; let me suggest that perhaps it is not the peace which extends
throughout the world that ruins great natures, but
much rather this boundless war, which represses our
desires,—nay, and these passions, which like an army
of occupation, have entered into the life of today and
are putting it utterly to sack. For the love of money,
for which we have all by now a sick and insatiable
desire, and the love of pleasure, lead us away as their
slaves, or rather, one might say, like pirates, plunge

---

[16] The text is corrupt here. "Keep their bodies inactive," "per-
vert their growth" and "make them smaller" have been suggested as
possible readings.

our lives and ourselves with them, to the bottom: the love of wealth is a disease that makes for meanness, and the love of pleasure, one that is most ignoble.

I am unable then, on consideration, to discover any possibility for us who esteem unlimited wealth so highly, or to speak more truly, make a god of it, to shut the gates of our souls to the influx of evils which nature has made inseparable from it. For on immoderate and unchecked Wealth follows, as the phrase goes, "with equal stride," its constant associate, Extravagance, and as the former opens the entrance into our cities and homes, the latter straightway enters in and takes its abode with us. And when these two have been settled for some time in our lives, they "build nests," (as the philosophers say) and presently devoting themselves to procreation, they bring forth Vainglory and Vanity and Luxury, no supposititious brood but true offspring of their own. And if a man suffer the progeny of this Wealth too to remain and reach full growth, it speedily engenders in the soul inexorable masters, Insolence and Violation of Law and Absence of Shame. These things must arise as I have said, and men must no longer raise their glances upward nor reck of their fame among posterity, but for such as these the ruination of their lives is gradually brought to pass in a downward cycle; and the great things in the soul must waste and wither away, and cease to deserve emulation or to provoke it, when men look with the highest admiration on their mortal parts, and neglect to make grow that in them which is immortal. For in a simple case in court, a man who has been bribed can no longer be a free and sound judge of what is just and fair—the taker of bribes is bound to consider conduct like his own fair and just—; now when bribery and corruption have come to preside over the entire lives of each and every one of us, and the pursuit of the death of strangers,[17] and we set traps to capture inheritances that are none of ours, and purchase such indiscriminate profiting at the cost of our own souls, enslaved as we are by . . .[18] in such a widespread havoc of our lives, a havoc that assumes the proportions of a plague, do we imagine that there is left among us any free and uncorrupted judge of what is

---

[17] An allusion to the practice, common in imperial Rome, of sycophancy toward elderly and childless persons of wealth for the purpose of being remembered in their wills.

[18] A word or phrase has dropped out. "Greed," "our own souls," "our own cupidity" have been suggested to complete the sense.

great and endures beyond our time to all eternity, who could attain to office in the face of the machinations of the desire for profit at any price? No; perhaps for such as we, it is better to be ruled than to be free, since once our greed for ill-gotten gain were let loose, as from a prison, against our neighbors, it would inundate the whole inhabited earth with ill.

And in general (I said), the natures of the men born in these days have an indolence of spirit that is all-consuming, in which indolence all of us save a few spend their lives, working at a task or taking it up only to get praise or pleasure, and never doing so for that conferring of benefits on others which deserves our ardent efforts and men's honor.

But "it is best to let these matters lie" and pass to the next point.

[The remainder is lost.]

St. Augustine on a Christian Style

ERICH AUERBACH

AUGUSTINE'S VIEWS IN the matter become readily understandable if we bear in mind that his aim was to provide practical pointers for the use of the classical style levels and that he closely followed Cicero, especially Cicero's definition of the low *sermo,* formulated entirely with a view to political or forensic oratory. But their basic assumptions were entirely different. When Cicero (*Orator* 101) writes (as Augustine quotes him *On Christian Doctrine* 4.17): "He therefore will be eloquent who can speak of small things in a simple manner, of middling things in the intermediate style, and of great things in the grand manner," he takes these gradations in an absolute sense; *small* designates something absolutely base, such as the financial transactions and commonplace occurrences that an orator addressing a court of law is obliged to speak of. A Christian orator recognizes no absolute levels of subject matter; only the immediate context and purpose

From Literary Language and Its Public in Latin Antiquity and in the Middle Ages by Erich Auerbach. Bollingen Series LXXIV, pp. 34-39, distributed by Pantheon Books. Reprinted by permission of Bollingen Foundation and Francke Verlag.

(whether his aim is to teach, to admonish, or to deliver an impassioned appeal) can tell him which level of style to employ. A Christian orator's subject is always Christian revelation, and this can never be base or in-between. When Augustine teaches that Christian themes should sometimes be expounded in the intermediate or lowly style, he is referring solely to the form of presentation, which must be varied if it is to be understandable and effective; the pagan gradations of subject matter have lost their validity. The sublime or pleasingly "middling" subjects of pagan literature are un-Christian and reprehensible; Augustine is visibly embarrassed by a passage in which Cyprian employs an idyllic style in dealing with an "intermediate" theme. But it is in Chapter 18, immediately after the quotation from Cicero, that he takes his most explicit stand against the ancient gradations of subject matter. I shall paraphrase the passage in slightly abridged form.

Cicero's threefold classification, he writes, is appropriate to legal matters, but not to the spiritual matters with which we are concerned. Where financial dealings are involved, Cicero calls the subject matter "low"; he calls it "lofty" where men's lives and well-being are at stake; the intermediate lies in between. We Christians cannot accept such a distinction: for us all themes are sublime, especially when we are addressing the people from the pulpit; for we are always concerned with the welfare of men, and not only their worldly welfare but their eternal salvation; so that even the gain and loss of money become important, regardless of whether the sum involved is large or small; the justice we must assuredly observe even in trifling money matters is of no small importance, for the Lord has said: "He that is faithful in that which is least is faithful also in much" (Luke 16:10). The least is very little; but it is great to keep faith in little things. (Augustine goes on to cite I Cor. 6:1-9, where Paul rebukes the members of the congregation who have laid legal disputes among themselves before the heathen courts). Why is the Apostle indignant? Why does he react so violently? Why does he vituperate, rebuke, and threaten? What is the reason for the agitation manifested by his bitter invective and frequent changes of tone? Why, in short, does he adopt so lofty and impassioned a style in speaking of such insignificant matters? Are earthly affairs so important to him? Not at all. He does so for the sake of justice, charity, piety; no man of sound mind can doubt that these are sublime even in connection with the most paltry affairs. . . . Wherever we may speak of those things that save us from eternal damnation and lead us to eternal beatitude, whether to the people or in private conversation, whether addressing one or many, friends or enemies, in continuous discourse or in dialogue, in sermons or in books, they remain sublime. A cup of cold water is assuredly a small and worthless thing; but does this mean that the Lord said something small and worthless when he promised that whosoever should give a cup of cold water to the least of his servants would in no wise lose his reward (cf. Matt. 10:42)? And should a preacher who refers to this incident in church suppose that because it is trivial he should employ not the intermediate nor the lofty, but the lowly form of discourse? Has it not transpired that while we were speaking of this to the people (and not ineptly because God was with us), there burst from that cold water something akin to a flame, which, through hopes of heavenly reward, fired the cold hearts of men to works of mercy?

Only after this remonstrance, which is itself delivered in an impassioned, lofty style, does Augustine proceed to explain how the doctrine of the three levels may nevertheless prove useful to a Christian orator. The remonstrance is of fundamental importance: in the Christian context humble everyday things, money matters or a cup of cold water, lose their baseness and become compatible with the lofty style; and conversely, as is made clear in Augustine's subsequent remarks, the highest mysteries of the faith may be set forth in the simple words of the lowly style which everyone can understand. This was a radical departure from the rhetorical, and indeed from the entire literary, tradition. It was a fundamental tenet of this tradition that each style level or literary genre must deal with a corresponding level of subject matter; thus a classification of themes was essential. A wide variety of subjects were assigned to the lowest class; in general it embraced factual information, all things regarded as insignificant and unimpressive, personal matters, daily life, the comic and frivolously erotic, the satirical, realistic, and obscene; genres associated with such subject matter were satire, mime, iambus, legal oratory when it dealt with private and economic interests, and usually the animal fable. The dividing line between low and intermediate was fluid.

The descriptions of the lowly style are as varied as the subject matter, and there are subgradations. As we have seen, Augustine takes Cicero's account of it in *Orator* as his starting point; Cicero describes the low style as unadorned yet pure and elegant, seemingly easy but requiring true mastery; his conception of it is barely distinguishable from the Attic ideal.

But in the most widespread view the low style implied sharp realism and homespun vigor. The style levels are particularly evident in the ancient theater; in comedy persons and events of daily life are treated in the low, and occasionally in the intermediate, style; in tragedy legendary figures, princes, and heroes in extraordinary situations are made to speak with lofty dignity. In every case the greatest importance is attached to compatibility between subject matter and expression. It is held to be ridiculous and in monstrous bad taste to treat of sublime matters in base, everyday, realistic words or of commonplace matters in the sublime style. This idea is expressed time and time again by Cicero, Horace, Quintilian, by the author of *On the Sublime,* and later by the innumerable rhetoricians who copied out the works of the classical theoreticians. The doctrine of the style levels led a phantom existence throughout the Middle Ages and awoke to new life in the era of Humanism. It should not be thought that the great orators and critics of late antiquity were petty pedants; they were flexible enough to recognize that a crass, realistic expression could occasionally be used effectively even in a "sublime" setting; and it was sometimes with admiration that they noted changes of level in a single work with one and the same overall style. But even this attitude presupposed a gradation of themes and a correspondence between subject matter and expression.

In Augustine, however, the principle of the three levels hinged exclusively on the author's specific purpose, accordingly as he wished to teach, to condemn or to praise, or to persuade. He found a similar view in Cicero; but he rejected Cicero's assumption that each level of style corresponded to a class of subject matter. The themes of Christian literature, he held, are all sublime; whatever lowly thing it may touch upon is elevated by its contact with Christianity. Nevertheless, the theory of the three levels of expression is useful to Christian teachers and orators; for Christian doctrine is not only sublime, but also obscure and difficult; yet since it is

intended for all, since it is desirable that all should understand it and live in accordance with it, it should be set
forth in the lowly, intermediate, or sublime style as the
situation requires.

III. THE TRADITION RENEWED

A Delight in Their Manner of Style and Phrase

FRANCIS BACON

MARTIN LUTHER, CONDUCTED no doubt by a higher providence, but in discourse of reason finding what a province he had undertaken against the bishop of Rome and the degenerate traditions of the church and finding his own solitude being no ways aided by the opinions of his own time, was enforced to awake all antiquity, and to call former times to his succours to make a party against the present time. So that the ancient authors, both in divinity and in humanity, which had long time slept in libraries, began generally to be read and revolved. This by consequence did draw on a necessity of a more exquisite travail in the languages original, wherein those authors did write, for the better understanding of those authors, and the better advantage of pressing and applying their words. And thereof grew again a delight in their manner of style and phrase, and an admiration of that kind of writing; which was much furthered and precipitated by the enmity and opposition that the propounders of those primitive but seeming new opinions had against the schoolmen; who were generally of the contrary part, and whose writings were altogether in a different style and form; taking liberty to coin and frame new terms of art to express their own sense, and to avoid circuit of speech, without regard to the pureness, pleasantness, and, as I may call it, lawfulness of the phrase or word. And again, because the great labour that then was with the people (of whom the Pharisees were wont to say, *Execrabilis ista turba, quae non*

From The Advancement of Learning, Book 1.

novit legem) ¹, for the winning and persuading of them, there grew of necessity in chief price and request eloquence and variety of discourse, as the fittest and forciblest access into the capacity of the vulgar sort: so that these four causes concurring, the admiration of ancient authors, the hate of the schoolmen, the exact study of languages, and the efficacy of preaching, did bring in an affectionate study of eloquence and copy of speech, which then began to flourish. This grew speedily to an excess; for men began to hunt more after words than matter; more after the choiceness of the phrase, and the round and clean composition of the sentence, and the sweet falling of the clauses, and the varying and illustration of their words with tropes and figures, than after the weight of matter, worth of subject, soundness of argument, life of invention, or depth of judgement. Then grew the flowing and watery vein of Osorius, the Portugal bishop, to be in price. Then did Sturmius spend such infinite and curious pains upon Cicero the Orator, and Hermogenes the Rhetorician, besides his own books of periods and imitation, and the like. Then did Car of Cambridge, and Ascham with their lectures and writings almost deify Cicero and Demosthenes, and allure all young men that were studious unto that delicate and polished kind of learning. Then did Erasmus take occasion to make the scoffing Echo: *Decem annos consumpsi in legendo Cicerone*²; and the Echo answered in Greek, "One Asine."³ Then grew the learning of the schoolmen to be utterly despised as barbarous. In sum, the whole inclination and bent of those times was rather towards copy than weight.

Latin and the Vernacular Tongues: 1575-1625

MORRIS W. CROLL

THE LAST QUARTER of the sixteenth century was the period when the literary claims and pretensions of Latin and the

¹ "This cursed people who knoweth not the law." *Ed.*
² "I have spent ten years in reading Cicero." *Ed.*
³ "Ass." *Ed.*

From Section III of "Attic Prose: Lipsius, Montaigne, Bacon," in Style, Rhetoric, and Rhythm, ed. by T. M. Patrick et al., Princeton, pp. 181-184. 1965. Also in Schelling Anniversary Papers, pp. 130-133. Reprinted by permission of Princeton University Press and Appleton-Century-Crofts.

modern languages were most evenly balanced, when it was easiest to pass from one to the other without a change of subject matter or style. Before that time there had been a fairly clear, though by no means a deliberate, differentiation of their uses. The chief artistic use of the vernacular in the sixteenth century had been to express the surviving medieval-ism of the culture of that age. It was the language, for in-stance, of what had been perhaps the most general medium of medieval literary expression, the sermon; it was the lan-guage of a multitude of romantically-retold tales of both antiquities, in which the fading ideals and customs of chivalry were adapted to an age of courtiers; it was the language of courtly ceremonial and show; it was the medium in which the medieval book of etiquette and universal instruction enjoyed a brief revival. It reflected, in brief, the customs of a courtly life which had not been modified in its essential features by the intellectual effort of the Renaissance. On the other hand, whatever was really new and forward-looking in the Renaissance found its prose expression in the ancient tongue. Some humanists, it is true, foresaw the modern uses of their mother-languages: Bembo, DuBellay, Ascham, for instance. Yet their writings are not representative of the usual vernacular prose of their time; and there is little distortion in the statement that in 1550 all serious, modern thought was expressed in Latin, and all that was tradition, or merely popular, in its character tended to find its way into vernacular prose.

One hundred years after that date the progress of modern-ism had reversed these relations in most respects. The usual language of serious criticism, and even of philosophy, had become English, French, or Italian; and, what is more important, the *subject* of literary criticism had become chiefly the vernacular languages and their usages; Latin was already the language of a dead literature, whose chief value was to enrich the native styles with romantic allusion, heroic images, and far-echoing rhythms.

In these observations there is of course nothing new, and the purpose of reviving them here is to call attention to a fact which scholarship has not yet clearly enough taken account of—that between the two *termini* that have just been mentioned there was a most interesting period in which the two languages, or the two kinds of languages, the ancient and the vernacular, were present in the minds of most well-educated people in relations of almost exact balance and

equality, and there were no real differences whatever between the uses of the one and the other. This period, which
extended over about two generations, one before the turn
of the century, one after, was the hinge on which the great
change turned, a quiet revolution, effected unconsciously in
the main, it would seem, and participated in by many who
would have regretted it if they had known what they were
doing, but of vastly more importance than most of the
changes which have been the subject of literary controversy.
This period should be more carefully studied by literary
historians with reference to the history of the modern languages than it has yet been; and there are the two comments
on it which are directly suggested by the study of "Attic"
prose.

The first has to do with the effect of the equalization of
the languages upon the vernacular literatures, and is to the
effect that out of this passing state of equilibrium emerged
a standard form of literary prose in every modern language,
upon which all later forms are founded and out of which they
have developed without radical or revolutionary change.

Italian, English, and French prose of the preceding periods
has various merits which antiquarians love to point out for
the reproof or exhortation of writers of the present day. But
none of it is quite *standard* prose. Some of it is too popular
and crude and violent. Some of it is too highly wrought and
fantastically mannered. And a third kind—the smallest class
—though pure and correct, is too poverty-stricken, thin, and
limited in its expressive resources. The explanation of this
fact of course is that, as we have just observed, men of
ideas reserved all the serious, progressive, and modern uses
of their intellects for expression in Latin; they felt that the
spoken languages had not been sufficiently conventionalized
to carry the definite meanings and logical processes of continued exposition. It was good for *concrete* uses alone. And
as long as this sort of differentiation continued in force
there could not be a standard prose style in either Latin or
the various vernaculars, for a standard form of prose is
determined by the *general* thought of the age which it expresses, its collective widsom and experience; it is neither
remotely and professionally intellectual, on the one hand,
nor a simple record of facts and sensations, on the other; its
function is rather to relate the varied phenomena of the external life of each period to its dominant ideas and the general philosophic trend of its mind. It is clear that no such

style could make its appearance in an age when the intellect spoke one language, the senses another.

On the other hand, when these two languages had become virtually interchangeable in the minds of a great many writers, as they were, for example, in the minds of Montaigne and Bacon, when one and the other came with equal ease and idiomatic freedom from their pens, it made little difference in fact which one they used, for each would have some of the characteristic quality of the other. A writer in Latin would show the colloquial and concrete qualities of his speech in his own language; a writer in French or English would derive from his Latin the rhetorical firmness, the exact use of abstraction, the logical process which the learned language imposes.

This is the phenomenon that we observe in fact in the period of Montaigne and Bacon. These are the first writers in the vernacular languages who employ a style which renders the process of thought and portrays the picturesque actuality of life with equal effect and constantly relates the one to the other; and it is in this sense that we may justify the statement that the Anti-Circeronian leaders—Montaigne, Charron, and Pasquier in France, Bacon, Hall, Jonson, Wotton in England—are the actual founders of modern prose style in their respective languages. In the works of these authors, and in none of those that precede them, we can find a style in the popular language which is at once firm, uniform, and level enough to be called a style and also adaptable enough to adjust itself to the changing life of the modern world—a style which may grow and change in later generations without losing its recognizable features.

Lyric Style in the 1590's

J. V. CUNNINGHAM

WORDSWORTH IN THE Preface to the *Lyrical Ballads* speaks of the formal engagement an author makes in the act of writing verse that "he will gratify certain known habits of association . . . that certain classes of ideas and expressions will be found in his book . . . that others will be carefully excluded." Now, the inclusion and exclusion of certain classes of ideas and expressions, and in verse of certain meters and metrical practices, constitutes a style. And in any literary situation certain attitudes and experiences, "certain known habits of association," are available to a particular style, and the exploration of other attitudes and experiences requires a new and different style, for a style is itself a principle of selection and order. This is what Wordsworth implies when he says in the sentence that follows: "This exponent or symbol held forth by metrical language must in different eras of literature have excited very different expectations; for example, . . . in the age of Shakespeare and Beaumont and Fletcher, and that of Donne and Cowley . . ." What we are concerned with here is the discrimination of certain kinds, or traditions, or styles of metrical language in a given literary situation, the 1590's in England, and the indication, so far as our clumsy means permit, of the exponent or symbol that these hold forth.

Now I need not tell this audience that the age of Shakespeare and Beaumont and Fletcher is the age of Donne, and that the age of Cowley is something else again. For Shakespeare and Donne, if we restrict ourselves to the evidence, appear on the literary scene at about the same time, around 1592, and Fletcher died five or six years before Donne. But the chronological dislocation that Wordsworth endorses still persists: it has distorted literary history, and consequently the interpretation of the relevant texts. In the Pelican guide to English Literature, for example, the works of the 1590's are distributed through the first three volumes: Spenser in volume I, Shakespeare and Jonson the dramatist in volume II, Donne and Jonson the poet in volume III, and there are only seven volumes for the whole of English literature from Chaucer to the present day.

Let us imagine, then, a young man, probably of good family and possibly a younger son—Campian or Wotton or Davies or Donne—who comes to London around 1590. He has, perhaps, a small patrimony, has had a thorough grammar school education, a year or two at Oxford or Cambridge, and has now entered the third university of England, one of the Inns of Court. He is, in brief, Lorenzo, Jr. alias Edward Knowell, of Ben Jonson's *Every Man in His Humour*.[1] And, indeed, that character is quite possibly modeled on Donne,

---

[1] The character is called Lorenzo, Jr. in the 1601 edition of the play (produced 1598), Edward Knowell in the revised 1616 edition.

for not only did Jonson later write a dialogue on poetry in which Donne was the principal speaker, but also Donne's *First Satire* furnishes the "invention" of the play: a scholarly young man of good family, interested in poetry, is invited by a friend and goes out on the town to observe and describe the follies of various social types. Our poet, then, is something of a wit, and is ambitious. He will write some toys in verse, partly to display his wit, and partly in the hope he will be noticed by someone in power, some official of the state who might further his ambitions—Lord Essex, let us say, or Sir Thomas Egerton. What will he write, and in what way will he write it? What styles were available? What styles could he reject?

There were notably two. The first is the one commonly associated with the Elizabethan lyric, what C. S. Lewis has called the Golden. It is, he says, a "poetry which is, so to speak, innocent or ingenuous. In a Golden Age the right thing to do is obvious; 'good is as visible as green.' . . . Men have at last learned how to write; for a few years nothing more is needed than to play out again and again the strong simple music of the uncontorted line and to load one's poem with all that is naturally delightful—with flowers and swans, with ladies' hair, hands, lips, breasts, and eyes, with silver and gold, woods and waters, the stars, the moon, and the sun."[2] It is a style I would prefer to call the sweet or pleasant style, *"dulce . . . orationis genus et solutum et fluens, sententiis argutum, verbis sonans"*—"sweet, fluent, and copious, with bright conceits and sounding phrases,"[3] the style of epideictic oratory. Its exemplar in its octosyllabic form is "The Passionate Shepherd to His Love:"

> Come live with me and be my love,
> And we will all the pleasures prove
> That valleys, groves, hills and fields,
> Woods or steepy mountain yields.

It is a poetry in which one sits

> By shallow rivers to whose falls
> Melodious birds sing madrigals.

Indeed, "The Passionate Shepherd" attains the perfection of

[2] C. S. Lewis, *English Literature in the Sixteenth Century* (Oxford, 1954), pp. 64-5.

[3] Cicero, *Orator*, 42.

which the sweet style is capable, for that style aims at a harmonious arrangement of elements that have already a preestablished harmony. It is really an abstract style, like a Navaho rug, dependent on design, and its triumphs are quite impersonal. Such a poem is written by no man but by a tradition.

But more basic and native at this time is another style, what Lewis calls the drab, and I the moral style. It is the style of "The Nymph's Reply to the Shepherd," ascribed quite plausibly to Ralegh:

> Time drives the flocks from field to fold,
> When rivers rage and rocks grow cold.
> And Philomel becometh dumb.
> The rest complains of cares to come.

It is relentlessly iambic; the line is organized in two distinct halves, with two four-syllable phrases bound into internal unity by structural alliteration of stressed syllables, or, for variation, the flat music of

> And Philomel becometh dumb.

It is a central, a limited, and an impressive style:

> But could youth last and love still breed,
> Had joys no date and age no need . . .

The locus classicus in decasyllabic form, of course, is:

> O eyes! no eyes, but fountains fraught with tears;
> O life! no life, but lively form of death;
> O world! no world, but mass of public wrongs,
> Confused and filled with murder and misdeeds! [4]

In poulter's measure it is the style of Father Southwell's "The Burning Babe," for the old habit of vision goes comfortably with it. It is the way in which one writes in the Tower on the eve of execution. "Even such is time that takes in trust," or "Tichbourne's Elegy" (1586):

> I sought my death and found it in my womb,
> I looked for life and saw it was a shade,
> I trod the earth and knew it was my tomb,
> And now I die, and now I was but made.
> My glass is full, and now my glass is run,
> And now I live, and now my life is done.

[4] Thomas Kyd, *The Spanish Tragedy*, 3. 2. 1-4.

"Tichbourne's Elegy" belongs to a particular literary kind, what I call the moral poem, which is the exemplar and pattern of the moral style. It is a small but sturdy genre that flourished in the late middle ages, and continued to thrive until the last decade of the sixteenth century: Chaucer's "Flee fro the press, and dwelle with sothfastnesse," and Dunbar's "Be mirry, man, and tak nocht far in mynd," are examples of this style. It consists of a sequence in serial order of *sententiae,* maxims, proverbs, or propositions of a similar kind, usually one to a line, sometimes two, and occasionally a single *sententia* over two lines, commonly in decasyllables and in an extended stanza, often in ballade form. The decasyllable is normally phrased in fours and sixes in iambic pattern, though sometimes in reverse order of six and four, and the phrases are bound by alliteration of stressed syllables:

> The life is long that loathsomely doth last,
> The doleful days draw slowly to their date,
> The present pangs and painful plagues forpast
> Yield grief aye green to stablish this estate,
> So that I feel in this great storm and strife
> The death is sweet that endeth such a life.

Thus line is piled on line in unvarying units. When successful, as in "Tichbourne's Elegy," the moral poem expresses a cumulative experience of serious insistence. For it is moral, in the simple, old-fashioned meaning of that term.

Hence the exponent or symbol of this particular and quite limited tradition is easy to describe: a heavy-handed seriousness, a scorn of urbanity, a deliberate rejection of that delicacy which would discriminate shades of white and of black. It is a morally ruthless, secure, and overpowering style. And so Sidney in the *Astrophil* series, as he accumulates compliments, exploits sentiment, and dallies with the potentialities of adultery, is ever vigilant against the stable four and six structure and the firm advancing beat of the "drumming decasyllabon":

> Dear, therefore be not jealous over me
> If you hear that they seem my heart to move.
> Not them, oh no, but you in them I love.

In contrast, when he expresses the old morality in those sonnets that are often appended by editors at the end of *Astrophil,* he does it in the moral style:

> Band of all evils, cradle of causeless care,
> Thou web of will whose end is never wrought,
> Desire, desire! I have too dearly bought
> With price of mangled mind thy worthless ware.

And:

> Then farewell world, thy uttermost I see.
> Eternal love, maintain thy life in me.

By the end of the decade the moral style had lost for the most part its productive vigor; only Matheo and Bobadilla of *Every Man in His Humour* in 1598 think the "O eyes! no eyes!" passage "simply the best that ever you heard." Yet on an apt occasion, with an obvious subject and direct feelings about it, those who grew up with the style can return to it, as Donne did in "A Hymn to God the Father," with verbal repetition instead of structural alliteration:

> Wilt thou forgive that sin where I begun,
> Which was my sin though it were done before?
> Wilt thou forgive those sins through which I run
> And do run still though still I do deplore?

It is a poem from an earlier age.

The sweet and the moral, then, were available to the young man in 1590; they were styles he could accept or reject, and those we are concerned with here for the most part rejected them. And the new style? It is said to be "metaphysical," and to have been innovated by Donne. Now much has been said of this style, and much that has been said is untrue. It is said to be colloquial, which it is not, except in rare passages of dialogue, as in the "First Satire." But *colloquial* is not really a descriptive term in current criticism but a term of praise, like *subtle* and *complex,* and like those terms in need of definition. By *colloquial,* I take it, one means that in the sort of situation sketched or implied in the poem what is said is what could be said somewhat casually by one person to another without seeming to be affected, or indeed insane. One has only to visualize the situations in Donne's lyrics and try acting them out to have unappeasable doubts about his colloquiality:

> I wonder, by my troth, what thou and I
> Did till we loved?

This could possibly be said musingly, though hardly in reply to some remark of the partner. But what will the lady make of:

> Were we not weaned till then?
> But sucked on country pleasures childishly?
> Or snorted we in the seven sleepers' den?

No, the style is not really colloquial, for these are not dialogues. They are in part written in the familiar style of the familiar letter, as perhaps here, and in a variety of different styles. For the genuinely colloquial in the lyric you will do better with Sidney who sometimes writes a shorter poem in dialogue form:

> "Take me to thee and thee to me."
> "No, no, no, no, my dear, let be."

The truth is, the work of Donne that would be available to his circle at this time does not offer a consistent model of style. His answer to "The Passionate Shepherd," for example, opens in the pleasant style:

> And we will some new pleasures prove
> Of golden sands and crystal brooks,

proceeds by way of a light line to a Petrarchan hyperbole:

> There will the river whispering run,
> Warmed by thy eyes more than the sun.

then to a Gorgianic figure of the "living sepulcher" type:

> When thou wilt swim in that live bath,

developed now by the qualification of philosophic exactness:

> Each fish which every channel hath

and ending with a juxtaposition of grammatical words which one may call colloquial but which defies the enunciation of common speech:

> Will amorously to thee swim,
> Gladder to catch thee than thou him.

Actually, this is probably an attempt to do what Latin permits and English resists. A little further on we get rather simple bad writing, the jammed-up line:

> Let coarse, bold hands from slimy nest
> The bedded fish in banks out-wrest.

And the poem concludes with an easy, and pleasing enough, urbanity:

> That fish that is not catched thereby,
> Alas, is wiser far than I.

This is not a style but a heterogeneity of styles.

A similar stylistic uncertainty can be seen in a much better poem, "The Calm," written in 1597 during the Islands expedition, and one of the poems we have reason to believe would have been available as a model in this decade. It begins:

> Our storm is past, and that storm's tyrannous rage
> A stupid calm, but nothing it, doth swage.

The couplet is troubled by a tight idiomatic qualification, "but nothing it," which is not needed by the rationale of the poem; it is a metaphysical side-reflection, an operation on a term. There follows an allusion to an obscure fable. Then in a few lines:

> As steady as I can wish that my thoughts were,
> Smooth as thy mistress' glass, or what shines there,
> The sea is now.

This is random ingenuity. The young Donne is an improvisatory genius, an extemporal wit, a better born Thomas Nashe. As Samuel Butler the elder put it: "Dr. Donne's writings are like Voluntary or Prelude, in which a man is not tied to any particular design of Air, but may change his Key or mode at pleasure. So his compositions seem to have been written without any particular scope," that is, end in view.

Yet he does in another sense have an end in view. His motive is clear and explicit; it is the desire for novelty:

> And we will some new pleasures prove.

Now, the charm of "The Passionate Shepherd" lies precisely in its lack of novelty; it is the almost accidental issue of an apparently stable tradition. Again, the force and weight of "The Nymph's Reply" is grounded on the age-old wisdom of her sentences. Novelty, however, is no positive principle; it stipulates only a something else. It is a principle of rejection rather than of selection. The author of "The Bait" will go neither Marlowe's way nor Ralegh's; but if he goes he must go some way, and we may ask, Where does he find it? In the detail of style, as we have seen, he goes uncertainly. And as for the invention? His shepherd is not a shepherd but a fisherman, and that is the clue. For at the end of the last century Sannazaro sought to treat the pastoral convention under a novel guise, and wrote his Latin piscatory eclogues. That is, Donne goes for his invention to that vast, once living though now dead, body of contemporary literature, the current Latin poetry of the Renaissance. And not only in this instance. The whole body of his early work, with the partial exception, and it is partial only, of the *Songs and Sonnets,* is an attempt to realize in English the contemporary forms of occasional poetry in Latin, and especially those that admitted the particularities of sexual or of disreputable experience, and the details of everyday life. He writes epigram, not in the tradition of Heywood, but in that of Martial, and satires on the model of Horace. He uses the verse letter as the humanist poets used it. He naturalizes the subjective-erotic elegy of Propertius and Ovid, and writes an heroical epistle whose subject is Lesbianism; as, also, an epithalamium which, if you compare it with Spenser's, is clearly the epithalamium of a Latinist.

But Donne was not alone in turning his interest to the erotic experience of Latin elegy and the realistic social description of satire and epigram. It is an interest that suddenly appears, and at precisely this time, in several other men of his own age, and one somewhat older, at the Inns of Court as he was. The older poet was Thomas Campian, whose elegies and epigrams in Latin were printed in 1595, but whose *Observations in the Art of English Poesy,* containing fully realized English epigrams in the Latin mode, and one elegy, may be the book entered in the Stationer's Register on October 12, 1591.[5] If the text entered in 1591 was substantially the text printed in 1602, Campian may have given the hint, though to Ben Jonson, some years later, Donne is the innovator:

> Whose every work of thy most early wit
> Came forth example, and remains so yet.

But to realize new genres, to explore hitherto unexploited areas of experience, involves the problem of style. Neither the pleasant nor the moral style would do; the material was inherently repugnant to them. What was needed was the

[5] I owe this date to Professor Walter R. Davis of the University of Notre Dame.

English equivalent of the Classical plain style in Latin. This John Davies, among others, attempted to supply in his *Epigrams,* datable about 1594. It is a plain style, but it is the plainest of plain styles, the *genus humile* rather than the *genus tenue.* However, it can handle the sights and sounds and characters and place names of the streets of London, directly and without disguise:

> See yonder melancholy gentleman
> Which hoodwinked with his hat alone doth sit,
> Think what he thinks, and tell me if you can
> What great affairs trouble his little wit.
> He thinks not of the war 'twixt France and Spain. . .
> But he doth seriously bethink him whether
> Of the gulled people he be more esteemed
> For his long cloak or his great black feather,
> By which each gull is now a gallant deemed.
> Or of a journey he deliberates
> To Paris Garden, Cockpit, or the play,
> Or how to steal a dog he meditates,
> Or what he shall unto his mistress say.

Here is no alliterative phrasing, or phrasing by fours and sixes. Here is nothing that is naturally delightful. It is a prosaic style; it has, in fact, the characteristics of good workaday prose, in which what interest there is is in what is being talked of. But it is workaday prose in metrical form at a time when there was little workaday prose in literary prose. It can handle any subject so long as it can be handled in its proper terms and without adornment. It is the flat style. It aims at a unassuming lack of distinction, and with appropriate material has its own rightness, as in Hoskyns' epitaph "On a Man for Doing Nothing":

> Here lies the man was born and cried,
> Told threescore years, fell sick, and died.

But the difficulty with the flat style, of course, is that it is flat. This is what Jonson had in mind when he told Sir John Harington that his epigrams "were narrations and not epigrams," or said of Owen's that they were "bare narrations." That is, to translate the remarks into our English, Harington's epigrams and Owen's are unadorned exposition, without distinction of style. So Shakespeare in an experiment in the flat style and its attendant attitudes and subjects seeks to relieve

or transform the flatness by introducing some verbal figures
that might be thought congruent with the style:

> When my love swears that she is made of truth
> I do believe her though I know she lies,
> That she might think me some untutored youth
> Unlearned in the world's false subtleties.

So far all is flat, except for the slight rhetorical touch of
"untutored," "unlearned." But now he introduces more point-
edness:

> Thus vainly thinking that she thinks me young,
> Although she knows my days are past the best,
> Simply I credit her false-speaking tongue;
> On both sides thus is simple truth suppressed.

And concludes with an epigrammatic pun:

> Therefore I lie with her and she with me,
> And in our faults by lies we flattered be.

By such means, by a sparse use of the elementary verbal
figures, together with a tightness of metrical form, there
was developed what I call the English plain style. The chief
technical difference between this and the Classical plain style,
which I shall next discuss, is the bareness of its diction
and the regular coincidence of grammatical and metrical
units, whereas in the classical style, especially when written
in decasyllabic couplets, the lines are often run-over, or, as
Jonson says, "broken like hexameters." Small masterpieces
of the English plain style are Hoskyns' "Absence" and Ay-
toun's "Upon Love":

> I loved thee once, I'll love no more,
> Thine be the grief as is the blame,
> Thou art not what thou wast before,
> What reason I should be the same?
> He who can love unloved again
> Hath better store of love than brain.
> God send me love my debts to pay,
> While unthrifts fool their love away.

Styles are noticeable or unnoticeable. The sweet and the
moral are noticeable; the flat is unnoticeable but undistinguished. What is needed is a noticeably unnoticeable style,
the style of Cicero's Attic orator, "a directness of speech

that seems to one judging easily imitable, to one trying it nothing less so." *"Nam orationis subtilitas imitabilis illa videtur esse existimanti, sed nihil est experienti minus."*[6] Such a style first appears in this particular literary situation scattered here and there in Sidney's *Astrophil and Stella,* as in the passage quoted earlier:

> Dear, therefore be not jealous over me
> If you hear that they seem my heart to move.
> Not them, oh no, but you in them I love.

If Campian's "The Writer to His Book" was written by 1591 there was a fully realized model in blank verse available to the poets we are concerned with:

> "Whither thus hastes my little book so fast?"
> "To Paul's Churchyard." "What! in those cells to stand
> With one leaf like a rider's cloak put up
> To catch a termer?"

How close this is to Jonson:

> Nor have my title-leaf on posts or walls
> Or in cleft sticks advanced to make calls
> For termers . . .

It is the style of Donne's early poetry at its best. A style that can handle circumstantiality and detail, can accommodate in poetry what we think of as the material of prose, and yet without modulation of manner can strike through to the heart of human feeling. In Donne's early poetry it appears intermittently, amid a debris of other incongruous and indecorous manners, but when it appears it is absolute, unrevisably right. It appears in the verse letter, "The Calm," to which we alluded earlier, in the couplet Jonson pointed out to Drummond of Hawthornden:

> No use of lanterns [ventilators] and in one place lay
> Feathers and dust, today and yesterday.

a kind of exact and minute particularity almost unknown to the poetry of the preceding decades. Or:

> Whether a rotten state, and hope of gain,
> Or to disuse me from the queasy pain
> Of being beloved, and loving, or the thirst

[6] *Orator,* 76.

> Of honor or fair death out pushed me first,
> I lose my end.

Or again:

> What are we then? How little more, alas,
> Is man now than before he was. He was
> Nothing. For us, we are for nothing fit:
> Chance or ourselves still disproportion it.

Where did Donne get this style? Possibly from Sidney, possibly from Campian, but certainly from the effort to realize in English the forms of Latin poetry, and their appropriate styles. There remained only for a Ben Jonson to recognize it, perfect and establish it, and in the forms that Donne had pioneered: epigram, elegy, satire, verse letter, epithalamium, and in the same tradition of Latin learning. The relationship of Jonson and Donne is that of Horace to Lucillius, perfector to inventor.

THE PASSIONATE SHEPHERD TO HIS LOVE

CHRISTOPHER MARLOWE

> Come live with me and be my love,
> And we will all the pleasures prove
> That valleys, groves, hills and fields,
> Woods or steepy mountain yields.
>
> And we will sit upon the rocks,
> Seeing the shepherds feed their flocks
> By shallow rivers to whose falls
> Melodious birds sing madrigals.
>
> And I will make thee beds of roses
> And a thousand fragrant posies,
> A cap of flowers, and a kirtle
> Embroidered all with leaves of myrtle,
>
> A gown made of the finest wool
> Which from our pretty lambs we pull,
> Fair-linèd slippers for the cold,
> With buckles of the purest gold.
>
> A belt of straw and ivy-buds
> With coral clasps and amber studs:
> And if these pleasures may thee move,
> Come live with me and be my love.

The shepherds' swains shall dance and sing
For thy delight each May morning:
If these delights thy mind may move,
Then live with me and be my love.

THE NYMPH'S REPLY TO THE SHEPHERD

WALTER RALEGH

If all the world and love were young,
And truth in every shepherd's tongue,
These pretty pleasures might me move
To live with thee and be thy Love.

Time drives the flocks from field to fold
When rivers rage and rocks grow cold
And Philomel becometh dumb;
The rest complains of cares to come.

The flowers do fade, and wanton fields
To wayward Winter reckoning yields.
A honey tongue, a heart of gall,
Is fancy's spring, but sorrow's fall.

Thy gowns, thy shoes, thy beds of roses,
Thy cap, thy kirtle, and thy posies,
Soon break, soon wither, soon forgotten,
In folly ripe, in reason rotten.

Thy belt of straw and ivy-buds,
Thy coral clasps and amber studs,
All these in me no means can move
To come to thee, and by thy love.

But could youth last, and love still breed,
Had joys no date nor age no need,
Then these delights my mind might move
To live with thee, and be thy Love.

THE BAIT

JOHN DONNE

Come live with me and be my love,
And we will some new pleasures prove
Of golden sands and crystal brooks,
With silken lines and silver hooks.
There will the river whispering run,

Warmed by thine eyes more than the sun,
And there the enamored fish will stay,
Begging themselves they may betray.

When thou wilt swim in that live bath,
Each fish which every channel hath
Will amorously to thee swim,
Gladder to catch thee than thou him.

If thou to be so seen be'st loath,
By sun or moon, thou darkenest both,
And if myself have leave to see,
I need not their light, having thee.

Let others freeze with angling reeds,
And cut their legs with shells and weeds,
Or treacherously poor fish beset
With strangling snare or windowy net;

Let coarse bold hands from slimy nest
The bedded fish in banks outwrest,
Or curious traitors, sleave-silk flies,
Bewitch poor fishes' wandering eyes.

For thee, thou need'st no such deceit,
For thou thyself art thine own bait;
That fish that is not catched thereby,
Alas, is wiser far than I.

On Sound and Diction

PIERRE NICOLE

As Cicero so notably says, time that erases the fictions of opinion only confirms the judgments of nature.[1]

If we may apply this maxim to literature we may say that that is truly beautiful which agrees both with the nature of things themselves and with the inclinations of our senses and of our soul. And since in a work of literature one takes account of sound, diction, and idea, the agreement of all these

From **An Essay on True and Apparent Beauty**, by Pierre Nicole, translated by J. V. Cunningham. Augustan Reprint Society, No. 24, University of California, Los Angeles, 1950. The original, Paris, 1659.

[1] *On the Nature of the Gods*, 2.2.5.

with nature in its two aspects is required for beauty. Hence we will take these up one by one, beginning with sound.

ON SOUND

HOW SELDOM IT CHARMS IN ECHOING THE SENSE, HOW COMMONLY BY SWEETNESS. ITS NATURAL MEASURE IN THE EAR.

We have assigned the first division of natural beauty to sound, which we distinguish from diction in that propriety and force of meaning are looked to in this; in sound it is the pleasantness or harshness that is regarded, flattering or offending the ear, or it is a kind of imitation of the subject matter—sad things recited tearfully, excited rapidly, or harsh harshly. This is common enough in the spoken word; in writing, however, with which we are chiefly concerned here, it is uncommon, though Virgil sometimes quite happily represents the sound of things themselves, their swiftness and slowness, in the sound of his verse. When you hear, for example, the well-known *procumbit humi bos,* do you not seem to hear the blunt sound of the falling bull? Or when you read the line *Quadrupedante putrem sonitu quatit ungula campum,*[2] doesn't the sound of running horses strike your ears? But this effect, as I said, is uncommon, and hardly to be found in any other poet than Virgil. Thus the chief potentiality of sound, and the most common, lies in charming the ear. It is a slight beauty, yet it is of nature, and for this reason especially agreeable to all classes of people. For there is scarcely any person so uneducated as not to be naturally displeased at what is incomplete and botched, or not to perceive what is full, ordered, and defined. Hence Cicero says justly in the *Orator:*

> The ear, or the soul at the injunction of the ears, possesses a natural way of measuring sounds, by this judges some longer, some shorter, and ever anticipates the completion of a measure. It feels hurt when a rhythm is maimed or curtailed as if it had been defrauded of due payment. It dislikes even more whatever is prolonged and runs on beyond the proper bounds, since too much is more offensive than too little. Not that everyone knows the metrical feet, or understands anything about rhythm, or is aware of

[2] *Aeneid,* 5.481 and 8.596.

what offends him, or where, or why; it is rather that nature has set in our ears a power of judging the length and brevity of sound, as also the acute and grave accent of words.[3]

PLEASANTNESS OF SOUNDS IS JUSTLY EXACTED OF POETS. THE HARSHNESS OF MANY POETS, PARTICULARLY THE GERMAN. SOME ARE TOO MELODIOUS.

Hence it is that anyone who wishes to conform to nature must necessarily strive for pleasantness of sound. This is the more justly exacted of poets since poetry itself is nothing other than measured language, bound into fixed numbers and feet, for the purpose of charming the ear. Consequently, those poets are justly censured who rest content with rounding off their words in six feet and altogether neglect to accommodate the ear. A good many epigrammatists are constant offenders in this kind, especially those who have rendered the Greek Anthology in Latin and the German poets.

For example, who can tolerate this German epigram?

> He who made all that nothing was of nothing,
> Who'll make that nothing that now something is,
> Made you who nothing were what you now are
> From nothing, will make nothing what you are—
> Yes, or if something, being but sin from sin,
> From sin must form something for heaven fit.

Again, what is harsher than this epigram?

> You from your soul could not but know mine that
> That gave up in your ghost but just now his:
> As soul is known from soul so is your ghost
> Known to the Muses by my muse that's yours.

Or than this distich?

> Forward, nor turn from the old path one bit:
> This that you are I while I live shall be.

But just as it is a considerable fault in diction wholly to neglect the pleasure of the ear, since verse, as we said, was devised to flatter it, so on the other hand those writers make a grievous mistake who have an immoderate regard for the ear, and pay no attention to the thought so long as they are satisfied with the sound. Out of such concern we

[3] Orators, 177-8, 173.

get tuneful trifles and verses empty of substance. Writers who have by an attentive consideration of the poets achieved the faculty of poetic diction and rhythm quite often fall into this error. They abound in choice phrases and so are in effect content to smooth over the commonplace with a not indecorous makeup. You can see this in many poems and epigrams of Buchanan, Borbonius, and Barleius. If the reader is not quite attentive such poems will often deceive him, but being reread and examined they beget a kind of distaste because of the thinness of the matter. Consequently, we have looked carefully for this fault, and have eliminated many poems that are melodious in this way and have nothing inside.

HOW DICTION SHOULD BE SUITED TO SUBJECT MATTER.

We come now to the question of conforming the diction and subject matter to nature, in which, as was said above, nature must be considered in its double aspect: namely, in relation to the subjects of which we speak, and in relation to the audience by whom we are heard or read.

The agreement of words and subject consists in this: that lofty words should be fitted to lofty subjects, and lowly to lowly. It is true, of course, that every kind of writing demands simplicity, but the simplicity meant is such as does not exclude sublimity or vehemence. In fact, it is no less faulty to treat high and weighty subjects in a slight and unassuming style than it is to treat what is slight and unassuming in a high and weighty style. In both of these ways one departs from that agreement with nature in which, we have said, beauty resides. Therefore, not every piece of writing admits the rhetorical figures and ornaments, and likewise not every one excludes them. The answer lies wholly in whether there is throughout a complete harmony between diction and subject.

In addition, I wish you would carefully observe something that few do—namely, when you temper your diction to the subject, to regard it not only as it is in itself or in the mind of the writer, but also as it has been formed by your speech in the minds of your audience. Thus, the reader is assumed to be unacquainted with what you have to say at the beginning of a work, and hence you must use simple language to initiate him into your lines of thought. Afterward you may build upon this foundation what you can. It follows that if you are to speak of some outrageous crime, you should not inveigh against it with a comparable violence of diction until your audience has achieved such a notion of the crime as will not be at odds with such force and violence.

Thus Virgil begins in the best way with simple diction:

> Arms and the man I sing who first from Troy
> Banished by fate came to the Italian shore.

And Homer too, who was praised for this by Horace:

> Speak to me, Muse, of him, when Troy had fallen,
> Who saw the ways of many and their cities.

But Statius begins badly, and sweeps the reader away too suddenly in these verses:

> Fraternal arms, and alternate rule by hate
> Profane contested, and the guilt of Thebes
> I sing, moved by the fiery Muse.

Claudian is even more at fault, and thrusts these bombastic lines on our unprepared attention:

> The horses of Hell's rapist, the stars blown
> By the Taenarian chariot, chambers dark
> Of lower Juno . . .

But this rule should particularly be observed in the use of adjectives, which are always ill-joined with their noun when they disaccord with the impression the reader has in his mind. I have seen the opening of Lucan censured on this point:

> Wars through Emathian fields, wars worse than civil,
> And crime made legal is my song.

The critics urge that the epithet "worse than civil" could justly be employed after the depiction of the slaughter at Pharsalia, but that here it is out of order and suddenly attacks the reader who was thinking of no such thing. It offends against the precept of Horace:

> Not smoke from brightness is his aim, but light
> He gives from smoke.

IN WHAT WAY DICTION SHOULD ANSWER TO MAN'S INNER NATURE. FIRST, THE GROUNDS OF THE NATURAL DISAFFECTION WITH UNUSUAL DICTION: HOW FAR THIS SHOULD BE OBSERVED.

But it is not sufficient that diction answer to the subject matter unless it also answers to the nature of man, in which may be discerned a kind of aversion to obsolete, low, and inappropriate words. I prefer to call this aversion a natural one rather than a result of opinion, though it is in a way based on opinion. For although the feeling that a particular word is more in common use and more civilized than another is purely a matter of men's judgment, nevertheless it is as natural to be displeased by the unusual and inappropriate as it is to be pleased with the usual and proper. Whatever is contrary to reason offends by the very fact that it is seen to lack reason. Certainly, to leave aside familiar terms and to search out unusual ones is wholly foreign to reason. However, there is added to this natural source of offense another that proceeds from opinion. Since such words are commonly condemned, there is associated with them a certain distaste and contempt such that it is scarcely possible to pronounce them without immediately arousing the associated feelings.

Consequently, the intelligent writer will willingly comply with usage so as not to give grounds for displeasure—whether this displeasure springs from nature or opinion. Though he is aware that usage is unstable and changes day by day, nevertheless he will prefer rather to please at one time than never. He will be careful, however, in his written work not to make use of the current jargon, especially of the French court and women's circles, or of any locutions that are not yet generally received. For the life of such expressions is too short to be bound into a lasting work—not to speak of the detestable affectation which detracts from the weight and dignity of the writing.

To conclude, there is a beauty and charm in propriety and elegance of diction which is not to be scorned, though it is but of a time, and, since it rests on opinion, by which usage is determined, will pass away with a change of opinion. Hence those who write not for an age but for all time should try to attain something else, something that has no admixture of opinion: such is the agreement of words with nature, which we will now explain.

THE INNER AND MORE INTIMATE AGREEMENT OF WORDS AND NATURE.

If one wishes to look deeply into the nature of the human mind and to search out its inner sources of delight, he will find there something of strength conjoined with something of weakness, and out of this circumstance arises variety and irregularity. The mind's vexation with a continual relaxation derives from its strength, while from its weakness stems the fact that it cannot bear a continual straining. Hence it is that nothing pleases the human mind very long, nothing that is all of one piece. So in music it rejects a wholly perfect harmony, and for this reason musicians deliberately intercalate discordant sounds—what are technically called dissonances. So, finally, it happens that physical exercise, even if it was at first undertaken for pleasure, becomes torture when continued without interruption.

This point has its pertinence to literature, the more so since in that field nature reveals the greatest delicacy and cannot long endure what is lofty and excited. Yet on the other hand, whatever creeps close to earth and never lifts its head is, if it be prolonged, wearisome. To stand, to rest, to rise up, to be thrown down, this is what every reader or listener desires, and from this derives the driving necessity for variety, for the mingling of the majestic and slight, excited and calm, high and low. But it may seem that this consideration has little pertinence to the epigram, which is brief and so in less need of variety. However, I need not apologize for introducing these more general considerations since others of more immediate pertinence to the course of our discussion are derived from them, and particularly the question of the discriminate use of metaphors, which are of considerable effect in adorning or vitiating poetry.

For if we consider attentively why men are pleased with metaphors we will find no other reason than that already stated: the weakness of nature which is wearied by the inflexibility of truth and plain statement and must be refreshed by an admixture of metaphors which depart somewhat from the truth. This gives the clue to the proper and legitimate use of metaphors: they are to be employed specifically, as musicians employ discordant sounds, to relieve the distaste of perfect harmony. But how frequently and at what point they should be introduced is a matter of considerable caution and skill. One warning will suffice for the present: that metaphors, hyperboles, and whatever varies from the plain and natural way of saying something should not be sought for their own sakes but as a kind of relief for nauseated nature. They are to be accepted on grounds of necessity, and consequently a good deal of moderation must be observed in their use. Thus Quintilian rightly says, "A sparing and opportune use of these figures gives luster to speech: frequent use obscures and fills with disgust." [4] You will discover this fault often in many epigrams, especially in those of contemporary writers, as I shall show by several examples later on. However, lest this doctrine should issue in too strict an austerity of diction, it should be noted that only those expressions are to be taken as metaphors that are remote from ordinary usage and offer the mind a double idea. Hence if a metaphor is so commonplace that it no longer has a figurative connotation and suggests nothing other than the notion itself for which it is used, then it should be numbered among proper rather than metaphorical expressions and does not fall in that class of tropes whose too frequent use is here censured.

ON A TOO METAPHORICAL STYLE. CERTAIN EPIGRAMS REJECTED FOR THIS REASON.

Though poets are granted a greater indulgence in the use of tropes, nevertheless they have their own mean, or, as Cicero says, their own modesty, and there is ever an especial ornament to be derived from simplicity. Consequently those writers stray pretty far from beauty for whom, as it were, all nature plays the ham to the point that they say nothing in an ordinary way, imagine nothing in the way in which it is perceived outside of poems, but instead elevate, debase, alter, and clothe everything in a theatrical mask. For this reason we have excluded from this anthology a number of epigrams as too metaphorical: for example, these two by Daniel Heinsius, a man otherwise eminent in scholarship and letters:

> Driver of light, courier of the bright pole,
> Surveyor of the sky, and hour-divider,
> Servant of time, circler perpetual,
> Cleanser of earth, disperser of the clouds,
> Ever your chariot, fiery four-in-hand,
> You curb fast; you who bear on the bright day
> Steal from the world once more your countenance
> And of your glowing hair conceal the flame;
> Tomorrow from the arms of Tethys you
> Return once more: but night has sealed my sun.

By "my sun" he means Douza. And again:

> Sweet children of the night, brothers of fire,
> Small cohorts, citizens of the fiery pole,
> Who wandering through the cloudless fields of air
> Lead the soft choruses with a light foot
> When our tired bodies are stretched softly out
> And gentle sleep invades our conquered sense,
> Why now as then through the enameled halls
> From the recesses, still, and the clear windows
> Of the gold arch bear off his hallowed face?
> Farewell, at last; you shall not see your Douza. [5]

In these epigrams, apart from the metaphors heaped up *ad nauseam,* and each of them harsh and absurd, a keen critic has noted another fault: namely, that nothing is more distant from the spirit of a man grieving and mourning for the death of a friend—and this is what Heinsius intended to depict—than such a wantonness of epithets. And so much for diction.

Pulpit Style

JONATHAN SWIFT

I COULD LIKEWISE have been glad, if you had applied yourself a little more to the study of the English language than I fear you have done; the neglect whereof is one of the most general defects among the scholars of this kingdom, who seem to have not the least conception of a style, but run on in a flat kind of phraseology, often mingled with barbarous terms and expressions, peculiar to the nation. Neither do I perceive that any person either finds or acknowledges his

---

[5] Nicole's criticism of these poems is just but superficial. The difficulty with such poems lies in the method, which consists in the establishment by amplification of one pole, followed by the briefest statement of the contrary pole. But the latter is of personal concern and is the essential subject of the poem. Thus the subject is deliberately avoided for the greater part of the poem, and hence there is in the amplification no principle of order to control the detail and its accumulation. This accounts for the features Nicole censures; however, he himself makes a similar point below in condemning negative descriptions.

From A Letter to a Young Gentleman Lately Entered into Holy Orders.

wants upon this head, or in the least desires to have them supplied. Proper words in proper places, makes the true definition of a style. But this would require too ample a disquisition to be now dwelt on: however, I shall venture to name one or two faults, which are easy to be remedied, with a very small portion of ability.

The first is the frequent use of obscure terms, which by the women are called *hard words*, and by the better sort of vulgar, *fine language;* than which I do not know a more universal, inexcusable, and unnecessary mistake, among the clergy of all distinctions, but especially the younger practitioners. I have been curious enough to take a list of several hundred words in a sermon of a new beginner, which not one of his hearers among a hundred could possibly understand; neither can I easily call to mind any clergyman of my own acquaintance who is wholly exempt from this error, although many of them agree with me in the dislike of the thing. But I am apt to put myself in the place of the vulgar, and think many words difficult or obscure, which the preacher will not allow to be so, because those words are obvious to scholars. I believe the method observed by the famous Lord Falkland in some of his writings, would not be an ill one for young divines: I was assured by an old person of quality who knew him well, that when he doubted whether a word was perfectly intelligible or no, he used to consult one of his lady's chambermaids (not the waiting woman, because it was possible she might be conversant in romances), and by her judgement was guided whether to receive or reject it. And if that great person thought such a caution necessary in treatises offered to the learned world, it will be sure at least as proper in sermons, where the meanest hearer is supposed to be concerned, and where very often a lady's chambermaid may be allowed to equal half the congregation, both as to quality and understanding. But I know not how it comes to pass, that professors in most arts and sciences are generally the worst qualified to explain their meanings to those who are not of their tribe. A common farmer should make you understand in three words, *that his foot is out of joint, or his collarbone broken,* wherein a surgeon, after a hundred terms of art, if you are not a scholar, shall leave you to seek. It is frequently the same case in law, physic, and even many of the meaner arts.

And upon this account it is, that among *hard words,* I number likewise those which are peculiar to divinity as it is a science; because I have observed several clergymen, other-

wise little fond of obscure terms, yet in their sermons very
liberal of those which they find in ecclesiastical writers, as if
it were our duty to understand them; which I am sure it is
not. And I defy the greatest divine to produce any law either
of God or man, which obliges me to comprehend the meaning
of *omniscience, omnipresence, ubiquity, attribute, beatific
vision,* with a thousand others so frequent in pulpits, any
more than that of *eccentric, idiosyncrasy, entity* and the like.
I believe I may venture to insist further, that many terms
used in Holy Writ, particularly by St. Paul, might with
more discretion be changed into plainer speech, except when
they are introduced as part of a quotation.

I am the more earnest in this matter, because it is a general
complaint, and the justest in the world. For a divine has nothing to say to the wisest congregation of any parish in this
kingdom, which he may not express in a manner to be understood by the meanest among them. And this assertion must
be true, or else God requires from us more than we are
able to perform. However, not to contend whether a logician
might possibly put a case that would serve for an exception,
I will appeal to any man of letters, whether at least nineteen
in twenty of those perplexing words might not be changed
into easy ones, such as naturally first occur to ordinary men,
and probably did so at first to those very gentlemen who are
so fond of the former.

We are often reproved by divines from the pulpits, on account of our ignorance in things sacred, and perhaps with
justice enough. However, it is not very reasonable for them
to expect, that *common men* should understand expressions
which are never made use of in *common life.* No gentleman
thinks it safe or prudent to send a servant with a message,
without repeating it more than once, and endeavouring to put
it into terms brought down to the capacity of the bearer. Yet
after all this care, it is frequent for servants to mistake, and
sometimes to occasion misunderstandings between friends, although the common domestics in some gentlemen's families
may have more opportunities of improving their minds than
the ordinary sort of tradesmen.

It is usual for clergymen who are taxed with this learned
defect, to quote Dr. Tillotson, and other famous divines, in
their defense, without considering the difference between
elaborate discourses upon important occasions, delivered to
princes or parliaments, written with a view of being made
public, and a plain sermon intended for the middle or

lower size of people. Neither do they seem to remember the many alterations, additions, and expungings, made by great authors in those treatises which they prepare for the public. Besides, that excellent prelate above-mentioned was known to preach after a much more popular manner in the city congregations: and if in those parts of his works he be anywhere too obscure for the understandings of many who may be supposed to have been his hearers, it ought to be numbered among his omissions.

The fear of being thought pedants hath been of pernicious consequence to young divines. This hath wholly taken many of them off from their severer studies in the university, which they have exchanged for plays, poems, and pamphlets, in order to qualify them for tea tables and coffeehouses. This they usually call *polite conversation; knowing the world;* and *reading men instead of books.* These accomplishments when applied in the pulpit, appear by a quaint, terse, florid style, rounded into periods and cadences, commonly without either propriety or meaning. I have listened with my utmost attention for half an hour to an orator of this species, without being able to understand, much less to carry away one single sentence out of a whole sermon. Others, to show that their studies have not been confined to sciences, or ancient authors, will talk in the style of a gaming ordinary, and Whitefriars, where I suppose the hearers can be little edified by the terms of *palming, shuffling, biting, bamboozling,* and the like, if they have not been sometimes conversant among pickpockets and sharpers. And truly, as they say, a man is known by his company, so it should seem that a man's company may be known by his manner of expressing himself, either in public assemblies, or private conversation.

It would be endless to run over the several defects of style among us; I shall therefore say nothing of the *mean* and *paltry* (which are usually attended by the *fustian*), much less of the *slovenly* or *indecent.* Two things I will just warn you against: the first is the frequency of flat unnecessary epithets; and the other is the folly of using old threadbare phrases, which will often make you go out of your way to find and apply them, are nauseous to rational hearers, and will seldom express your meaning as well as your own natural words.

Although, as I have already observed, our English tongue is too little cultivated in this kingdom, yet the faults are nine in ten owing to affectation, and not to the want of understanding. When a man's thoughts are clear, the properest words will generally offer themselves first, and his own judgement will direct him in what order to place them, so as they may be best understood. Where men err against this method, it is usually on purpose, and to show their learning, their oratory, their politeness, or their knowledge of the world. In short, that simplicity without which no human performance can arrive to any great perfection, is nowhere more eminently useful than in this.

Some Notes on English Prose Style

JAMES SLEDD

An Example

We all know the usual English translation of the report which Caesar made about a victory in battle: "I came, I saw, I conquered." It is a good translation; and since we need a simple example to begin our discussion, we will use it to suggest some of the things that the word *style* can mean.

Speech or writing?

Our first question must be whether we are talking about marks on paper or about human speech. It is possible to talk sensibly about either, or about the relations between the two; but sensible talk is *not* possible if we try to talk about both at once without distinguishing one from the other. If we try to talk about speech, moreover, we immediately face another difficulty: the same marks on paper would not prompt all of us to make the same speech sounds.

I came, I saw, I conquered.

The writer of this book, if he were given these marks to read, would read them thus;

$$^{12}\text{ài} + {}^{2}\text{ké:m}^{2}\nearrow{}^{2}\text{ài} + {}_{2}\text{s}\acute{\text{ɔ}}{:}^{2}\nearrow{}^{2}\text{ài} + {}^{3}\text{ká}\eta\text{kʃd}^{1}\searrow$$

Few of his colleagues would read the marks in just this way; for example, most of them would "pronounce the r" in *conquered* (/³kánkʃd¹↘./) in a way which they consider quite natural and colorless but which the writer would use only for comic or satirical effects. Plainly we must not only decide whether to talk about speech or about writing; a decision to

From *A Short Introduction to English Grammar* by James Sledd. Copyright © 1959 by Scott, Foresman and Company. Reprinted by permission of the publisher.

talk wholly or partly about speech will force us also to decide *whose* speech.

One content in two forms

Postponing this group of questions about speech and writing for a while, we may tentatively proceed to consider the utterance which we have transcribed:

$$^{1:2}\text{ài} + {}^{2}\text{ké:m}^{2\,\nearrow\,2}\text{ài} + {}^{2}\text{s\'o:}^{2\,\nearrow\,2}\text{ài} + {}^{3}\text{kánkšd}^{1}\searrow$$

What does it mean? Presumably something like this—that the general arrived on the scene of battle, observed the situation, and won the victory. We now have two statements, the original utterance and our paraphrase of it, that mean much the same thing; or, if anyone should find our paraphrase inaccurate, we at least have the recognition that we can usefully ask what a statement means and expect an answer in other words than those of the statement itself. In short we can say the same thing in different ways.

Style as manner

This conclusion, though it seems painfully obvious, is very useful and important. It allows us to suggest what will ultimately be our definition of style, and it reminds us that we can ask stylistic questions both about the content of our utterances and about our expression of that content. Style, that is, will be for us the manner of saying what is said, but we will recognize that there is style in thought as well as style in language; and if sometimes we must separate matter and manner in our studies, we must always be able to put them together again. All that we shall say about style is implicit in these few remarks.

CONTENT. Turning again to our transcribed utterance, we note that its matter represents a very careful choice of detail. From a communiqué reporting victory in battle, the battle itself has been left out, as if victory were the easiest and most natural thing in the world for the omnipotent Me who had only to arrive and survey the field in order to win it. The battle has been left out, and the armies have been

---

[1] Professor Sledd uses, as he must, a phonetic notation to describe the actual sounds of speech since conventional writing inadequately represents it. The letters representing vowels are given roughly the values they have in the Romance languages: the vowel in *came* is represented by *e:*, the colon indicating that it is long. The representation of consonants in this sentence offers no difficulty except that the sign　ŋ　is used to represent the sound of the

left out: *I came, I saw;* and a successful climax to the action is made to appear as inevitable as the rhetorically effective climax in the reporting of it.

EXPRESSION. The manner of the utterance is as essential to its effect as the carefully chosen details which are its matter. There are three clauses, *I came, I saw,* and *I conquered;* and though they are exactly parallel grammatically, the contrast between the dissyllabic verb in the third clause and the monosyllabic verbs in the first and second fits the climax in the matter of the report. Each clause, again, is as bare as possible, the unexpanded combination of a nominal (three times repeated) and a verbal; while between the clauses, intonation patterns provide the connections which conjunctions might have helped provide. The tight concision of the whole is enhanced by the arrangement of the stresses and by the alliteration in /ké:m/ and /káŋkšd/.

Importance of style

Before going on, now, to develop one by one the topics which these introductory paragraphs have hinted at, we may say a word to the skeptic who doubts the wisdom of giving two paragraphs to a single sentence. It is easy to pretend that style does not matter, that it neither helps nor hinders communication or that it takes care of itself if the writer takes care that he has something to say. The pretense is easy, but it is only pretense, and experience destroys it. To show the importance of style, we may simply compare our paraphrase and the utterance with which we began:

> I came, I saw, I conquered.
> I arrived on the scene of battle, I observed the situation, I won the victory.

The paraphrase is as accurate as we can make it, but though the two statements are almost indistinguishable in their mean-

---

medial consonant in *singer.* The pitch levels are represented by numbers. The sentence begins on 2, the second-lowest of the four levels of pitch in English, sustains that pitch until it rises on the next to last syllable to 3, and then falls to 1. The sign / indicates the strongest stress (there is one, and only one, in each phrase); ﹨ middle stress; and ﹈ the weakest stress. The sign + indicates what is called "open transition" between syllables (*slyness* as opposed to *minus*). The arrow ↗ represents a terminal (or pause) marked by a slight rise in pitch, not enough to reach the next higher pitch level; ↘ represents the quick dying away of the voice at the end of an utterance.

ing, they are altogether different in their total effects. When we say the same thing in different ways, the total effects of what we say will depend to a considerable extent on how we say it; and the best style is often hard to find.

Definition

Recognizing that there is style in thought as well as style in language, we have yet suggested that style for us will be the manner of saying what is said. In this section, we must expand our definition and point out some of the things which it implies.

Separability of matter and manner

The first implication, of course, is that matter and manner are separable, that what we say and the way we say it are different things. We make this assumption every day. We make it when we write or read a translation, a paraphrase, or a summary; when, in deductive logic, we say that one proposition is equivalent to another; or when we ask a friend what a third person has said and accept, as our answer, an indirect quotation. Indeed, if we did not assume that matter and manner are separable, language and communication would be impossible; for a man could explain himself only by repeating the words he said before, and if we did not understand him after the repetition, nothing more could be done. Our understanding of a lecture, for example, would end when we could no longer remember the precise manner of its delivery, and could be demonstrated or communicated only if we were perfect mimics. Such absurd consequences would follow directly from the denial that what we say and how we say it are different things.

Style in thought

If style is the manner of saying what is said, then it follows that style is possible only because there *are* more ways of saying a thing than one. In one sense we can say that the same thing has been said in different ways when the same conclusion has been established on different premises or when different modes of persuasion have moved an audience to take the same action or entertain the same belief. It is in this sense of the word *manner* that we can talk about different styles of thought. We could say, for instance, that two men have different styles of thought if one prefers to argue deductively, from first principles, and the other reasons inductively, from empirical observations; or we could find different rhetorical styles in a closely reasoned appeal to the intellect and a gaudy play for the feelings of an audience. Style in this sense is less a matter of expression than of content, as when we spoke of the choice of detail in Caesar's arrogantly calm *I came, I saw, I conquered.*

Style as linguistic choice

Style in this sense, however, is not our prime concern in this book. We want to talk mainly about style in its other connotation, style in language. Style in language is possible because all of us, fortunately, command more than one kind of English and because, even within a *single* kind of English, there are synonymous expressions from which we may make our choice. Illustrations are plentiful. Since few Americans spend all their lives in a single area and since no area is safe from the verbal barrage laid down by our talkative compatriots, we all recognize different regional dialects and have at least some facility in their use or abuse; and since the flexibility of our class structure allows us to move rather freely among the classes which we pretend not to recognize, we quietly make it our business to learn the lingo of more than one group. Regionally, the average American can at least give a bad imitation of Brooklynese or the "Southern drawl"; and socially, he is much too canny to talk to his preacher and his teacher, his boss and his barkeeper in just the same way.

Even the mythical unfortunate who might be confined to a single regional and social dialect would still face the linguistic choices which make style in language possible. Within each dialect, the same thing can be said in ways which differ in sounds, in inflections, in syntax, or in choice of words. Thus some Chicagoans can pronounce *park* as either /párk/ or /páərk/ ; as the plural of *index,* the writer of this book can use either *indexes* or *indices;* our teachers may have allowed us to say either "A big crowd of people *was* there" or "A big crowd of people *were* there"; and some of us have probably heard discussions of "synonyms at three levels," like *rise—mount—ascend* or *time—age—epoch.* We constantly choose among the lexical and grammatical variants which our dialects make available to us.

EFFECTS OF SUCH CHOICE. Why do we bother to make a choice among synonymous expressions, among different ways of saying the same thing? That we do bother to choose is plain, and for a very good reason: different ways of saying the same thing may produce effects which are even more strikingly different. For example, both /párk/ and /páərk/; can refer to the same expanse of lawn, covered with shrubs, trees, and couples lying on newspapers; they can point to the same thing. That is not to say that the total effects of the use of these two forms will also be identical. To the quaint people who dislike or pretend to dislike the "Midwestern *r*," both might be objectionable when compared to an elegant /pá:k/; but of the two, ‖ might be the more painful. Or, if this example seems far fetched, we need only remember the consternation which *I ain't got none* would cause in circles where *I haven't any* is expected, or the anguish which a four-letter word would cause to people who never blink an eye at its scientific synonym. Unless we know how to say the same thing in different ways, some of our efforts at communication are bound to fail; we will lose influence and make enemies.

NECESSITY OF COMPARISONS. It should be plain, by this point that style in language is itself synonymous with linguistic choice; and choice implies rejection. Here our concept of style has important consequences for our method of studying it. We must recognize that if we want to talk about a man's style, we must know both how he said things and how he *might* have said them but chose not to; and we must also recognize that no one can *cultivate* his style unless he somehow knows enough about the resources of his language to choose those which he needs. A teacher, for example, considering a student's papers, might suggest to him that he was hurting his style by writing too many choppy sentences. The remark would have no point if *all* English sentences were choppy; and the student could do nothing to improve his work unless he was familiar, or could become familiar, with more fluent writing. Both critically and creatively, the study of style is basically comparative.

The necessary comparisons cannot be made, in any economical or systematic way, without a set of terms and distinctions by which to analyze, describe, and prescribe stylistic choices. If we are going to talk about choppy sentences and fluent sentences as features of contrasting style, or if we are to profit from instructions to choose the one and avoid the other, we must first know what makes a sentence and what makes a sentence either fluent or choppy. That is, we must have a grammar; and a little reflection on the problems of word choice will show that we must also have a dictionary or its equivalent. The mere possession of grammars and dictionaries will not make us creative stylists or competent analysts of style; linguistic choice is not the whole of style; but the normally intelligent student, although he will concentrate during most of his school years on the content of his writing, may well give a little direct attention to its manner; and among his most valuable resources will be a grammar, a dictionary, and a shelfful of good books for models.

Plain talk vs. speech for writing

Two basic facts to remember as we go about this job are that the reader of presumably serious prose does not expect to be presented with unconsidered chitchat and that the writer of any kind of discourse, so long as he uses the conventional orthography, cannot present his reader with a full representation of that discourse—he cannot write everything he says. The writer must find means to escape the resultant embarrassments and ambiguities.

A few quotations will clarify the statement that educated people do not and should not write as they casually talk. Here are two fragments of a telephone conversation which was recently recorded in an American academic community (the speaker is obviously a person of some education):

1. "he suggested that we go down and get Mrs. R——— and tell her who we are and that he sent us and try the fourteen-inch typewriters and see if our stencils would work with such type and if we can use them to get them right away because they have those in stock and we won't have to wait"

2. "we're short and we want to get rid of those rentals but they are expecting within two weeks or so to be receiving—ah—to start receiving their orders on eleven-inch machines with pica type and of course pica type has always been best for our stencils but I rather think there might be a chance that we can work with elite type." [2]

As oral communication, these utterances were apparently successful. The responses of the other party to the conversation were also recorded, and they consist largely of "Yes" and

[2] From *The Structure of English* by Charles Carpenter Fries, copyright, 1952, by Harcourt, Brace and Company, Inc.

"I see." Nor is there any reason to feel that the speaker was somehow debasing the English language. He was talking as we all talk, perhaps somewhat better than most of us; but for our present purpose, that is just the point. He was talking as educated people *talk,* not as they are expected to *write,* and so his remarks, when they are written down, strike us at once as awkward, incoherent, perhaps "illiterate." They show, indeed, some of the characteristics which we regularly associate with "Vulgar English," notably the very long and formless "sentences" loosely connected by repeated *and.* The suggestion again is obvious that much of our difficulty in learning to write results from differences between oral and written styles; the elements and expectations involved in oral and written discourse are not altogether the same.

The differences, although they are relatively small in comparison with the shared elements, nonetheless appear in every aspect of our language, perhaps most obviously in the construction of sentences and the choice of words. The writer of the immediately preceding sentence would never speak it in plain talk. In conversation he would not be likely to put an adverbial clause, like *although . . . elements,* between the simple subject, *differences,* and the simple predicate, *appear;* he would not tack on the concluding adverbial phrase, *perhaps . . . words;* and he would not choose phrases like *nonetheless* and *perhaps most obviously.* The kind of speech of which our writing is a secondary representation typically differs, in such ways as these, from the speech of daily life; convention dictates different selections from the resources of our language when we write a book and when we talk to our family.

Balance, parallelism, and antithesis

We will complete our remarks on sentences and clauses as structural elements of style by making some remarks on balance, parallelism, and antithesis. By parallelism we shall mean similarity of grammatical structures; by balance we shall mean similarity of grammatical structures expressing similar ideas; and by antithesis we shall mean similarity of grammatical structures expressing opposed ideas. The similarity and opposition of ideas which distinguish balance from antithesis are of course created by the words that compose the grammatical structures; for since the structures are by definition similar, a basic likeness of structural ideas must underlie both the opposition of antithesis and the similarity of balance.

The simplest forms of balance and parallelism, as we have defined them, can hardly be avoided by speakers of English. All coordinate constructions are parallel, and the language provides special markers of parallelism in forms like *both . . . and, either . . . or,* and *neither . . . nor.* With the inevitable, however, we are no more concerned in a discussion of style as linguistic choice than we are with the simple blunders which are commonly labeled as unnecessary shifts or faulty parallelism. Our subjects are the balance and antithesis which speakers and writers deliberately create.

THEIR ELEMENTS AND EXTENT. The elements of balance and antithesis may be sentences, clauses, or parts of clauses (including, naturally, stress patterns and intonation patterns), and the grammatical parallelism involved may be so slight that it pairs only two words or so extensive that each form in one of the balanced or antithetical constructions has its grammatical equivalent in the other. In certain kinds of verse, the parallelism between sentences can approach completeness, as in the following lines by Alexander Pope:

> Steel could labour of the gods destroy,
> And strike to dust th' imperial towers of Troy;
> Steel could the works of mortal pride confound
> And hew triumphal arches to the ground.

The interest of the example lies not only in the relatively precise balance of the first couplet against the second but also in the punctuation. If we ask how many sentences the four lines contain, we will get one answer in terms of speech and another in terms of marks on paper. A sentence ends, according to the definition in our grammar, with the word *Troy;* but if we judge by punctuation, there is only one sentence, ending with the period after *ground.* Like the parallelism between the couplets, the semicolon after the first and the period after the second help to indicate a semantic unity; but gramatically each couplet is a separate sentence. In other words, it is impossible to establish an exact correspondence between punctuation and linguistic form. Punctuation belongs to writing and can be learned only by the study of writing, so that the verses we have quoted reinforce our earlier statement: nobody ever learned to write without reading.

Exact parallelism is not so common in most prose as it is

in the kind of verse which we have quoted, but even in prose
some fairly elaborate specimens can be found, as in the following stylistic discussion:

> They [certain prefaces] have not the formality of
> a settled style, in which the first half of the sentence
> betrays the other. The clauses are never balanced, nor
> the periods modelled; every word seems to drop by
> chance, though it falls into its proper place. Nothing
> is cold or languid; the whole is airy, animated, and
> vigorous; what is little, is gay; what is great is splendid.

CHANGING TASTE. To most modern readers, this sort of
thing is a little too much. The passage is certainly clear and
emphatic, and the writer's skill in expressing his balanced or
opposed ideas in parallel forms gives some pleasure in itself;
but the vigor of these sentences is certainly not an airy vigor,
and no word seems to drop by chance, though all are properly placed.

Many writers today, if they make two sentences elaborately
parallel, are likely to qualify the effect by some means, perhaps by a contrast between the elaboration of the grammar
and the colloquial tone of the vocabulary or between the high-
flown expression and the humble content. Here is a paragraph from a recent description of a drive through New
England:

> Stay with me on 62 and it will take you into Concord.
> As I say, it was a delicious evening. The snake had
> come forth to die in a bloody S on the highway, the
> wheel upon its head, its bowels flat now and exposed.
> The turtle had come up too to cross the road and die
> in the attempt, its hard shell smashed under the rubber
> blow, its intestinal yearning (for the other side of the
> road) forever squashed. There was a sign by the way-
> side which announced that the road had a "cotton sur-
> face." You wouldn't know what that is, but neither,
> for that matter, did I. There is a cryptic ingredient in
> many of our modern improvements—we are awed and
> pleased without knowing quite what we are enjoying.
> It is something to be traveling on a road with a cotton
> surface.[3]

The sentences about the snake and the turtle are closely
parallel, but the writer is half teasing. Though he has serious
things to say, he will not say them stuffily.

---

[3] From "Walden" by E. B. White, in *One Man's Meat* (New
York: Harper & Brothers, 1942). Copyright, 1939, by E. B. White.

MODERATION. The danger of stuffiness may be less when the parallelism does not extend so far as sentences but is limited to clauses or their parts. Nothing is stuffier than self-admiration in a political discussion, yet one modern writer has managed to give two cheers for democracy without sounding like a commissar or a congressman. The following paragraph is not one of his most distinguished, but it does illustrate some quieter uses of balance and antithesis rather well:

> I believe in aristocracy, though—if that is the right word, and if a democrat may use it. Not an aristocracy of power, based upon rank and influence, but an aristocracy of the sensitive, the considerate and the plucky. Its members are to be found in all nations and classes, and all through the ages, and there is a secret understanding between them when they meet. They represent the true human tradition, the one permanent victory of our queer race over cruelty and chaos. Thouands of them perish in obscurity, a few are great names. They are sensitive for others as well as for themselves, they are considerate without being fussy, their pluck is not swankiness but the power to endure, and they can take a joke.[4]

The last four clauses show the possibility of using balance and antithesis without monotony. They are all parallel in meaning, since they all state qualities of the "aristocracy," and the subject of three of them is *they;* but in the third clause of the four, the subject is not *they* but one of *their* qualities. Again, the fourth clause breaks the pattern of internal opposition which has been established in the first three, where qualities which the aristocrats do have are set off against qualities which they lack. Even the individual oppositions between virtues and their corresponding vices are expressed in grammatical forms which vary from clause to clause: *for others, for themselves; considerable, fussy; swankiness, the power to endure.*

SUMMARY. To speak of a contrast between virtues and vices is, of course, to speak of matter as well as manner. Although grammatical parallelism can be discussed in purely formal terms, the definitions themselves of balance and antithesis

[4] From "What I Believe," copyright, 1939, by E. M. Forster. Reprinted from *Two Cheers for Democracy* by E. M. Forster by permission of Harcourt, Brace and Company, Inc. By permission also of Edward Arnold, Ltd.

involve both content and expression, and our remarks on these devices have plainly not been limited to style in language. Indeed, in so far as balance and antithesis depend on the choice of particular words as well as the choice of particular structures, our remarks have not been limited to structural elements of style. This is as it should be. Matter and manner *are* separable; structures *can* remain while words come and go; but the items that fit into grammatical structures are meaningful individual forms, and we choose both the single forms and the larger structures primarily to express meanings. "Style, that is, will be for us the manner of saying what is said, but we will recognize that there is style in thought as well as style in language; and if sometimes we must separate matter and manner in our studies, we must always be able to put them together again."

Sounds and Sound Effects

Concerning sound and sound effects, there is an ancient tradition of description and prescription in which sense and nonsense are elaborately intermingled; but we will give here only the briefest of notes on a subject which after all is of relatively slight importance for exposition and argument. It would do us no good to catalogue some dozens of tricky sound patterns and give them Greek or Latin names, and it would do us actual harm to talk about the symbolic values of individual sounds, the shapes and colors of vowels, the ten most beautiful words in the language, the coo of /u:/ in *croon* and the roll of /o:/ in *tone*. Such talk is not an infallible sign of charlatanism, but it comes close to being one.

SUPERFIXES AND INTONATION PATTERNS. A few practical suggestions still can and should be made. The primary elements by which sound effects are produced are of course the sounds we described in the first chapter of our grammar, *not* marks on paper; and as we suggested by our very first example (*I came, I saw, I conquered*) and as we should all know from experience of English poetry, stress patterns and intonation patterns are particularly important. To be sure, we want our prose to be prose. Nobody wants to keep stumbling over bits of unintended verse, because to do so leads his mind astray and makes him conscious that the careless writer had let his own mind quietly go to sleep. On the other hand, even in prose the controlled repetition of stress patterns and intonation patterns can be effective. Here is part of the very moving conclusion of a modern story:

> Snow was general all over Ireland. It was falling on every part of the dark central plain, on the treeless hills, falling softly upon the Bog of Allen and, farther westward, softly falling into the dark mutinous Shannon waves. It was falling, too, upon every part of the lonely churchyard on the hill where Michael Furey lay buried. It lay thickly drifted on the crooked crosses and headstones, on the spears of the little gate, on the barren thorns.[5]

If we scanned the three final prepositional phrases, using the symbol [1] for a metrically stressed syllable and the symbol for a metrically unstressed syllable, we would discover the following pattern:

        on the crooked crosses and headstones

        on the spears of the little gate

        on the barren thorns

Each phrase, we note, begins with two metrically unstressed syllables followed by a metrically stressed syllable; the first two phrases have three metrically stressed syllables, the last phrase only two; and no two metrically stressed syllables come together without a metrically unstressed syllable between them. The phrases, finally, are marked off by terminals, of which the last would certainly be /↘/.

THE SPACING OF TERMINALS. Since *full* metrical regularity is an undesirable intrusion into prose, sound effects there can be considered as examples not only of controlled repitition but of controlled variation, and the last example suggests one of the techniques of varying. By varying the length of sentences, clauses, and important parts of clauses, we vary also the length of the stretches between terminals, especially between successive occurrences of the terminal /↘/, with its connotations of finality. In this way, sound can sometimes be made to combine with sense in the marking off of

[5] From "The Dead" by James Joyce, included in *The Portable James Joyce,* copyright 1946, 1947, by The Viking Press, Inc. Reprinted by permission of The Viking Press, Inc., New York. By permission also of Jonathan Cape, Ltd., London, and the Executors of the James Joyce Estate.

paragraphs by something less superficial than a mere in-
dentation on the page. Note that each of the three paragraphs
which are quoted just below begins with a relatively short
sentence or a short phrase—a sentence or phrase which is
shorter than the one that precedes or follows it. These
short units would each be closed, in almost any reading, by
the terminal   /↘/,   and quite possibly there would be no
second occurrence of this terminal until the end of the
following longer sentence. In the third paragraph, however,
with its very short opening phrase, the sentences or phrases
that would close with. /↘/ are much shorter than the
long sentences in the first and second paragraphs. The result
is a keener irony in the jibe at soldiers.

> The desire for fame is rooted in the hearts of men.
> It is one of the most powerful of all human desires,
> and perhaps for that very reason, and because it is so
> deep and secret, it is the desire that men are most un-
> willing to admit, particularly those who feel most sharp-
> ly its keen and piercing spur.
> The politician, for example, would never have us
> think that it is love of office, the desire for the no-
> torious elevation of public place, that drives him on.
> No, the thing that governs him is his pure devotion to
> the common weal, his selfless and high-souled states-
> manship, his love of his fellow man, and his burning
> idealism to turn out the rascal who usurps the office
> and betrays the public trust which he himself, as he
> assures us, would so gloriously and so devotedly main-
> tain.
> So, too, the soldier. It is never love of glory that
> inspires him to his profession. It is never love of battle,
> love of war, love of all the resounding titles and the
> proud emoluments of the heroic conqueror. Oh, no. It
> is devotion to duty that makes him a soldier. There is
> no personal motive in it. He is inspired simply by the
> selfless ardor of his patriotic abnegation. He regrets
> that he has but one life to give for his country.[6]

PACE. Of the patterns of stress and pitch, therefore, those
that occur before instances of the terminal /↘/ are certainly not the least ·important; but none of the patterns are
negligible, since they largely determine the rhythms of English prose, as of English verse. If terminals are widely spaced

---

[6] From Thomas Wolfe, *You Can't Go Home Again* (New
York: Harper & Brothers, 1940). By permission of Harper &
Brothers.

and if the stronger stresses do not immediately succeed one another, the pace is likely to be quick; but the movement is clogged if the stronger stresses are not separated by weaks or if terminals are placed close together. In the following sentences, it is quite hard to read the underlined bits quickly:

He has learnt to prefer real longlived things.[7]
Is it something . . . for use to me today here?
Their manners, speech, dress, friendships . . . are un-
rhymed poetry.
Of all nations the United States with veins full of
poetical stuff most needs poets.
Out of him speaks the spirit of peace, large, rich,
thrifty.

The next lot of examples, on the other hand, move faster:

Some of them were professional conformists who found it simply impossible to violate the established code.
Great masses of people appear to be unable to abstain from it.
He had a genius for committing imbecilities comparable to that possessed by Herman.
He sometimes called it "the credibility of the commonplace."
As the essential situation in the East is the tension that we have already observed, our policy must be an attempt at a series of interventions.

A HORRIBLE EXAMPLE. Neither batch of sentences, slower or faster, has been cited for any other quality than its relative speed; but since we began this discussion of sound effects with an admirably rhythmic passage, we will balance that fine example with an abominable one. It would take some effort to produce an uglier sentence than the following:

Then may we attain to a poetry worthy the immortal soul of man, and which, while absorbing materials, and, in their own sense, the shows of Nature, will, above all, have, both directly and indirectly, a freeing, fluidizing, expanding, religious character, exulting with science, fructifying the moral elements, and stimulating aspirations, and meditations on the unknown.[8]

The ugliness of this particular sentence is due largely to

[7] Walt Whitman, Preface to *Leaves of Grass*. The next four examples are from the same source.

[8] Walt Whitman, *Democratic Vistas*.

its complete failure in rhythm, though *fluidizing* deserves some credit, too. Other kinds of ugliness may be unwarily produced by careless handling of vowels and consonants. Among the most common blunders are the use of rare sequences, like the consonant clusters in *glimpsed streams;* aimless alliteration; and aimless rhymes or jingles (including the aimless repetition of the same word, especially under stress or in similar grammatical positions). The word *aimless* has been deliberately repeated. Both alliteration and the repetition of a word can be used to good effect, but they are seldom pleasing when the writer has merely stumbled into them by accident.

A PRECAUTION. He is not likely to stumble if he takes the elementary precaution of reading his prose aloud or of having it read to him by a competent friend. For most expository and argumentative writing, it is enough that the speech sounds should not force themselves on our attention or that, if we do notice them, we find their arrangement purposeful. Reading an essay aloud will warn us if it does not meet these elementary requirements, and *hearing* it may do more. If your meaning does not come through in someone else's reading, or if our competent reader falters and has to go back, we can be sure that we have blundered in something more serious than euphony and rhythm.

Figures of Speech

The use of a word in an unusual sense is often called a figure of speech. The reader or hearer understands the intended, *unusual* meaning from the usual meaning, the rest of the utterance, and the external situation. (In a book, of course, there is no external situation, only a longer utterance than we have to guide us in ordinary speech.) It would be possible, therefore, to describe and classify figures in terms of the clues which make the intended meaning clear, but the usual basis of classification is the relation between the literal and figurative meanings. Among the numerous figures which have been classified in this way, we will mention only four: understatement and overstatement, irony, and metaphor.

OVERSTATEMENT, UNDERSTATEMENT, IRONY. Understatement and overstatement are simple devices. A statement can be made weaker than the situation would justify, or it can be made stronger. Often the restraint of understatement results in quiet emphasis, sometimes in humorous diminution. Overstatement, which is a poor means to emphasis, had best be funny or it will grow tiresome. In either case, the effect of the figure depends on the discrepancy between the content and the way the content is expressed, and the same thing may be said of irony. An ironic statement is one in which the literal and figurative meanings are opposites, as possibly in the sentence, *The duty of the schools is to help everybody get ahead of the Joneses.*

The example rightly suggests that irony, like climax and anticlimax, presupposes a scale of values. If speaker and hearer, writer and reader share the same values, irony is easily used either in derision or in fun; but when values are so thoroughly confused as they are at the present day, irony can result in various complications. It may fall quite flat if the literal meaning is naïvely accepted; it may be used to puzzle an audience which does not quite know what is intended but smells a rat somewhere; it can startle and astonish if an audience can be brought to accept the literal meaning for a while and then suddenly forced to recognize the true intention. The possibilities for both success and failure are greater than with understatement and overstatement.

METAPHOR. Like irony, metaphor is a complex and powerful device, but the term has been so loosely employed and the thing itself has been so fancifully examined that sensible discussion is very difficult. Traditionally, metaphor has been defined as an implied comparison, the application to one thing of a linguistic form which literally means another thing. More commonly in recent years, any transfer of meaning and hence any figure of speech has been called a metaphor, and on the basis of this pretended definition elaborate theories of the importance of metaphor have been built. Metaphor, it is said, it not mere decoration or illustration but essential statement, shaping our attitudes, interpreting our experience, and giving us kinds of truth which we can get in no other way. Such theories often begin or end by contrasting the literal language of science with the metaphorical language of poetry—always to the advantage of poetry.

ITS POWER AND USES. We will not entangle ourselves in these complexities, which have little practical value in the teaching of exposition or argument. Undoubtedly, metaphor as traditionally defined can be used to enliven an otherwise dull piece of writing. An example is the last sentence of Sinclair Lewis's *Babbitt.* Ted Babbitt and Eunice Littlefield

have slipped off from a dance one Saturday night and have
got married without their parents' knowledge or consent, and
the next morning the families have gathered to see what
can be done about the marriage. Ted is surprised when his
father takes him out of the room and tells him he was
right to marry if that was what he wanted to do. The last
sentence of the book describes Ted's return with his father
to the living room:

> Arms about each other's shoulders, the Babbitt men
> marched into the living-room and faced the swooping
> family.[9]

Most readers remember this sentence because of the one
metaphorical word, *swooping,* which suggests a comparison
between the scolding, chattering adults and a noisy flock of
smaller birds attacking a hawk. Very few of Lewis's sentences are so well remembered.

The same example indicates that metaphor may not only
give life to otherwise dull prose. If we give the name of
one thing, A, to another, B, we suggest so close a resemblance that our attitudes and feelings toward A are transferred to B: since a skunk is a smelly little beast, a man who
gets called a skunk may be treated with wary contempt.
Metaphor can thus be very moving. It can shape attitudes
by implying and stimulating judgments of value, and the
judgments can be all the more persuasive because they are
not argued but assumed and are conveyed directly in the
metaphoric word. During a recent governmental crisis, for
example, a columnist wrote that the administration would
be "free from the miasmic conniving which took place during
the illness of Wilson." [10] To connive is to work together
sneakingly, and a miasma is a poison floating in the air,
especially in the night mists. The metaphorical *miasmic* implied that when President Wilson was ill, sneaking plotters
in the government were like a poison in the very air the
nation breathed; in contrast, the present administration was
represented as healthy and healthful, clean and honest. The
metaphor directly conveyed a sweeping judgment on the two
American parties and nudged the voter ungently away from
one and toward the other.

Whether metaphor in this instance was wisely or foolishly

---

[9] Sinclair Lewis, *Babbitt* (New York: Harcourt, Brace and
Company, Inc., 1922), p. 401.

[10] *Chicago Sun-Times,* October 2, 1955.

used is a matter for the reader's own decision. The point is simply that metaphor can be used, with or without reasoned argument, to prepare an audience for reasonable or unreasonable action. It can also be used, in an equally a-rational way, to give the feel of direct experience, as when a poet spoke of "swallows with spools of dark thread sewing the shadows together": [11] reading the line, we get the feel of the thing as if we ourselves were watching the birds in the gathering darkness. Similarly, in the following lines, blowing and falling leaves in autumn are not so much described as presented:

> Leaves, summer's coinage spent, golden are all to-gether whirled, sent spinning, dipping, slipping, shuffled by heavy-handed wind, shifted sideways, sifted, lifted, and in swarms made to fly, spent sun-flies, gorgeous tatters, airdrift, pinions of trees.[12]

METAPHOR AS A GUIDE TO INQUIRY. Metaphors like *summer's coinage, heavy-handed wind,* and *pinions of trees* would often be out of place in expository or argumentative prose, but there is another use of metaphor which is extremely important to the prose writer. When we try to explain something, we try to put it into a *class* of things, to say that it is like something else with which it shares some quality. That is just what metaphors do, and so they can serve not only as illustrations but as guides to inquiry, like the models which chemists use to represent molecules. Political scientists, for example, often talk of institutions as if they were living organisms. Their metaphor gives them a way of explaining the relations of one institution to another, since it allows them to talk about changes with environment; but it also invites them to pursue certain lines of inquiry. Are there parallels between organic evolution and the development of institutions, or between the development of institutions and the life cycle of organisms? Since many living creatures act from unreasoned habit, would it be just to say that formal law is less important to the conduct of a

[11] From "Bat" by D. H. Lawrence, in *Collected Poems of D. H. Lawrence.* Copyright 1929 by Jonathan Cape and Harrison Smith, Inc. Reprinted by permission of The Viking Press, Inc., New York. By permission also of the Estate of the late Mrs. Frieda Lawrence.

[12] From "Lapwing" by R. E. Warner in W. H. Auden and John Garrett, *The Poet's Tongue* (London: G. Bell & Sons, Ltd., 1937), II, pp. 78-79.

society than customs and traditions are? What are the illnesses of institutions, their symptoms, and their cures? Considering metaphor as an aid to reflection, we might very well insist that it is no more at home in poetry than in science.

The strength and the weakness of metaphor in exposition and argument is, as we have suggested, that the metaphoric use of a single word may embody or conceal a whole series of statements which need examination. An institution is not really a living organism; but to call it one, on the basis of a few obvious resemblances, is an invitation to hunt for likeness and to ignore plain difference. Metaphors are strongly persuasive, and not only to truth.

ABUSES OF METAPHOR. If that is the inherent strength and weakness of metaphor, there are also abuses of it which are not inherent but which result from the user's ignorance or disregard of linguistic differences between himself and his audience. Since we have defined a figure of speech as the use of a word in an unusual meaning, we cannot be quite sure what particular uses a particular individual will regard as figurative unless we know in advance what he accepts as the normal meanings of our words. For us, a metaphor may be *dead;* that is, what was formerly the unusual meaning may have become the usual meaning. This is what had happened for the city child who said, when she first saw a pig and learned its name, that it was very properly called a pig, since it was so dirty. The child's normal meaning for *pig* was not "swine" or "hog" but "dirty child, dirty beast"; and for her the use of *pig* which most speakers take as normal had become metaphoric. Similar explanations can probably be given for most *mixed* metaphors, of which the following is a somewhat gaudy instance:

His whole picture will be a house of cards which will collapse at the first breeze of methodological rigor.

The writer of this sentence was not thinking about a real house of cards or a real picture. He was using *picture* to mean "explanation or account" and *house of cards* to mean "flimsy structure of argument." He did not stop to think that for many readers the literal meanings of his phrases would be so very different that the whole sentence would be absurd.

IV.   THE TRADITION
DENIED

Indivisibility of Expression into Modes or Degrees
and Criticism of Rhetoric

BENEDETTO CROCE

Criticism of the rhetorical categories

THE ILLEGITIMATE DIVISION of expressions into various grades
is known in literature by the name of doctrine of *ornament*
or of *rhetorical categories*. But similar attempts at distinctions in other artistic groups are not wanting: suffice it to
recall the *realistic* and *symbolic* forms, so often mentioned
in relation to painting and sculpture.

Realistic and *symbolic, objective* and *subjective, classical*
and *romantic, simple* and *ornate, proper* and *metaphorical,*
the fourteen forms of metaphor, the figures of *word* and
sentence, pleonasm, ellipse, inversion, repetition, synonyms
and *homonyms,* these and all other determinations of modes
or degrees of expression reveal their philosophical nullity
when the attempt is made to develop them in precise definitions, because they either grasp the void or fall into the absurd. A typical example of this is the very common definition
of metaphor as of *another word used in place of the proper
word.* Now why give oneself this trouble? Why substitute the
improper for the proper word? Why take the worse and longer
road when you know the shorter and better road? Perhaps, as
is commonly said, because the proper word is in certain cases
not so *expressive* as the so-called improper word or metaphor?
But if this be so the metaphor is exactly the proper word in
that case, and the so-called "proper" word, if it were used,
would be *inexpressive* and therefore most improper. Similar

From **Aesthetic** by Benedetto Croce, translated by Douglas Ainslie, The Noonday Press,
1953. Reprinted by permission of Farrar, Straus & Giroux, Inc. and of Vision Press Ltd.
and Peter Owen Ltd.

observations of elementary good sense can be made regarding the other categories, as, for example, the general one of the *ornate*. Here for instance it may be asked how an ornament can be joined to expression. Externally? In that case it is always separated from the expression. Internally? In that case, either it does not assist the expression and mars it; or it does form part of it and is not an ornament, but a constituent element of the expression, indivisible and indistinguishable in its unity.

It is needless to say how much harm has been done by rhetorical distinctions. Rhetoric has often been declaimed against, but although there has been rebellion against its consequences, its principles have, at the same time, been carefully preserved (perhaps in order to show proof of philosophic consistency). In literature the rhetorical categories have contributed, if not to make dominant, at least to justify theoretically, that particular kind of *bad writing* which is called *fine writing* or writing according to rhetoric.

Empirical sense of the rhetorical categories

The terms above mentioned would never have gone beyond the schools, where we all of us learned them (only we never found an opportunity of using them in strictly aesthetic discussions, or at most of doing so jocosely and with a comic intention), were it not that they can sometimes be employed in one of the following significations: as *verbal variants* of the aesthetic concept; as indications of the *anti-aesthetic*, or finally (and this is their most important use), no longer in the service of art and aesthetic, but of *science* and *logic*.

Use of these categories as synonyms of the aesthetic fact

First. Expressions considered directly or positively are not divisible into classes, but some are successful, others half-successful, others failures. There are perfect and imperfect, successful and unsuccessful expressions. The words recorded, and others of the same sort, may therefore sometimes indicate the successful expression, and the various forms of the failures. But they do this in the most inconstant and capricious manner, so much so that the same word serves sometimes to proclaim the perfect, sometimes to condemn the imperfect.

For example, some will say of two pictures—one without inspiration, in which the author has copied natural objects

without intelligence; the other inspired, but without close relation to existing objects—that the first is *realistic,* the second
symbolic. Others, on the contrary, utter the word *realistic*
before a picture strongly felt representing a scene of ordinary
life, while they apply that of *symbolic* to another picture that
is but a cold allegory. It is evident that in the first case
symbolic means artistic and realistic inartistic, while in the
second, realistic is synonymous with artistic and symbolic
with inartistic. What wonder, then, that some hotly maintain
the true art form is the symbolic, and that the realistic is
inartistic; others, that the realistic is artistic and the symbolic
inartistic? We cannot but grant that both are right, since
each uses the same words in such a different sense.

The great disputes about *classicism* and *romanticism* were
frequently based upon such equivocations. Sometimes the
former was understood as the artistically perfect, and the
second as lacking balance and imperfect; at others "classic"
meant cold and artificial, "romantic," pure, warm, powerful,
truly expressive. Thus it was always possible reasonably to
take the side of the classic against the romantic, or of the
romantic against the classic.

The same thing happens as regards the word *style.* Sometimes it is said that every writer must have style. Here style
is synonymous with form of expression. At others the form of
a code of laws or of a mathematical work is said to be
without style. Here the error is again committed of admitting
diverse modes of expression, an ornate and a naked form,
because, if style is form, the code and the mathematical
treatise must also be asserted, strictly speaking, to have each
its style. At other times, one hears the critics blaming someone for "having too much style" or for "writing a style."
Here it is clear that style signifies, not the form, nor a mode
of it, but improper and pretentious expression, a form of the
inartistic.

Their use to indicate various aesthetic imperfections

Second. The second not altogether meaningless use of these
words and distinctions is to be found when we hear in the
examination of a literary composition such remarks as these:
here is a pleonasm, here an ellipse, there a metaphor, here
again a synonym or an ambiguity. The meaning is: Here is
an error consisting of using a larger number of words than
necessary (pleonasm); here, on the other hand, the error

arises from too few having been used (ellipse), here from the use of an unsuitable word (metaphor), here of two words which seem to say two different things (ambiguity). This depreciatory and pathological use of the terms is, however, less common than the preceding.

Their use in a sense transcending aesthetic, in the service of science

Thirdly and finally, when rhetorical terminology possesses no aesthetic signification similar or analogous to those passed in review, and yet one feels that it is not void of meaning and designates something that deserves to be noted, this means that it is used in the service of logic and of science. Granted that a concept used by a writer in a scientific sense is designated by a definite term, it is natural that other terms found in use to signify the same thought, become *in respect to* the vocabulary fixed upon by him as true, metaphors, synecdoches, synonyms, elliptical forms, and the like. We ourselves in the course of this treatise have several times made use of, and intend again to make use of such language, in order to make clear the sense of the words we employ, or may find employed. But this proceeding, which is of value in discussions pertaining to the criticism of science and philosophy, has none whatever in literary and artistic criticism. There are words and metaphors proper to science: the same concept may be psychologically formed in various circumstances and therefore differ in its intuitional expression. When the scientific terminology of a given writer has been established and one of these modes fixed as correct, then all other uses of it become improper or tropical. But in the aesthetic fact there are none but proper words: the same intuition can be expressed in one way only, precisely because it is intuition and not concept.

Rhetoric in the schools

Some, while admitting the aesthetic non-existence of the rhetorical categories, yet make a reservation as to their utility and the service they are supposed to render, especially in schools of literature. We confess that we fail to understand how error and confusion can educate the mind to logical distinction, or aid the teaching of a science which they disturb and obscure. Perhaps what is meant is that such distinctions, as empirical classes, can aid memory and learning, as was admitted above for literary and artistic kinds. To this there is no objection. There is certainly another purpose for which the rhetorical categories should continue to appear in schools: to be criticized there. The errors of the past must not be forgotten and no more said, and truths cannot be kept alive save by making them combat errors. Unless an account of the rhetorical categories be given, accompanied by a criticism of them, there is a risk of their springing up again, and it may be said that they are already springing up among certain philologists as the latest *psychological* discoveries.

The resemblances of expressions

It might seem that we thus wished to deny all bond of resemblance between different expressions and works of art. Resemblances exist, and by means of them, works of art can be arranged in this or that group. But they are likenesses such as are observed among individuals, and can never be rendered with abstract determinations. That is to say, it would be incorrect to apply identification, subordination, coordination and the other relations of concepts to these resemblances, which consist wholly of what is called a *family likeness,* derived from the historical conditions in which the various works have appeared and from relationship of soul among the artists.

The relative possibility of translations

It is in these resemblances that lies the relative possibility of translations; not as reproductions of the same original expressions (which it would be vain to attempt), but as productions of similar expressions more or less nearly resembling the originals. The translation called good is an approximation which has original value as a work of art and can stand by itself.

V. PARTICULARITIES

On Sound and Sense

SAMUEL JOHNSON

Let me likewise dwell a little on the celebrated paragraph,[1] in which it is directed that "the sound should seem an echo to the sense," a precept which Pope is allowed to have observed beyond any other English poet.

This notion of representative meter, and the desire of discovering frequent adaptations of the sound to the sense, have produced, in my opinion, many wild conceits and imaginary beauties. All that can furnish this representation are the sounds of the words considered singly, and the time in which they are pronounced. Every language has some words framed to exhibit the noises which they express, as *thump, rattle, growl, hiss*. These, however, are but few, and the poet cannot make them more, nor can they be of any use but when sound is to be mentioned. The time of pronunciation was in the dactylic measures of the learned languages capable of considerable variety; but that variety could be accommodated only to motion or duration, and different degrees of motion were perhaps expressed by verses rapid or slow, without much attention of the writer, when the image had full possession of his fancy; but our language having little flexibility, our verses can differ very little in their cadence. The fancied resemblances, I fear, arise sometimes merely from the ambiguity of words; there is supposed to be some relation between a *soft* line and a *soft* couch, or between *hard* syllables and *hard* fortune.

Motion, however, may be in some sort exemplified; and yet it may be suspected that even in such resemblances the mind often governs the ear, and the sounds are estimated by their

[1] Pope, *Essay on Criticism*, 337-83.

From "The Life of Pope."

meaning. One of the most successful attempts has been to describe the labor of Sisyphus:

> With many a weary step, and many a groan,
> Up a high hill he heaves a huge round stone;
> The huge round stone, resulting with a bound,
> Thunders impetuous down, and smokes along
>   the ground.[2]

Who does not perceive the stone to move slowly upward, and roll violently back? But set the same numbers to another sense:

> While many a merry tale, and many a song,
> Cheered the rough road, we wished the rough road
>   long.
> The rough road then, returning in a round,
> Mocked our impatient steps, for all was fairy
>   ground.

We have now surely lost much of the delay, and much of the rapidity.

But to show how little the greatest master of numbers can fix the principles of representative harmony, it will be sufficient to remark that the poet, who tells us that

> When Ajax strives some rock's vast weight to throw,
> The line too labors, and the words move slow;
> Not so when swift Camilla scours the plain,
> Flies o'er th' unbending corn, and skims along
>   the main,[3]

when he had enjoyed for about thirty years the praise of Camilla's lightness of foot, tried another experiment upon *sound* and *time,* and produced this memorable triplet:

> Waller was smooth; but Dryden taught to join
> The varying verse, the full resounding line,
> The long majestic march, and energy divine.[4]

Here are the swiftness of the rapid race and the march of slow-paced majesty exhibited by the same poet in the same sequence of syllables, except that the exact prosodist will find the line of *swiftness* by one time longer than that of *tardiness.*

[2] Pope, *Odyssey,* XI, 735-38.
[3] *Essay on Criticism,* 370-73.
[4] *Imitations of Horace,* Epistles, II. i. 267-69.

Beauties of this kind are commonly fancied, and when real are technical and nugatory, not to be rejected and not to be solicited.

Poetic Diction

WILLIAM WORDSWORTH

HAVING DWELT THUS long on the subjects and aim of these Poems, I shall request the Reader's permission to apprise him of a few circumstances relating to their *style,* in order, among other reasons, that he may not censure me for not having performed what I never attempted. The Reader will find that personifications of abstract ideas rarely occur in these volumes; and are utterly rejected, as an ordinary device to elevate the style, and raise it above prose. My purpose was to imitate, and, as far as possible, to adopt the very language of men; and assuredly such personifications do not make any natural or regular part of that language. They are, indeed, a figure of speech occasionally prompted by passion, and I have made use of them as such; but have endeavoured utterly to reject them as a mechanical device of style, or as a family language which Writers in metre seem to lay claim to by prescription. I have wished to keep the Reader in the company of flesh and blood, persuaded that by so doing I shall interest him. Others who pursue a different track will interest him likewise; I do not interfere with their claim, but wish to prefer a claim of my own. There will also be found in these volumes little of what is usually called poetic diction; as much pains has been taken to avoid it as is ordinarily taken to produce it; this has been done for the reason already alleged, to bring my language near to the language of men; and further, because the pleasure which I have proposed to myself to impart, is of a kind very different from that which is supposed by many persons to be the proper object of poetry. Without being culpably particular, I do not know how to give my Reader a more exact notion of the style in which it was my wish and intention to write, than by informing him that I have at all times endeavoured to look steadily at my subject; consequently, there is I hope in these Poems little falsehood of description, and my ideas are expressed in lan-

From the "Preface to the Lyrical Ballads" (1802).

guage fitted to their respective importance. Something must have been gained by this practice, as it is friendly to one property of all good poetry, namely, good sense: but it has necessarily cut me off from a large portion of phrases and figures of speech which from father to son have long been regarded as the common inheritance of Poets. I have also thought it expedient to restrict myself still further, having abstained from the use of many expressions, in themselves proper and beautiful, but which have been foolishly repeated by bad Poets, till such feelings of disgust are connected with them as it is scarcely possible by any art of association to overpower.

If in a poem there should be found a series of lines, or even a single line, in which the language, though naturally arranged, and according to the strict laws of metre, does not differ from that of prose, there is a numerous class of critics, who, when they stumble upon these prosaisms, as they call them, imagine that they have made a notable discovery, and exult over the Poet as over a man ignorant of his own profession. Now these men would establish a canon of criticism which the Reader will conclude he must utterly reject, if he wishes to be pleased with these volumes. And it would be a most easy task to prove to him, that not only the language of a large portion of every good poem, even of the most elevated character, must necessarily, except with reference to the metre, in no respect differ from that of good prose, but likewise that some of the most interesting parts of the best poems will be found to be strictly the language of prose when prose is well written. The truth of this assertion might be demonstrated by innumerable passages from almost all the poetical writings, even of Milton himself. To illustrate the subject in a general manner, I will here adduce a short composition of Gray, who was at the head of those who, by their reasonings, have attempted to widen the space of separation betwixt Prose and Metrical composition, and was more than any other man curiously elaborate in the structure of his own poetic diction.

> In vain to me the smiling mornings shine,
> And reddening Phoebus lifts his golden fire:
> The birds in vain their amorous descant join,
> Or cheerful fields resume their green attire.
> These ears, alas! for other notes repine;
> *A different object do these eyes require;*

My lonely anguish melts no heart but mine;
And in my breast the imperfect joys expire;
Yet morning smiles the busy race to cheer,
And new-born pleasure brings to happier men;
The fields to all their wonted tribute bear;
To warm their little loves the birds complain,
I fruitless mourn to him that cannot hear,
And weep the more because I weep in vain.

It will easily be perceived, that the only part of this Sonnet which is of any value is the lines printed in Italics; it is equally obvious, that, except in the rhyme, and in the use of the single word "fruitless" for fruitlessly, which is so far a defect, the language of these lines does in no respect differ from that of prose.

By the foregoing quotation it has been shown that language of Prose may yet be well adapted to Poetry; and it was previously asserted, that a large portion of the language of every good poem can in no respect differ from that of good Prose. We will go further. It may be safely affirmed, that there neither is, nor can be, any *essential* difference between the language of prose and metrical composition. We are fond of tracing the resemblance between Poetry and Painting, and, accordingly, we call them Sisters: but where shall we find bonds of connexion sufficiently strict to typify the affinity betwixt metrical and prose composition? They both speak by and to the same organs; the bodies in which both of them are clothed may be said to be of the same substance, their affections are kindred, and almost identical, not necessarily differing even in degree; Poetry [1] sheds no tears "such as Angels weep," but natural and human tears; she can boast of no celestial ichor that distinguishes her vital juices from those of prose; the same human blood circulates through the veins of them both.

If it be affirmed that rhyme and metrical arrangement of themselves constitute a distinction which overturns what has

---

[1] I here use the word "Poetry" (though against my own judgment) as opposed to the word Prose, and synonymous with metrical composition. But much confusion has been introduced into criticism by this contradistinction of Poetry and Prose, instead of the more philosophical one of Poetry and Matter of Fact, or Science. The only strict antithesis to Prose is Metre; nor is this, in truth, a *strict* antithesis, because lines and passages of metre so naturally occur in writing prose, that it would be scarcely possible to avoid them, even were it desirable.

just been said on the strict affinity of metrical language with that of prose, and paves the way for other artificial distinctions which the mind voluntarily admits, I answer that the language of such Poetry as is here recommended is, as far as is possible, a selection of the language really spoken by men; that this selection, wherever it is made with true taste and feeling, will of itself form a distinction far greater than would at first be imagined, and will entirely separate the composition from the vulgarity and meanness of ordinary life; and, if metre be superadded thereto, I believe that a dissimilitude will be produced altogether sufficient for the gratification of a rational mind. What other distinction would we have? Whence is it to come? And where is it to exist? Not, surely, where the Poet speaks through the mouths of his characters: it cannot be necessary here, either for elevation of style, or any of its supposed ornaments: for, if the Poet's subject be judiciously chosen, it will naturally, and upon fit occasion, lead him to passions the language of which, if selected truly and judiciously, must necessarily be dignified and variegated, and alive with metaphors and figures. I forbear to speak of an incongruity which would shock the intelligent Reader, should the Poet interweave any foreign splendour of his own with that which the passion naturally suggests: it is sufficient to say that such addition is unnecessary. And, surely, it is more probable that those passages, which with propriety abound with metaphors and figures, will have their due effect, if, upon other occasions where the passions are of a milder character, the style also be subdued and temperate.

Poetic Diction

SAMUEL TAYLOR COLERIDGE

The language, too, of these men has been adopted (purified indeed from what appear to be its real defects, from all lasting and rational causes of dislike or disgust) because such men hourly communicate with the best objects from which the best part of language is originally derived; and because, from their rank in society and the sameness and narrow circle of their intercourse, being less under the action of social vanity, they convey their feelings and notions in simple and unelaborated expressions.[1]

From Biographia Literaria.

TO THIS I reply that a rustic's language, purified from all provincialism and grossness, and so far reconstructed as to be made consistent with the rules of grammar—(which are in essence no other than the laws of universal logic, applied to psychological materials)—will not differ from the language of any other man of common sense, however learned or refined he may be, except as far as the notions, which the rustic has to convey, are fewer and more indiscriminate. This will become still clearer, if we add the consideration—(equally important though less obvious—that the rustic, from the more imperfect development of his faculties, and from the lower state of their cultivation, aims almost solely to convey insulated facts, either those of his scanty experience or his traditional belief; while the educated man chiefly seeks to discover and express those connections of things, or those relative bearings of fact to fact, from which some more or less general law is deducible. For facts are valuable to a wise man, chiefly as they lead to the discovery of the indwelling law, which is the true being of things, the sole solution of their modes of existence, and in the knowledge of which consists our dignity and our power.

As little can I agree with the assertion, that from the objects with which the rustic hourly communicates the best part of language is formed. For first, if to communicate with an object implies such an acquaintance with it, as renders it capable of being discriminately reflected on, the distinct knowledge of an uneducated rustic would furnish a very scanty vocabulary. The few things and modes of action requisite for his bodily conveniences would alone be individualized; while all the rest of nature would be expressed by a small number of confused general terms. Secondly, I deny that the words and combinations of words derived from the objects, with which the rustic is familiar, whether with distinct or confused knowledge, can be justly said tó form the best part of language. It is more than probable, that many classes of the brute creation possess discriminating sounds, by which they can convey to each other notices of such objects as concern their food, shelter, or safety. Yet we hesitate to call the aggregate of such sounds a language, otherwise than metaphorically. The best part of human language, properly so called, is derived from reflection on the acts of the mind it-

[1] Wordsworth, *Observations Prefixed to "Lyrical Ballads"* (1800).

self. It is formed by a voluntary appropriation of fixed symbols to internal acts, to processes and results of imagination, the greater part of which have no place in the consciousness of uneducated man; though in civilized society, by imitation and passive remembrance of what they hear from their religious instructors and other superiors, the most uneducated share in the harvest which they neither sowed, nor reaped. If the history of the phrases in hourly currency among our peasants were traced, a person not previously aware of the fact would be surprised at finding so large a number, which three or four centuries ago were the exclusive property of the universities and the schools; and, at the commencement of the Reformation, had been transferred from the school to the pulpit, and thus gradually passed into common life. The extreme difficulty, and often the impossibility, of finding words for the simplest moral and intellectual processes of the languages of uncivilized tribes has proved perhaps the weightiest obstacle to the progress of our most zealous and adroit missionaries. Yet these tribes are surrounded by the same nature as our peasants are; but in still more impressive forms; and they are, moreover, obliged to particularize many more of them. When, therefore, Mr. Wordsworth adds, "accordingly, such a language"—(meaning, as before, the language of rustic life purified from provincialism)—"arising out of repeated experience and regular feelings, is a more permanent, and a far more philosophical language, than that which is frequently substituted for it by Poets, who think that they are conferring honour upon themselves and their art in proportion as they indulge in arbitrary and capricious habits of expression;" it may be answered, that the language, which he has in view, can be attributed to rustics with no greater right, than the style of Hooker or Bacon to Tom Brown or Sir Roger L'Estrange. Doubtless, if what is peculiar to each were omitted in each, the result must needs be the same. Further, that the poet, who uses an illogical diction, or a style fitted to excite only the low and changeable pleasure of wonder by means of groundless novelty, substitutes a language of folly and vanity, not for that of the rustic, but for that of good sense and natural feeling.

Here let me be permitted to remind the reader, that the positions, which I controvert, are contained in the sentences —"a selection of the real language of men;"—"the language of these men" (that is, men in low and rustic life) "has been adopted; I have proposed to myself to imitate, and, as far as possible, to adopt the very language of men." "Between the language of prose and that of metrical composition, there neither is, nor can be, any *essential difference*:" it is against these exclusively that my opposition is directed.

I object, in the very first instance, to an equivocation in the use of the word "real." Every man's language varies, according to the extent of his knowledge, the activity of his faculties, and the depth or quickness of his feelings. Every man's language has, first, its individualities; secondly, the common properties of the class to which he belongs; and thirdly, words and phrases of universal use. The language of Hooker, Bacon, Bishop Taylor, and Burke differs from the common language of the learned class only by the superior number and novelty of the thoughts and relations which they had to convey. The language of Algernon Sidney differs not at all from that, which every well-educated gentleman would wish to write, and (with due allowances for the undeliberateness, and less connected train, of thinking natural and proper to conversation) such as he would wish to talk. Neither one nor the other differ half as much from the general language of cultivated society, as the language of Mr. Wordsworth's homeliest composition differs from that of a common peasant. For "real" therefore, we must substitute ordinary, or *lingua communis*. And this, we have proved, is no more to be found in the phraseology of low and rustic life than in that of any other class. Omit the peculiarities of each and the result of course must be common to all. And assuredly the omissions and changes to be made in the language of rustics, before it could be transferred to any species of poem, except the drama or other professed imitation, are at least as numerous and weighty, as would be required in adapting to the same purpose the ordinary language of tradesmen and manufacturers. Not to mention, that the language so highly extolled by Mr. Wordsworth varies in every county, nay in every village, according to the accidental character of the clergyman, the existence or non-existence of schools; or even, perhaps, as the exciseman, publican, and barber happen to be, or not to be, zealous politicians, and readers of the weekly newspaper *pro bono publico*. Anterior to cultivation the *lingua communis* of every country, as Dante has well observed, exists everywhere in parts, and nowhere as a whole.

Neither is the case rendered at all more tenable by the addition of the words, "in a state of excitement." For the nature of a man's words, where he is strongly affected by joy, grief, or anger, must necessarily depend on the number and quality of the general truths, conceptions and images, and of the words expressing them, with which his mind had been previously stored. For the property of passion is not to create; but to set in increased activity. At least, whatever new connections of thoughts or images, or—(which is equally, if not more than equally, the appropriate effect of strong excitement)—whatever generalizations of truth or experience the heat of passion may produce; yet the terms of their conveyance must have pre-existed in his former conversations, and are only collected and crowded together by the unusual stimulation. It is indeed very possible to adopt in a poem the unmeaning repetitions, habitual phrases, and other blank counters, which an unfurnished or confused understanding interposes at short intervals, in order to keep hold of his subject, which is still slipping from him, and to give him time for recollection; or in mere aid of vacancy, as in the scanty companies of a country stage the same player pops backwards and forwards, in order to prevent the appearance of empty spaces, in the procession of Macbeth, or Henry VIII. But what assistance to the poet, or ornament to the poem, these can supply, I am at a loss to conjecture. Nothing assuredly can differ either in origin or in mode more widely from the apparent tautologies of intense and turbulent feeling, in which the passion is greater and of longer endurance than to be exhausted or satisfied by a single representation of the image or incident exciting it. Such repetitions I admit to be a beauty of the highest kind; as illustrated by Mr. Wordsworth himself from the song of Deborah. *At her feet he bowed, he fell, he lay down: at her feet he bowed, he fell: where he bowed, there he fell down dead.* Judges v.27.

The Problem of an American Style

JAMES RUSSELL LOWELL

IN CHOOSING THE Yankee dialect, [1] I did not act without thought. It had long seemed to me that the great vice of

---

[1] For example: "We're curus critters: Now ain't jes' the minute Thet ever fits us easy while we're in it." Ed.

From the Preface to the **Bigelow Papers**, Second Series.

American writing and speaking was a studied want of simplicity, that we were in danger of coming to look on our mother-tongue as a dead language, to be sought in the grammar and dictionary rather than in the heart, and that our only chance of escape was by seeking it at its living sources among those who were, as Scottowe says of Major-General Gibbons, "divinely illiterate." President Lincoln, the only really great public man whom these latter days have seen, was great also in this, that he was master—witness his speech at Gettysburg—of a truly masculine English, classic because it was of no special period, and level at once to the highest and lowest of his countrymen. I learn from the highest authority that his favorite reading was in Shakespeare and Milton, to which, of course, the Bible should be added. But whoever should read the debates in Congress might fancy himself present at a meeting of the city council of some city of Southern Gaul in the decline of the Empire, where barbarians with a Latin varnish emulated each other in being more than Ciceronian. Whether it be want of culture, for the highest outcome of that is simplicity, or for whatever reason, it is certain that very few American writers or speakers wield their native language with the directness, precision, and force that are common as the day in the mother country. We use it like Scotsmen, not as if it belonged to us, but as if we wished to prove that we belonged to it, by showing our intimacy with its written rather than with its spoken dialect. And yet all the while our popular idiom is racy with life and vigor and originality, bucksome (as Milton used the word) to our new occasions, and proves itself no mere graft by sending up new suckers from the old root in spite of us. It is only from its roots in the living generations of men that a language can be reinforced with fresh vigor for its needs; what may be called a literate dialect grows ever more and more pedantic and foreign, till it becomes at last as unfitting a vehicle for living thought as monkish Latin. That we should all be made to talk like books is the danger with which we are threatened by the Universal Schoolmaster, who does his best to enslave the minds and memories of his victims to what he esteems the best models of English composition, that is to say, to the writers whose style is faultily correct and has no blood-warmth in it. No language after it has faded into *diction*, none that cannot suck up the feeding juices secreted for it in the rich mother-earth of common folk, can bring forth a sound and lusty book. True vigor and heartiness of phrase do not pass from page to page, but from man to man, where the brain is kindled and the lips suppled by downright living interests and by passion in its very throe. Language is the soil of thought, and our own especially is a rich leaf-mould, the slow deposit of ages, the shed foliage of feeling, fancy, and imagination, which has suffered an earth-change, that the vocal forest, as Howell called it, may clothe itself anew with living green. There is death in the dictionary; and, where language is too strictly limited by convention, the ground for expression to grow in is limited also; and we get a *potted* literature, Chinese dwarfs instead of healthy trees.

But while the schoolmaster has been busy starching our language and smoothing it flat with the mangle of a supposed classical authority, the newspaper reporter has been doing even more harm by stretching and swelling it to suit his occasions. A dozen years ago I began a list, which I have added to from time to time, of some of the changes which may be fairly laid at his door. I give a few of them as showing their tendency, all the more dangerous that their effect, like that of some poisons, is insensibly cumulative, and that they are sure at last of effect among a people whose chief reading is the daily paper. I give in two columns the old style and its modern equivalent.

OLD STYLE	NEW STYLE
Was hanged.	Was launched into eternity.
When the halter was put around his neck.	When the fatal noose was adjusted about the neck of the unfortunate victim of his own unbridled passions.
A great crowd came to see.	A vast concourse was assembled to witness . . .

The quality of exaggeration has often been remarked on as typical of American character, and especially of American humor. In Dr. Petri's *Gedrängtes Handbuch der Fremdwörter,* we are told that the word *humbug* is commonly used for the exaggerations of the North-Americans. To be sure, one would be tempted to think the dream of Columbus half fulfilled, and that Europe had found in the West a nearer way to Orientalism, at least in diction. But it seems to me that a great deal of what is set down as mere extravagance is more fitly to be called intensity and picturesqueness, symptoms of the imaginative faculty in full health and strength, though producing, as yet, only the raw and formless material in which poetry is to work. By and by, perhaps, the world will see it fashioned into poem and picture, and Europe, which will be hard pushed for originality erelong, may have to thank us for a new sensation. The French continue to find Shakespeare exaggerated because he treated English just as our country-folk do when they speak of a "steep price," or say that they "freeze to" a thing. The first postulate of an original literature is that a people should use their language instinctively and unconsciously, as if it were a lively part of their growth and personality, not as the mere torpid boon of education or inheritance.

American Style

GEORGE PHILIP KRAPP

IF A NEW SOUL and a new style were born in America, one finds it difficult to settle upon a fixed date for this important event. It remains a matter of debate who is rightly to be called the first American man of letters. Early colonial writers like Captain John Smith and the Puritan recorders and historians were neither Americans nor men of letters in any just sense of these terms. Not until one approaches the Revolution in the third quarter of the eighteenth century can one reasonably speak of writers in America as being American. Of these first American writers, the chief historical place is unquestionably occupied by Benjamin Franklin. Franklin was much more than a man of letters, and indeed has come to be regarded in the latter light not because he made a direct bid for literary fame but, like Bacon, whom he in several respects resembled, because his larger activities could not be carried on without the assistance of a literary method and technic. After many generations of Americans have lived, Franklin's own personal life also seems in many respects prophetic of what a definitely typical literary American was to be. In rough outline the story of the poor printer's boy who emerges by rigorous self-discipline and native wit into the

From **The English Language in America**, Volume I.

bright light of public success might serve for numerous American authors.

American in spirit and in choice of theme Franklin may have been, but when one examines the details of his literary method, one finds no peculiar Americanism in style. It could not have been otherwise with the spiritual background which Franklin has described near the beginning of his *Autobiography*. "From a child," he says, "I was fond of reading, and all the little money that came into my hands was ever laid out in books. Pleased with *Pilgrim's Progress,* my first collection was of John Bunyan's works in separate little volumes. I afterwards sold them to enable me to buy R. Burton's *Historical Collections.* . . . My father's library consisted chiefly of books in polemic divinity, most of which I read. . . . Plutarch's *Lives* there was in which I read abundantly and I still think that time spent to great advantage. There was also a book of DeFoe's, called *An Essay on Projects,* and another of Dr. Mather's, called *Essays to do Good,* which perhaps gave me a form of thinking that had an influence on some of the principal future events of my life." After some excursions into the field of poetry, from which he was rescued by the ridicule of his father, Franklin devoted himself to prose writing. He describes a bad habit of disputatiousness which he had fallen into, caught by reading his father's religious books, and how he was brought to the realization of a more urbane manner of writing. "About this time, I met with an odd volume of the *Spectator*. It was the third. I had never before seen any of them. I bought it, read it over and over, and was much delighted with it. I thought the writing excellent, and wished, if possible, to imitate it. With this view I took some of the papers, and, making short hints of the sentiment in each sentence, laid them by a few days, and then, without looking at the book, tried to complete the papers again, by expressing each hinted sentiment at length, and as fully as it had been expressed before, in any suitable words that should come to hand. Then I compared my *Spectator* with the original, discovered some of my faults, and corrected them. But I found I wanted a stock of words, or a readiness in recollecting and using them, which I thought I should have acquired before that time if I had gone on making verses; since the continual occasion for words of the same import, but of different length, to suit the measure, or of different sound for the rhyme, would have laid me under a constant necessity of searching for variety, and also have tended to fix that variety in my mind, and made me master of it. Therefore I took some of the tales and turned them into verse; and, after a time, when I had pretty well forgotten the prose, turned them back again. I also sometimes jumbled my collections of hints into confusion, and after some weeks endeavored to reduce them into the best order, before I began to form the full sentences and complete the paper. This was to teach me method in the arrangement of thoughts. By comparing my work afterwards with the original, I discovered many faults and amended them; but I sometimes had the pleasure of fancying that, in certain particulars of small import, I had been lucky enough to improve the method or the language, and this encouraged me to think I might possibly in time come to be a tolerable English writer, of which I was extremely ambitious."

It has seemed worth while calling attention again to these well-known passages in Franklin's *Autobiography* because in kind they might stand for the normal experience of almost any American man of letters from the time they were written to the present day. What Franklin aspired to become was "a tolerable English writer," and he conceived that the best method of attaining this end was to discipline himself in the best literary traditions of the English language. The thought probably never occurred to Franklin that to be a true American writer he must renounce the whole or any part of British cultural tradition. Franklin's concern in writing was primarily with content, and so it is with every serious writer. Language is merely the mechanical means to convey the content effectively. If therefore one had at hand an adequate mechanical means, as any writer of English was convinced he had in Franklin's day in the language of Shakespeare and Milton and Addison, only a pedant or theorist would have refused to use this means. "Nicenesse in wordes," says the Preface to the King James translation of the Bible, "was always counted the next step to trifling." So the first writers of English in America thought when it came to the practical question of using or refusing the heritage of literary expression common to all whose native speech is English. Their purpose was not to escape the literary traditions of the past, but to utilize and to surpass them. The spirit of their endeavor was ambitiously expressed in the following lines from one of Samuel Low's *Poems* (1800), p. 135:

> The time will come, soon may that time arrive,
> When Roman greatness shall in us revive;

> When Homer's genius here sublime shall soar,
> And a new Virgil grace this western shore.

Homer and Virgil in these lines merely express figuratively respect for the accredited achievements of the past in English literature.

Charles Sanders Peirce on Technical Style

JAMES FEIBLEMAN

THE CHIEF TOOL that is employed by philosophy, and indeed by all thought, is language. ". . . the woof and warp of all thought and all research is symbols, and the life of thought and science is the life inherent in symbols; so that it is wrong to say that a good language is *important* to good thought, merely; for it is of the essence of it." Definition is the primary requisite of the proper use of language by any special science, such as philosophy aims to be. To fail in this regard with respect to any important term is to treat "a verbal definition as a doctrine." The secondary requisite is the use of new terms. ". . . the philosophist must be encouraged—yea, and required—to coin new terms to express such new scientific concepts as he may discover, just as his chemical and biological brethren are expected to do"; "he who introduces a new conception into philosophy is under an obligation to invent acceptable terms to express it . . . furthermore . . . once a conception has been supplied with suitable and sufficient words for its expression, no other *technical* terms denoting the same things, considered in the same relations, should be countenanced." "For in order that philosophy should become a successful science, it must, like biology, have its own vocabulary."

Of course, technical terms will tend to deprive philosophy of something of its literary charm. But "if philosophy is ever to stand in the ranks of the sciences, literary elegance must be sacrificed—like the soldier's old brilliant uniforms—to the stern requirements of efficiency." "Metaphysicians are a slow-thinking breed; but they seem duller than ordinary not

From **An Introduction to Peirce's Philosophy** by James Feibleman, Harper and Brothers, 1946. Quotations are from **The Collected Papers of Charles Sanders Peirce**, Harvard University Press, 1931-1935. Reprinted by permission of James Feibleman and The Belknap Press of Harvard University Press.

to perceive that a literary style in philosophy is an incongruity whose days are numbered." No study can become a science unless its "vocables have no such sweetness or charms as might tempt loose writers to abuse them—which is a virtue of scientific nomenclature too little appreciated": "In order to be deep it is requisite to be dull."

In philosophy, "A good style is one which approximates as closely as possible to a self-explaining diagram or a tabular array of familiar symbols." Philosophical method resembles scientific method in that ". . . language is but a kind of algebra. It would, certainly, in one sense be extravagant to say that we can never tell what we are talking about; yet, in another sense, it is quite true. The meanings of words ordinarily depend upon our tendencies to weld together qualities and our aptitudes to see resemblances, or, to use the received phrase, upon associations by *similarity;* while experience is bound together, and only recognizable, by forces acting upon us, or, to use an even worse chosen technical term, by means of associations by contiguity." In order to avoid all ambiguities and confusions, philosophy, like science, must aim at "an ideal philosophical terminology and system of logical symbols." "The ideal terminology will differ somewhat for different sciences. The case of philosophy is very peculiar in that it has positive need of popular words in popular senses—not as its own language (as it has too usually used those words), but as objects of its study. It thus has a peculiar need of a language distinct and detached from common speech, such a language as Aristotle, the scholastics, and Kant endeavored to supply, while Hegel endeavored to destroy it. It is good economy for philosophy to provide itself with a vocabulary so outlandish that loose thinkers shall not be tempted to borrow its words."

On the One Right Word

WALTER RALEIGH

LANGUAGE, IT HAS been shown, is to be fitted to thought; and, further, there are no synonyms. What more natural conclusion could be drawn by the enthusiasm of the artist

From **Style** by Sir Walter Raleigh.

than that there is some kind of preordained harmony between words and things, whereby expression and thought
tally exactly, like the halves of a puzzle? This illusion, called
in France the doctrine of the *mot propre*, is a will o' the
wisp which has kept many an artist dancing on its trail.
That there is one, and only one way of expressing one thing
has been the belief of other writers besides Gustave Flaubert,
inspiriting them to a desperate and fruitful industry. It is
an amiable fancy, like the dream of Michael Angelo, who
loved to imagine that the statue existed already in the block
of marble, and had only to be stripped of its superfluous
wrappings, or like the indolent fallacy of those economic
soothsayers to whom Malthus brought rough awakening,
that population and the means of subsistence move side by
side in harmonious progress. But hunger does not imply
food, and there may hover in the restless heads of poets,
as themselves testify—

> One thought, one grace, one wonder, at the least,
> Which into words no virtue can digest.

Matter and form are not so separable as the popular philosophy would have them; indeed, the very antithesis between
them is a cardinal instance of how language reacts on
thought, modifying and fixing a cloudy truth. The idea
pursues form not only that it may be known to others,
but that it may know itself, and the body in which it becomes incarnate is not to be distinguished from the informing soul. It is recorded of a famous Latin historian how he
declared that he would have made Pompey win the battle
of Pharsalia had the effective turn of the sentence required
it. He may stand for the true type of the literary artist.
The business of letters, howsoever simple it may seem to
those who think truth-telling a gift of nature, is in reality
two-fold, to find words for a meaning, and to find a meaning
for words. Now it is the words that refuse to yield, and now
the meaning, so that he who attempts to wed them is at the
same time altering his words to suit his meaning, and modifying and shaping his meaning to satisfy the requirements
of his words. The humblest processes of thought have had
their first education from language long before they took
shape in literature. So subtle is the connexion between the
two that it is equally possible to call language the form
given to the matter of thought, or, inverting the application
of the figure, to speak of thought as the formal principle

that shapes the raw material of language. It is not until the two become one that they can be known for two. The idea to be expressed is a kind of mutual recognition between thought and language, which here meet and claim each other for the first time, just as in the first glance exchanged by lovers, the unborn child opens its eyes on the world, and pleads for life. But thought, although it may indulge itself with the fancy of a predestined affiance, is not confined to one mate, but roves free and is the father of many children. A belief in the inevitable word is the last refuge of that stubborn mechanical theory of the universe which has been slowly driven from science, politics, and history. Amidst so much that is undulating, it has pleased writers to imagine that truth persists and is provided by heavenly munificence with an imperishable garb of language. But this also is vanity, there is one end appointed alike to all, fact goes the way of fiction, and what is known is no more perdurable than what is made. Not words nor works, but only that which is formless endures, the vitality that is another name for change, the breath that fills and shatters the bubbles of good and evil, of beauty and deformity, of truth and untruth.

On Quotation

WALTER RALEIGH

REAL NOVELTY OF vocabulary is impossible; in the matter of language we lead a parasitical existence, and are always quoting. Quotations, conscious or unconscious, vary in kind according as the mind is active to work upon them and make them its own. In its grossest and most servile form quotation is a lazy folly; a thought has received some signal or notorious expression, and as often as the old sense, or something like it, recurs, the old phrase rises to the lips. This degenerates to simple phrase-mongering, and those who practise it are not vigilantly jealous of their meaning. Such an expression as "fine by degrees and beautifully less" is often no more than a bloated equivalent for a single word—say "diminishing" or "shrinking." Quotations like this are the warts and excremental parts of language; the borrowings of

From *Style* by Sir Walter Raleigh.

good writers are never thus superfluous, their quotations are appropriations. Whether it be by some witty turn given to a well-known line, by an original setting for an old saw, or by a new and unlooked-for analogy, the stamp of the borrower is put upon the goods he borrows, and he becomes part owner. Plagiarism is a crime only where writing is a trade; expression need never be bound by the law of copyright while it follows thought, for thought, as some great thinker has observed, is free. The words were once Shakespeare's; if only you can feel them as he did, they are yours now no less than his. The best quotations, the best translations, the best thefts, are all equally new and original works.

From quotation, at least, there is no escape, inasmuch as we learn language from others. All common phrases that do the dirty work of the world are quotations—poor things, and not our own. Who first said that a book would "repay perusal," or that any gay scene was "bright with all the colours of the rainbow"? There is no need to condemn these phrases, for language has a vast deal of inferior work to do. The expression of thought, temperament, attitude, is not the whole of its business. It is only a literary fop or doctrinaire who will attempt to remint all the small defaced coinage that passes through his hands, only a lisping young fantastico who will refuse all conventional garments and all conventional speech. At a modern wedding the frock-coat is worn, the presents are "numerous and costly," and there is an "ovation accorded to the happy pair." These things are part of our public civilisation, a decorous and accessible uniform, not to be lightly set aside. But let it be a friend of your own who is to marry, a friend of your own who dies, and you are to express yourself—the problem is changed, you feel all the difficulties of the art of style, and fathom something of the depth of your unskill. Forbidden silence, we should be in a poor way indeed.

The Process

ROBERT LOUIS STEVENSON

A WORK OF art is first cloudily conceived in the mind; during the period of gestation it stands more clearly forward

From "A Note on Realism."

from these swaddling mists, puts on expressive lineaments, and becomes at length that most faultless, but also, alas! that incommunicable product of the human mind, a perfected design. On the approach to execution all is changed. The artist must now step down, don his working clothes, and become the artisan. He now resolutely commits his airy conception, his delicate Ariel, to the touch of matter; he must decide, almost in a breath, the scale, the style, the spirit, and the particularity of execution of his whole design.

The engendering idea of some works is stylistic; a technical preoccupation stands them instead of some robuster principle of life. And with these the execution is but play; for the stylistic problem is resolved beforehand, and all large originality of treatment wilfully foregone. Such are the verses, intricately designed, which we have learnt to admire, with a certain smiling admiration, at the hands of Mr. Lang and Mr. Dobson; such, too, are those canvases where dexterity or even breadth of plastic style takes the place of pictorial nobility of design. So, it may be remarked, it was easier to begin to write *Esmond* than *Vanity Fair*, since, in the first, the style was dictated by the nature of the plan; and Thackeray, a man probably of some indolence of mind, enjoyed and got good profit of this economy of effort. But the case is exceptional. Usually in all works of art that have been conceived from within outwards, and generously nourished from the author's mind, the moment in which he begins to execute is one of extreme perplexity and strain. Artists of indifferent energy and an imperfect devotion to their own ideal make this ungrateful effort once for all; and, having formed a style, adhere to it through life. But those of a higher order cannot rest content with a process which, as they continue to employ it, must infallibly degenerate towards the academic and the cut-and-dried. Every fresh work in which they embark is the signal for a fresh engagement of the whole forces of their mind; and the changing views which accompany the growth of their experience are marked by still more sweeping alterations in the manner of their art. So that criticism loves to dwell upon and distinguish the varying periods of a Raphael, a Shakespeare, or a Beethoven.

Style and Chronology: Shakespeare

WILLIAM ALLAN NEILSON AND
ASHLEY HORACE THORNDIKE

THE PURELY INTERNAL evidence [for dating Shakespeare's plays] is seldom as specific as the external, and requires to be handled with much judgment and caution. Most difficult in this class is the weighing of considerations of a moral or esthetic nature; for, though these are often powerful in their effect on the individual reader, they are usually incapable of proof to another person with different tastes and a different point of view. Of such tests, those afforded by a study of the methods used in the treatment of plot and in the development of character are perhaps the least subjective. Somewhat more palpable are the changing characteristics of style. The number and nature of classical allusions and Latin words and quotations; the kind and degree of elaboration of figures of speech, puns, conceits, and the like; diffuseness or concentration in the expression of thought; artificiality or lifelikeness in the treatment of dialogue; the use of prose or verse; the employment of oaths, checked by statute shortly after the accession of James I: these are the main aspects of style which can be used in determining, not exact dates, but the period of Shakespeare's activity within which a given work falls. More capable of mechanical calculation than the tests of either matter or style are those derived from changes in versification, though here too there is often a subjective element in the reckoning. The more important metrical tests include the following: the frequency of rhyme, whether in the heroic couplet or, as not uncommonly occurs in early plays, in alternates and even such elaborate arrangements as the sonnet; doggerel lines; alexandrines, or lines of twelve syllables; the presence of an extra syllable before a pause within the line; short lines, especially at the end of speeches; the substitution of other feet for the regular iambic movement of blank verse; weak and light endings; and, most valuable, the position of the pause in the line ("end-stopped" or "run on"), and feminine endings or hypermetrical lines, such as

These many summers in a sea of glor-y.

Many of these variable features were not consciously manipulated by the author; and, even when a general drift in a certain direction is clearly observable in his practice with regard to them, it is not to be assumed that his progress was perfectly regular, without leaps forward and occasional returns to an earlier usage. It is to be noted also that the subject and atmosphere of a particular play might induce a metrical treatment of a special kind, in which case the verse tests would yield evidence not primarily chronological at all. Nevertheless, when all allowances have been made and all due caution exercised, it will be found that the indications of the versification corroborate and supplement the external evidences in a valuable way.

The accompanying Tables [1] give the detailed results of investigations along these lines, and a study of the data therein contained will reveal both their possibilities and their limitations. In Table I the order of the plays is approximately that of the dates of their composition (virtually the same as the dates of first performance). The second and third columns cannot be regarded as giving any clue to chronology, except that they show that in the dramas written under the influence of Marlowe prose is comparatively rare. Elsewhere Shakespeare employed prose for a variety of purposes: for low comedy, as in the tavern scenes in *Henry IV,* and the scenes in which Sir Toby figures in *Twelfth Night;* for repartee, as in the wit-combats of Beatrice and Benedick; for purely intellectual and moralizing speeches, such as Hamlet's over the skull of Yorick. On the other hand, highly emotional scenes are usually in verse, as are romantic passages like the conversation of Lorenzo and Jessica in the moonlight at Belmont, or the dialogues of Fenton and Anne Page, which contrast with the realistic prose of the rest of the *Merry Wives* and also the artificial pastoralism of Silvius and Phœbe in *As You Like It.* Few absolute rules can be laid down in the matter, but study of Shakespeare's practice reveals an admirable tact in his choice of medium.

---

[1] The figures here given are based in columns 1, 2, 3, and 4 on the calculations of Fleay; in 5, 6, and 7 on those of König; and in 8 on those of Ingram.

TABLE I

	Total No. of Lines	Prose	Blank Verse	Pentameter Rhymes	% Blank Verse w. Fem. Endings	% Run-on Lines	% Speeches Ending within the Line	No. of Light and Weak Endings
L. L. L.	2785	1022	617	550	7.7	18.4	10.0	3
C. of E.	1777	226	1156	216	16.6	12.9	0.6	0
T. G. of V.	2292	659	1431	76	18.4	12.4	5.8	0
R. III F._1	3589	63	3278	152	19.5	13.1	2.9	4
Q.	3456	63	3099	142	....	....	....	....
K. J.	2553	0	2403	128	6.3	17.7	12.7	7
R. & J. Q._1	2156	259	1530	248	8.2	14.2	14.9	7
Q._2	3051	455	2052	417	....	....	....	....
M. N. D.	2166	493	729	574	7.3	13.2	17.3	1
R. II	2756	0	2174	525	11.0	19.9	7.3	4
Merch.	2656	604	1872	85	17.6	21.5	22.2	7
1 Hy. IV	3176	1464	1561	80	5.1	22.8	14.2	7
2 Hy. IV	3446	1857	1425	54	16.3	21.4	16.8	1
M. W. of W. Q._1	1586	1303	148	34	....	....	....	....
F._1	3029	2703	207	65	27.2	20.1	20.5	1
Hy. V.	3376	1367	1918	62	20.5	21.8	18.3	2
M. Ado	2825	2106	618	18	22.9	19.3	20.7	2
J. C.	2477	156	2181	32	19.7	19.3	20.3	10
A. Y. L. I.	2839	1679	871	58	25.5	17.1	21.6	2
T. N.	2690	1731	724	108	25.6	14.7	36.3	4
T. & C.	3496	1188	2065	176	23.8	27.4	31.3	6
A. W. W.	2966	1437	1176	251	29.4	28.4	74.0	13
Ham. Q_1	2068	609	1155	54	....	....	....	....
Q_2	3929	1200	2358	64	....	....	....	....
F._1	....	....	....	....	22.6	23.1	51.6	8
Meas.	2810	1134	1470	61	26.1	23.0	51.4	7
Oth.	3316	661	2549	78	28.1	19.5	41.4	2
Lear.	3328	952	2214	70	28.5	29.3	60.9	6
Mcb.	2108	158	1706	100	26.3	30.6	77.2	23
A. & C.	3059	287	2589	34	26.5	43.3	77.5	99
Cor.	3406	829	2413	28	28.4	45.9	79.0	104
Cym.	3339	535	2528	90	30.7	46.0	85.0	130
W. T.	3074	979	1946	34	32.9	37.5	87.6	100
Temp.	2062	458	1390	4	35.4	41.5	84.5	87

The frequency of rhyme, as shown in the fourth column, has more relation to date. While there is no very steady gradation, it is clear that in his earlier plays he used rhyme freely, while at the close of his career he had practically abandoned it. The large number of rhymes in *A Midsummer-Night's Dream* and *Romeo and Juliet* is accounted for mainly by the prevailing lyrical tone of a great part of these plays, while on the other hand, in *All's Well* it probably points to survivals of an earlier first form of this comedy. It ought to be noted that, in the figures given here, the rhyming lines in the play scene in *Hamlet*, the vision of *Cymbeline*, the masque in *The Tempest*, and the Prologue and Epilogue of *Henry VIII* are not reckoned.

More significant are the percentages in columns five, six, and seven. Before 1598, feminine endings never reach twenty per cent of the total number of pentameter lines; after that date they are practically always above that number, and show a fairly steady increase to the thirty-five per cent of *The Tempest*. The variations of run-on lines (which, of course, carry with them the frequency of pauses within the line, and inversely the growing rarity of end-stopped lines) are closely parallel to those of the feminine endings; while the increase in the proportion of speeches ending within the line is still more striking. In *The Comedy of Errors* this phenomenon hardly occurs at all; in *The Tempest* it happens in over eighty-four per cent of the speeches, the increase being especially regular after 1598. Yet in some cases other causes are operative. Thus cuts and revisions of plays were apt to leave broken lines at the ends of speeches, and the comparatively high percentages in *Love's Labour's Lost*, *Romeo and Juliet*, and *All's Well* are probably in part due to these causes.

The phenomena recorded in the last column are peculiar. Previous to the date of *Macbeth* it appears that Shakespeare practically avoided ending a line with light or weak words such as prepositions, conjunctions, and auxiliary verbs, but that from about 1606 to the end he employed them in proportions ranging from 3.53 per cent in *Antony and Cleopatra* to 7.14 per cent in his part of *Henry VIII*.

It will be observed that while the developments suggested by the different columns are fairly consistent, they do not absolutely agree in any two cases, and can obviously be used, as has been said, only to corroborate other evidence in placing a play in a period, not to fix a precise year.

Further, in the calculations involved, there are many doubtful cases calling for the exercise of individual judgment,
especially as to what constitutes a run-on line, or a light
or weak ending. Thus Professor Bradley differs from König
in several cases as to the figures given in the seventh column,
counting the percentage of speeches ending within the line
as 57 for *Hamlet*, 54 for *Othello*, 69 for *King Lear*, and 75
for *Macbeth*. For Acts III, IV, and I of *Pericles*, the 71
per cent is Bradley's, for which König's 17.1 is clearly a
mistake. Serious as are such discrepancies, and suggestive of
a need for a general re-counting of all the more significant
phenomena, they are not so great as to shake the faith of
any scholar who has seriously studied the matter in the usefulness of metrical tests as an aid in the settling of the
chronology.

Style and Authorship: Shakespeare

E. K. CHAMBERS

OF THE PLAYS as a whole, "the great majority are simply
not of Shakespeare's drafting." [1] Here, of course, common
sense revolts. After all, we have read the plays for ourselves,
and have learnt to recognize in them, through all their di-
versities, a continuous personality, of which style is only
one aspect. A single mind and a single hand dominate them.
They are the outcome of one man's critical reactions to
life, which make the stuff of comedy, and of one man's
emotional reactions to life, which make the stuff of tragedy.
Something must be wrong with the methods which have
led to such devastating conclusions.

Everything indeed is wrong with them. It would be both
tedious and unprofitable to follow Mr. Robertson's pains-
taking investigations in detail, when one's starting-point is a
complete rejection of the axioms by which they are governed.
And it is perhaps superfluous to stress the remarkable diversity between his reconstructions and those of other students who work, broadly speaking, upon the same lines.
The variant distributions of *Julius Caesar* among Marlowe,

[1] J. M. Robertson, *The Shakespeare Canon* (1922-30), iii, 100,
200.

From William Shakespeare: A Study of Facts and Problems by E. K. Chambers, Oxford, Clarendon Press, 1930, Volume I. Reprinted by permission of the Clarendon Press, Oxford.

Shakespeare, Jonson, Beaumont, Chapman, and Drayton furnish a noteworthy example. No doubt a method may be sound, and may be more skilfully applied by one practitioner than by another. But the conflicts do not inspire any great confidence in the critical principles which underlie them. The fundamental error lies in a misconception of the limits within which the discrimination of styles, as applied to the particular subject-matter of the Elizabethan drama, must operate. The percipience of style is a very real quality. It has its origin, I suppose, in the same natural feeling for the value of words and the rise and fall of rhythm, which is the starting-point of literary expression itself; and it may be trained, half-unconsciously, through reading and reflection and comparison into a valuable instrument of criticism. A quasi-intuitive sense is developed. It becomes effective in the presence of a writer who has a characteristic style and has room and inclination to give that style free play. It enables one, for instance, to dismiss some of the apocryphal plays ascribed to Shakespeare without more ado. It helps at least to disentangle collaborators, if their styles are sufficiently distinct, and their separate contributions of sufficient length. It must make allowance, of course, for many things; for the gradual evolution of styles, for influences, for experiments, for variations of interest and temper, for the adaptation of manner to subject-matter. It will be at a loss when a writer, as sometimes happens with Shakespeare, is bored, or in haste, or merely careless, and fails to hold his style. Moreover dramatic writing, and Elizabethan dramatic writing in particular, contains many bits of undistinguished joiner's work which may help the action along, but are in themselves colourless. One man might have written them as well as another. The most percipient critic cannot reasonably claim to have acquired a faculty which is fine enough to identify commonplace passages or very short passages. And he will be wise if he refrains, so far as possible, from detecting the small touches of a reviser. Now and then a phrasing seems to stand out in startling distinctness from its context, like the "poor worm" which "casts copp'd hills towards heaven" in the normally unShakespearean part of *Pericles* (1.1.100). But even in such cases attributions can rarely be made with conviction. It is said that the ultra-violet rays will reveal over-painting in pictures through different effects upon different pigments. The sense of style does not work like an ultra-violet ray. It must be added that the sense of style is itself ultimately dependent upon external evidence.

There is no way of getting at the characteristics of an individual writer, except from work of which his authorship is acknowledged. And if the acquired sense is then used to discredit the canon wholesale, a vicious circle is set up, of which the inevitable result is chaos.

The scholarly mind seeks to confirm its intuition by an analysis of the concrete features of style. A writer forms his own rhetorical habits in the building of lines and the linking of line to line, in the use of exclamation, antithesis, iteration, and cumulation, in the balance of noun against noun and verb against verb. He has his own small mannerisms of locution; his recurrent catch-phrases; his ellipses and inversions; his superfluous auxiliaries; his archaisms, it may be, and grammatical solecisms. These are the more characteristic, because they become unconscious, and are often at first sight unnoticeable. Such things can be observed and tabulated, with due regard to the risk of assuming monopolies in them. It is a matter of degree; one man may prefer "you" and another "ye," one " 'em" and another "them," if printers can be persuaded not to interfere. It is so too with rhythm. The normal iambic blank verse is capable of a great deal of variation, both in the structure of individual lines and in the grouping of lines into paragraphs. Stresses can be inverted; additional syllables can be introduced; pauses can come at the ends of lines or can break their flow; rhyme can be employed, sporadically, or with a clinching effect. Alliteration may be obvious or restrained. Writers acquire different habits of verse-manipulation, and many, like Shakespeare, follow different habits at different stages of their development. Many metrical variations can be expressed in statistics, but not all, and not the interplay of variations upon which the resultant rhythmical effect largely depends. Metrical analysis requires ample space, if it is to be significant, since a rhythmical habit is itself varied according to subjectmatter, and these variations only average out over long stretches of verse. Comparative figures for complete plays, perhaps for complete acts, may be of value, but not for single scenes and still less for single speeches. The method has proved useful in dividing the results of collaboration. The rhythm of Shakespeare's later verse, for example, differs markedly from that of Fletcher's; less so from that of Beaumont's or of Massinger's. Naturally each writer has also his individual range of thought, of dramatic situations, of imagery, of allusion, of vocabulary. But here there is much give and take, and there is nothing more dangerous than the attempt to determine authorship by the citation of parallels. Authors repeat their predecessors: their successors repeat them; they repeat themselves. Shakespeare's self-repetitions are innumerable. They are commonest between plays of approximately the same date, but common also between plays remote in time, especially when analogous themes recur. His younger contemporaries also repeat themselves freely and they repeat him just as freely. Parallels, therefore, are always open to a double interpretation, if chronology and lack of ascription permit; they may be from one pen or from two. It could hardly be otherwise. All literature is full of parallels, but especially the literature of the Elizabethans, because they had a far more restricted tradition behind them than the moderns, and especially the literature of the dramatic writers, because they were men of the theatre. Even if they were not actors themselves, they lived in a world of representations and rehearsals, and their minds were filled with auditory images of spoken words, which naturally came to the surface when they wrote. Parallels are of all degrees; they descend from elaborate passages involving a combination of common elements, through dramatic motives, similes and metaphors, historical and mythological allusions, special collocations of words, mannerisms, down to the mere occurrence of unusual words. They are in fact constantly brought forward by critics as evidence of common authorship. This they rarely can be. Where anonymous work is in question nothing better may be available, but conclusions so formed should at the most be held as possibilities. Probably the most striking parallels are the least evidential; it is the vivid idea or phrase which catches the imagination of another. There is a negative value in comprehensive collections of parallels, however slight, to a doubtful play. If none are found to a given writer, he is not likely to have written it. The converse does not hold true, but it may chime with other evidence. The collections made for *Pericles* and *Henry VIII* confirm distributions of shares arrived at on other grounds. It is, however, difficult, even when a concordance is available, to be sure that a collection is complete.

The history of Shakespeare's writing is one of the gradual development of a characteristic style or series of styles. In its matured flights it is often unmistakable. Its beginnings belong to a period in which the difficulties of style-discrimination are at their maximum. The dramatists of the 'eighties may reasonably be called a school.[2] They have largely a common style and a common vocabulary, which owe much to Spenser, to the Elizabethan translators of the classics, to Seneca and his court imitators. Marlowe is the dominant figure, with Peele, Greene, Lodge, and Nashe as his satellites; Kyd stands a little apart. There is a mass of anonymous work. There were other prolific writers, such as Thomas Watson, of whose plays we know nothing. Probably we should be able to differentiate some of the personalities a little better, if we had reliable canons. Even now, Marlowe's is more distinct than the rest. But there are no such canons. Only from two to seven plays are ascribed to any one man, and of these many have been transmitted in such corrupt texts that they are valueless. The style of non-dramatic work may be compared; the translations of Marlowe, the pamphlets of Greene, the ceremonial poems of Peele. But these only give limited help in judging the handling of dialogued verse. It is illegitimate to follow Mr. Robertson in expanding the canons by adding first one anonymous play, and then on the basis of this another, and then again another. There is no certainty in this process, which mainly rests on parallels, and the chain becomes weaker at every link. This school was Shakespeare's early environment, and his first plays were inevitably in its manner. The influence of Marlowe is discernible until well on in his career. Mr. Robertson, who has all the arts of the debater, except perhaps that of lucidity, abounds in pejorative terms for what he calls the "Imitation theory." He represents it as charging Shakespeare with a "passion for plagiarism," with "tranced" or "slavish" mimicry, with "abject parodies." If he repeated the phrase of a predecessor, he must have been an "avid copyist" or possessed by an "overwhelming impulse of apery." This is only beating the air. Young writers, even when they have done good work, do remain subject to influences, especially if they are of receptive, as well as creative, temperaments. There is no reason why Shakespeare should have been an exception. Very likely there was some deliberate imitation at first of admired models, but the issue is not primarily one of imitation. I have written above of parallels and repetitions. Psychologically, these may mean anything from plagiarism to quite unconscious echoing. A writer's mind is a well of subliminal memory, into which words and images

---

[2] Cf. *The Unrest in Shakespearean Studies* (1927, *Nineteenth Century*).

sink, and to the surface of which they arise again, unbidden, in the act of composition.[3] I do not think it would be possible to assert Shakespeare's authorship of, *2, 3 Henry VI* on internal evidence alone. They are school work and full of school echoes. There are many images drawn from country life, which set them a little apart, and may be marks of Shakespeare. Those which recall the sea are also noteworthy. Links of style with the plays to come, especially *Richard III,* are not wanting. Double endings are much more often used to vary the blank verse rhythm than in any of the ascertainable plays of Marlowe and his fellows, and Mr. Robertson does not really meet this point, either by citing the higher proportion of double endings in Marlowe's nondramatic translation of Lucan, or by the *a priori* argument that towards the end of their careers Marlowe, Kyd, and Greene must all have felt the need of some relief to the monotony of their earlier systems. Metrical evolution is not a *Zeitgeist* which all poets are alike bound to follow. We are not, however, left to internal evidence for *2, 3 Henry VI,* and there is certainly no such disparity of style as need compel us to abandon the authority of the First Folio. Ravenscroft's testimony puts *Titus Andronicus* upon a rather different footing. It may be that further study of the dramatic style of the 'eighties in relation to its origins will disclose lines of demarcation which are not at present apparent. At present it is tangled country, in which it is not much use to run like a hound through the undergrowth, catching a scent of Marlowe here, and whimpering there at a suspicion of Kyd or Peele. Complicated theories of collaboration and revision cannot be based upon such findings.

An Aristotelian Analysis of "The Gettysburg Address"

LANE COOPER

Fourscore and seven years ago our fathers brought forth on this continent a new nation, conceived in

---

[3] Cf. the admirable study of the working of Coleridge's imagination in J. L. Lowes, *The Road to Xanadu* (1927).

From **The Rhetoric of Aristotle** by Lane Cooper. Copyright, 1932 by Lane Cooper. Reprinted by permission of Appleton-Century-Crofts, Division of Meredith Publishing Company.

liberty, and dedicated to the proposition that all men are created equal.

Now we are engaged in a great civil war, testing whether that nation, or any nation so conceived and so dedicated, can long endure. We are met on a great battle-field of that war. We have come to dedicate a portion of that field as a final resting-place for those who here gave their lives that that nation might live. It is altogether fitting and proper that we should do this.

But, in a larger sense, we cannot dedicate—we cannot consecrate—we cannot hallow—this ground. The brave men, living and dead, who struggled here, have consecrated it far above our poor power to add or detract. The world will little note nor long remember what we say here, but it can never forget what they did here. It is for us, the living, rather, to be dedicated here to the unfinished work which they who fought here have thus far so nobly advanced. It is rather for us to be here dedicated to the great task remaining before us—that from these honored dead we take increased devotion to that cause for which they gave the last full measure of devotion; that we here highly resolve that these dead shall not have died in vain; that this nation, under God, shall have a new birth of freedom; and that government of the people, by the people, for the people, shall not perish from the earth.

As for style or diction, the speech is characterized by compactness, balance, and metaphor. The compactness is illustrated by two other cases of asyndeton: "we are engaged," "we are met," "we have come"; and "we cannot dedicate—we cannot consecrate—we cannot hallow—this ground." It would seem, too, by this method of expression that many things have been said, more, in fact, than have been said, though the speech is full of meaning. The balance in thought and phrase is easily detected by both eye and ear, and the use of antithesis is obvious, as in the contrast between then and now, birth and death, the living and the dead. The language is neither metrical nor yet without rhythm, indefinite. The basic foot is the iamb (or, according to the point where one begins to count, the trochee) as it was in spoken Greek; so, "shall not perish from the earth." Variation from this may be seen in the use of dactyls (or anapaests) and spondees: "We cannot dedicate—we cannot consecrate—we cannot hallow—this ground." It is the variation of the English Bible: "Though I speak with the tongues of men and of angels"; "The Lord is my shepherd, I shall not want." Compare also the language of Lincoln's *Second Inaugural Address:* "With malice toward none; with charity for all." There, too, the iambic basis and the dactylic variation from it are well-marked.

The metaphor of the dedication of a child runs through the speech, beginning with the violent figure of *sires* "conceiving," "bringing forth," and "dedicating"—dedicating the newly-born to something like a proposition in Euclid. Still, the violent metaphor has thus far escaped the notice of most readers. And the language of the speech as a whole is clear and appropriate, and dignified, the clearness arising from the use of customary words, dignity and vividness from an archaic flavor (as in "Fourscore and seven"), from the use of a special epithet like "fathers" for the founders of the nation, and from active metaphors, as when "brought forth" is echoed toward the close by "a new birth of freedom."

Biblical Style

BERGEN EVANS AND CORNELIA EVANS

BY BIBLICAL ENGLISH is usually meant English as used in the so-called Authorized Version of the Bible, published in 1611 by special command of King James I of England. It is this version of the Bible which has given to English speech and writing so many memorable phrases and distinctive rhythms. While later versions or translations often render the Hebrew or Greek originals more accurately, they rarely have a superior power or literary grace.

Compare, for instance, several versions of *Matthew 5:6*—

King James (1611): *Blessed are they which do hunger and thirst after righteousness: for they shall be filled.*

Smith and Goodspeed (1931): *Blessed are those who are hungry and thirsty for uprightness, for they will be satisfied!*

James Moffat (1935): *Blessed are those who hunger and thirst for goodness: they will be satisfied.*

American Revised Standard Version (1951): *Blessed are*

*those who hunger and thirst for righteousness, for they shall
be satisfied.*

It is difficult for the common reader to see in what
way these—and countless other—rewordings in the various
versions are an improvement. *Uprightness* is far less modern
than *righteousness*, and *goodness* has connotations that make
it a weak synonym for *righteousness*. The common, simple,
everyday word for having eaten enough is to be *full*. *Satisfied* suggests a desire to add a touch of gentility. Revising is
a difficult task and requires many things of the reviser. Some
of the most important are enumerated in *Psalms 24:4*.

The language of the King James Version *is* archaic. It was
archaic even when it first appeared, for its wording is sometimes that of the Wycliffite versions of the late fourteenth
century and often that of the various versions published
during the middle fifty years of the sixteenth century—
Tyndale's version, Coverdale's version, and the versions
known as the Geneva Bible and the Bishops' Bible. The in-
debtedness to Tyndale's version (1525-1535) is so great that
all Protestant versions of the books on which Tyndale worked
are more revisions of his version than independent translations. Thus *I Corinthians* 13:1 reads in Tyndale: *Though I
speake with the tonges of men and angels and yet had no
love I were even as soundynge brasse: and a tynklynge
Cymball.* In the King James Version it reads: *Though I speak
with the tongues of men and of angels, and have not charity,
I am become as sounding brass, or a tinkling cymbal.* The
King James Version is the more felicitous, but it is still only
a happy revision. In the Revised Standard Version (which
states in its preface that one of its aims is "to put the message
of the Bible in simple, enduring words") this passage reads:
*If I speak in the tongues of men and of angels, but have not
love, I am a noisy gong or a clanging cymbal.*

Although the literary quality of the Bible is uneven, certain
characteristics of its style may be noted.

1.   Throughout, there is an elevation of language. *"I am
Alpha and Omega, the beginning and the ending,"* saith the
Lord, *which is, and which was, and which is to come, the
Almighty.*

2.   The use of the word *and* at the beginning of sentences
gives a sense of continuity to narratives, but it also conveys
a feeling of the endlessness of existence, the rise and fall of

life. Of the twenty-five verses of the second chapter of *Second Kings,* only two do not begin with *and.*

3. Repetition of word or meaning is used to heighten effect: *Turn in, my lord, turn in to me. Bless me, even me also, O my father. Thou dost but hate me and lovest me not.*

4. Doublets and triplets contribute to the rhythms and enhance the poetry: *And gladness is taken away, and joy out of the plentiful field; and in the vineyards there shall be no singing, neither shall there be shouting. Let darkness and the shadow of death claim it for their own; let a cloud dwell upon it; let all that maketh black the day terrify it.*

5. The constant use of the question emphasizes the seeking quality in the Bible, the searching for the ways of God and answers to the mystery of life. It also often suggests sadness and plaintiveness: *What is man, that thou art mindful of him? and the son of man, that thou visitest him?* Or it may heighten anger or denunciation: *Wilt thou hunt prey for the lion? or fill the appetite of the young lions, when they couch in their dens, and abide in the covert to lie in wait?*

The imagery of the Bible draws on objects of daily use. Death is the pitcher broken at the fountain, the wheel broken at the cistern. Amos says that the sins of the people of Israel press upon him as a cart is pressed that is full of sheaves. Man is born unto trouble as the sparks fly upwards and his days are swifter than a weaver's shuttle.

The majority, accepted view is that the King James Version has offered a powerful and desirable stimulus to English prose style. And certainly it would be hard to find any English writer of stature whose style is wholly free from the influence of the Bible. Professor John Livingston Lowes, in an essay entitled "The Noblest Monument of English Prose," has spoken brilliantly in support of the majority view. A minority opinion is offered by Somerset Maugham in *The Summing Up* (1938): "To my mind King James's Bible has been a very harmful influence on English prose. I am not so stupid as to deny its great beauty. It is majestical. But the Bible is an oriental book. Its alien imagery has nothing to do with us. Those hyperboles, those luscious metaphors are foreign to our genius. I cannot but think that not the least of the misfortunes that the Secession from Rome brought upon the spiritual life of our country is that this work for so long a period became the daily, and with many, the only, reading of our people. Those rhythms, that powerful vocabulary, that grandiloquence, became part and parcel of the national sensibility. The plain, honest English speech was overwhelmed with ornament. Blunt Englishmen twisted their tongues to speak like Hebrew prophets . . . Ever since, English prose has had to struggle against the tendency to luxuriance." Maugham goes on to say that English writers have much to learn from Americans, since American writing has escaped the tyranny of the King James Bible and has formed its style on living speech.

The Cliché Expert Testifies on the Atom

FRANK SULLIVAN

Q—Mr. Arbuthnot, you're the very man I want to see. I've been longing to examine you on atomic energy.

A—Well, my boy, you've come to the right party. I believe I can say that I know all the clichés on the subject.

Q—How can you say that?

A—Without fear of successful contradiction.

Q—I'm glad to hear it. I suspected you would be making a study of the atomic cliché.

A—A study! Why I've been doing nothing since V-J Day but listen to the experts explain atomic energy and the bomb on the air, or editorialize about them in the newspapers. Indeed I *am* the cliché expert of the atom. You realize of course what the dropping of that test bomb in the stillness of the New Mexico night did.

Q—What did it do?

A—It ushered in the atomic age, that's what it did. You know what kind of discovery this is?

Q—What kind?

A—A tremendous scientific discovery.

Q—Could the atomic age have arrived by means of any other verb than "usher"?

A—No. "Usher" has the priority.

Q—Mr. Arbuthnot, what will never be the same?

A—The world.

From A Rock In Every Snowball by Frank Sullivan. Copyright 1946 by Frank Sullivan. Reprinted by permission of Little Brown and Co.

Q—Are you pleased?

A—I don't know. The splitting of the atom could prove a boon to mankind. It could pave the way for a bright new world. On the other hand it may spell the doom of civilization as we know it.

Q—You mean that it has—

A—Vast possibilities for good or evil.

Q—At any rate, Mr. Arbuthnot, as long as the bomb had to be discovered, I'm glad we got it first.

A—If you don't mind, I will be the one to recite the clichés here. You asked me to, you know.

Q—I'm sorry.

A—Quite all right. I shudder to think.

Q—What?

A—Of what might have happened if Germany or Japan had got the bomb first.

Q—What kind of race was it between the Allied and German scientists?

A—A close race.

Q—What pressed?

A—Time pressed.

Q—With what kind of energy did the scientists work in their race to get the bomb?

A—Feverish energy. Had the war lasted another six months the Germans might have had the bomb. It boggles.

Q—What boggles?

A—This tremendous scientific discovery boggles the imagination. Also stirs same.

Q—Where do we stand, Mr. Arbuthnot?

A—At the threshold of a new era.

Q—And humanity is where?

A—At the crossroads.

VI. NEW THRESHOLDS, NEW ANATOMIES

The Style of Oral Poetry: the Odyssey

DENYS PAGE

IF IT IS our desire to discover how the *Odyssey* was composed, to look into the minds and methods of Greek Epic poets in the centuries before the dawn of history, to understand and evaluate their achievement, it is absolutely necessary first to recognize how great a gulf divides two kinds of poetry—that which is composed and remembered in the mind, *without* the aid of writing, and that which is composed *with* the aid of writing. That the Homeric poems were composed and carried in the mind, and recited by word of mouth, and that this was the only method of their composition, and this for a long time the only mode of their publication to the audiences for which they were designed—the proof of these things is the outstanding achievement of an American scholar, Milman Parry, whose premature death extinguished the brightest light that has been shed on the Greek Epic in our time.

In societies where the art of writing is unknown, the poet makes his verses out of metrical formulas—fixed groups of words, traditional phrases descriptive of particular ideas and readily adaptable to similar ideas; the stock of such formulas, gradually accumulated over a long period of time, supplies the poet at need with a whole group of lines, or a single line, or a part of a line, all ready-made. He cannot stop to meditate while he recites; he cannot read over—let alone change—what he composed a few hundred lines ago; he cannot plan in advance except in very broad outline. But whatever he wants to say, within the limits of certain traditional themes, may (and often must) be expressed in phrases long ago designed for that purpose, and immediately suggested to him by his practised memory. He may or may not

From **The Homeric Odyssey** by Denys Page, Oxford, the Clarendon Press, 1955. Reprinted by permission of the Clarendon Press, Oxford.

be a good poet: he must be a good craftsman. There is a stock-in-trade, the vast number of traditional formulas, to be learnt only by long apprenticeship; and there is a technique, the craft of using and adapting formulas and systems of formulas, to be acquired only by long experience.

The Homeric Epic differs from all other Greek poetry, and from all poetry with which we (most of us) are familiar today, in just this respect: its elements are phrases, not words. It is largely composed of traditional formulas, fixed word-patterns, almost infinitely adaptable to the ideas suggested to the poet's imagination within the limits of his theme; and supplying lines, or parts of lines, more or less ready-made. In the *Iliad* and *Odyssey* this technique may be seen at a very advanced state of development, refined and thrifty, purified of superfluities, so that (in general) one formula cannot take the place of another, in the same part of the verse, without altering the meaning of what is being said. If the poet wishes to begin his verse with the thought "But when they arrived . . ." he has one way, and one only, of expressing this, *autar epei rh'ikonto,* "denying himself all other ways of expressing the idea." [1] The creation of the vast number of formulas, adaptable to almost all possible emergencies, must have been the work of many generations of poets; and from the refinement, thrift, and economy of the Homeric stock of phrases we are obliged to infer that we are at or near the culmination of a very long process.

Now the *Odyssey,* no less than the *Iliad,* is composed in this way: it reveals from start to finish the memory-technique of verse-making, the practice of composing from memory without the aid of writing. Whether the art of writing was known to its composers we may never know: what we do know, because we see it with our own eyes, is that the art of writing, if it was familiar, made little or no difference to the technique employed in the actual verse-making; that is still the formula-technique, the building of verses out of traditional phrases learnt by one generation from another and supplied to the poet by his practised memory at the moment required.

There is no longer any doubt about the fact; but one may well wonder whether it does not suggest some further questions of exceptional difficulty. Is not the complexity of the

[1] This, and the quotation two paragraphs later, are from articles by Milman Parry, *Harvard Studies in Classical Philology,* XLI (1930), 89, and XLIII (1932), 15. *Ed.*

structure of the *Odyssey*—its blend of three stories into one; its blend of episodes within one story—beyond the limit of what is possible for a man who has nothing but his memory to assist him? And would not a poem thus composed be continually changing? Would it not differ from one recitation to another, and would it not become unrecognizably transformed in the course of a generation or two? Modern analogies confirm what common sense suggests—that "the oral poem even in the mouth of the same singer is ever in a state of change; and it is the same when his poetry is sung by others."

These are difficult questions; I do no more than indicate the region in which their answer may be found. It is possible, or even likely, that the art of writing was practised (though not in general use) at the time when the first continuous *Odyssey* was composed. Now though that art played little or no part in the making of the poem, it might nevertheless be used to record the poem when made (or rather while making). If this were so, the boundaries of the poet's powers would be greatly extended: he could then build, as nobody before such a time could build, a structure of considerable size and some complexity, if each development was preserved in writing; and his admirers or apprentices would be able to reproduce their master's voice much more faithfully than before, not because they could learn it from the written record —that was merely the architect's plan, not his structure— but because the version which they heard from the master was more or less unvarying. This does not imply that the master himself (and others after him) would cease to expand or otherwise alter his poem in the course of time: the written record is nothing more than an aid to memory, a tool of the trade. The text of a poem was still the spoken, not the written, word; the whole conception of a static poem in a standard text is entirely foreign to the memory-technique of verse-making and to the manner of its transmission from one generation to another.

This conception of an oral poetry, composed in the mind and designed for preservation by memory alone, has—or rather ought to have—revolutionized our understanding of the *Iliad* and *Odyssey*. It should be obvious that many of the principles of criticism applicable to a Virgil or a Milton have no place here. Virgil and Milton may be expected to choose a particular word or phrase because it most accurately represents their thought in a particular context. However much they may owe to the past, they are seldom limited by tradition to a particular mode of expression; they are free to form an individual style. In the Homeric poems, whatever the context and whoever the person may be, the same act, thought, or emotion is likely to be described in the same words; not because those words are particularly suitable to that person or context, but because those words are the words which tradition supplies ready-made to the poet for the description of that act, thought, or emotion. His style is traditional and typical, not individual. He does not, as a rule, select or invent: he uses what his memory offers him, already adapted or readily adaptable to the part of his verse which he has to fill. It should be obvious too that the memory-technique of verse-composition and the employment of a traditional stock of phrases naturally impose severe limitations on the structure of the story and the characterization of the persons. It is very improbable that a poet who depends on nothing but his memory both for the making and for the preservation of his verses will so construct his plot that the true significance of an earlier part will emerge only in the light of a later part, and vice versa; except in very broad and simple conceptions integral to the main structure of his story. Delicate and subtle preparations *now* for what will follow in five hundred lines' time; veiled and indirect allusions *now* to what happened five hundred lines ago—such artifice lies beyond his power, even supposing that it lay within the bounds of his imagination. References backwards and forwards (over more than a short space) will be more or less explicit, and limited to the broad outlines of the story.

As with the plot, so with the characters. In poetry of this kind the characters will be—as indeed they are—envisaged in fairly broad outline. Their thoughts will be (for the most part) expressed in language which is traditional and typical, not specially designed for a given person in a given place; and the thoughts themselves (apart from their expression) will often be traditional and typical, not individual. Subtlety of soul, complexity of character, true portrayal of personality— for these we must wait until the practice of the art of writing affords the poet the necessary leisure and the necessary means for reflection, for planning the future in some detail, and for correcting the past.

Thus in answering the question how the *Odyssey* was composed we must start from the established position that this poem was composed in the mind, and destined for preserva-

tion by the memory alone, by a poet or poets highly skilled in
the use of a traditional language which had been gradually
developed over a very long period of time. Do not therefore
suppose that little or no room is left for the exercise of an
individual's poetic talent. A man may be either the master or
the slave of the rules by which he lives; the conventions of
an art have never yet confined genius and mediocrity in equal
chains. The meeting of Hector and Andromache, the em-
bassy to Achilles, the Doloneia, the ransom of Hector's body,
the stories of Nausicaa and of Polyphemus (to give only a
few examples) prove that those who worked within the limits
prescribed by the Greek Epic tradition could attain the highest point of excellence in the poetic art. Only we have wholly
misunderstood the nature of their achievement unless we recognize that they do, and must, work within those limits.
They are not free (except to a very limited extent) to frame
their own phraseology; they are not free (except, again, to a
very limited extent) to invent new characters or to depict
traditional characters in a mode contrary to tradition; they
are narrowly limited in their choice of theme, in what their
persons say and do; and there are some aspects of life and
manners which they may not reflect at all. "Homer" has often
been highly praised for doing what had been done before
him, and what he could have done in no other way. Intricacy
of design and subtleties of thought wholly alien to the oral
technique of composition have often been sought (and found)
in him. The road is open (since Milman Parry found it for us)
to a juster understanding of the distinction between the
traditional and the non-traditional elements in the *Iliad* and
Odyssey.

Nominal and Verbal Style

RULON WELLS

Description and Evaluation

PRONOUNCEMENTS ABOUT STYLE are of two sorts, descriptive
and evaluative. Description is logically prior to evaluation,
in that a reasoned description is possible without evaluation

From **Style in Language**, ed. by Thomas Sebeok. Copyright 1960 by the Massachusetts
Institute of Technology. Reprinted by permission of The M.I.T. Press.

whereas a reasoned evaluation is not possible without description. Some who do descriptive stylistics do it in deliberate abstraction from evaluation, that is, without the intention of proceeding to evaluate; others do the description primarily for the sake of the evaluation which they regard as the end to which description is a means.

What should be a mere distinction is widely regarded as an opposition; a division that should only divide subject from subject too often divides man from man. There is a reason for this. It is not the case, in practice, that the "describers" and the "appraisers" study the same things from different points of view. For the two intents—sheer description, on the one hand, and description conjoined with evaluation—lead to different selections. In principle the appraiser evaluates or appraises all texts, but in practice, in addition to the obvious specialties (texts in French, or English texts of the Elizabethan period, or Latin poetry), he tends to select for study the texts that he will evaluate *favorably*.[1] In particular, he is likely to shy away from spending his efforts on the meaner texts, those that do not even purport to be literature, and to concentrate on belles-lettres, which more vigorously exercise his powers. And equally, the sheer describer, who in principle describes all texts, tends in practice to focus on less pretentious texts precisely because they are less complicated. Experimentalists and statisticians, in particular, are likely to regard belles-lettres as too complicated for fruitful study. The time may come when this limitation is passed beyond, but I am speaking of the present day.

In general, then, appraiser and sheer describer tend to study mutually exclusive phenomena or aspects. But there are exceptions. One of these is the degree to which nouns and verbs are used in various styles. Here is a variable of style at once simple and interesting. Nominal (nominalizing) style, the tendency to use nouns in preference to verbs, and the opposite verbal or verbalizing style, which tends to use verbs rather than nouns, are two features that are fairly easy to describe yet are of great interest to appraisers. Those who appraise at all mostly appraise nominal style as inferior to verbal. And yet it crops up again and again, defended on the ground that it is adapted to its purpose.

---

[1] At least to the extent of finding them interesting. A critic may pronounce the style of some poem or essay a failure but add that it is a distinguished failure, or a significant experiment, or the like.

Nominal and Verbal Style

In this and the next two sections I shall confine my discussion to English, and to written English. The advice to shun the nominal style is sometimes put this way: "Don't use nouns where you could use verbs; don't shrink from the use of verbs." This way of putting it takes two things for granted: first, that nominality and verbality are matters of continuous degree, and second, that the continuum is characterized by the proportion of nouns to verbs in a given text. These presumptions, in turn, seem to indicate a "quantization" (quantitative measure) of our variable, by defining it as a ratio—the sort of thing that might be dubbed the Noun-Verb Quotient (NVQ). Before this indication can be precise, however, three points need to be settled.

1. What is a noun? (*a*) Shall we count pronouns and adjectives as nouns? They share many of the characters that distinguish nouns from verbs. (*b*) Shall a noun phrase count as a single noun? For example, shall "the foot of the mountain" be reckoned as containing one noun or two?

2. What is a verb? (*a*) Do nonfinite forms (infinitives, gerunds, participles) count as verbs, as nouns, as both, or as neither? (*b*) Shall a periphrastic verb like "will do" count as one verb or as two? (*c*) Shall the verb "to be" count the same as other verbs? (The feeling is sometimes expressed that the copula is not a true verb, since it has a purely logical function. On the other hand, it has person, tense, etc., like other verbs. Thus a discrepancy between its form and its meaning is felt. We might recognize this discrepancy by counting occurrences of forms of "to be" one-half, rather than one; or we might take the view that there is no quantitative way of recognizing the peculiar nature of the copula.)

3. The advice might be formulated a little differently. "Keep the proportion of nouns low and of verbs high." An index that would show whether this advice was being followed would have two parts: a Noun-Word Quotient (NWQ) *and* a Verb-Word Quotient (VWQ). For any given text the sum of these two quotients cannot exceed 1.0 and will only equal 1.0 if there are no other parts of speech in the text, but beyond that there is no necessary connection between the two quotients. It would be interesting to determine experimentally whether there is a consistent inverse relation between them.

The problem of quantizing nominality will not be pursued further here. It might well turn out that some of the questions raised are insignificant, for example, that the NVQ of scientific writers differs markedly from that of literary writers, no matter how noun and verb are delimited. But of course these facts could only be determined by experiment, for which reflections such as those of the present papers are a necessary preamble but no substitute.

There is a further consideration of which any treatment, quantitative or otherwise, should take account. Style is understood to be optional like vocabulary, as contrasted with grammar. So far as the writer of English has a choice, what he writes is *his* diction and *his* style; so far as he has none, it is the *English* language. A treatment that respects this optionality will somehow take account of whether, and in how many ways, a sentence with a certain degree of nominality could be replaced by one with a different degree, for example, a highly nominal by a highly verbal sentence. And of course it is understood that mere variation of style is made not to alter the substance or content of what is expressed but only the way of expressing it; underlying the very notion of style is a postulate of *independence of matter from manner*. If a given matter dictates a particular manner, that manner should not be called a style, at least not in the sense that I have been speaking of. But this postulate does not preclude that a certain matter shall favor or "call for" a certain manner—the so-called fitness of manner to matter, or consonance with it.

Consequences of Nominality

The advice to prefer verbs to nouns makes it sound as though it were a simple substitution, like the choice of familiar words in preference to rare ones, or of short words in preference to long ones. Occasionally this is so, but not in the usual case. In the more nominal phrase "the doctrine of the immortality of the human soul," the particles are different from those in the more verbal phrase "the doctrine that the human soul is immortal"; the one uses prepositions, the other a conjunction. In changing the verb of "He began to study it thoroughly" into the noun of "He began a thorough study of it," we must follow through by a corresponding change of adverb to adjective. The elementary fact of syntax that prepositions and adjectives go with nouns, conjunctions and adverbs with verbs, prevents the contrast of nominality and verbality from being *minimal*.

This fact has two consequences. (1) When nominality is evaluated good or bad, the ground may lie in whole or in part in features entailed by nominality, although distinct from it. (2) And so the nominal-verbal contrast is not a *pure dimension* of style, that is, it is not a variable which can vary without variation in the other basic factors of style.

The aforementioned consequences are necessary ones. Another class must be acknowledged, the probable consequences. From the statistical point of view, necessary consequences appear as those whose probability is 1.0, impossible consequence as those with probability .00, and the less or more probable consequences as those having intermediate probability values.

Even an impressionistic study can estimate some of these probabilities. To facilitate discussion, let us pretend—what is false, but not grossly false—that nominalizing and verbalizing sentences can be paired, so that we can speak of *the* nominal counterpart of such and such a verbal sentence and of the verbal counterpart of a given nominal sentence. The intent of this fiction is to concentrate our discussion on differences as near to minimal as is syntactically possible.

A nominal sentence is likely to be longer, in letters and in syllables, than its verbal counterpart. The greater length in the diction of those writers who favor nominal style results from the fact that the noun corresponding to the verb is likely to be longer than the verb—usually because it is derived from the verb stem by suffixes—and the entailed changes (loss of verb endings, replacement of conjunctions by prepositions, etc.) are not likely to compensate. Compare "when we arrive" with "at the time of our arrival"—fourteen letters (including word spaces) replaced by twenty-six, four syllables by eight.

Another likelihood is that the average number of clauses per sentence tends to decrease (the minimum being 1.0), for nominalization replaces conjunctions by prepositions. The sentence "If he does that, he will be sorry" has two clauses; its nominal counterpart "In the event of his doing that, he will be sorry" has only one.

A third likelihood, entailed by the second and also somewhat likely even in the absence of the second condition, is that the number of distinct sentence patterns will decrease. Compound sentences (both with coordinating and with subordinating conjunctions) tend to disappear, so that only simple (subject-predicate) sentences, more or less swollen by parentheses and modifiers, will be left.

Evaluation of Nominality

Nominality is judged bad by some, good by others.

1. Those who judge nominal style bad judge it so for one or more of the following reasons:

a. Nouns are more static, less vivid than verbs. Sometimes this view is defended on deep philosophical grounds. For example, Étienne Gilson sees in Aristotle's remark (*On Interpretation*, 3.16b19) that "verbs in and by themselves are substantival" a revealing clue to his philosophy; [2] not Aristotle but Thomas Aquinas is the one who gives to "is," to existence *in actu exercito*, its full due. And to the argument that the traditional, semantical definitions of noun and verb are of no avail because what one language considers an action, another may treat as a state, the rejoinder might be made that this is just the point: the contrast of action and state varies with the point of view, and one that does not reduce all actions to states is to be recommended. Something like this seems to be intended by Peter Hartmann.

b. Longer sentences are (on the whole) less vivid and less comprehensible than shorter ones.

c. A text whose sentences are all or mostly of one basic pattern will usually be monotonous. Verbal style allows more diversity, and a good style will exploit the genius of its language.

2. Those who judge nominal style good do so implicitly, for the most part; nominal style is practiced more than preached. The implicit reasons in its favor appear to be these:

a. It is easier to write. Thus it is natural for those who are more concerned with what they say than with how they say it to choose this style, or to drift into it.

b. It helps impersonality. In scientific writing ("scientific" in the broadest sense, including philosophy, and as contrasted with artistic and literary writing), expressions of personality are frowned upon. Now personality can be avoided in various ways. One is the use of the passive voice. Where the seven-

---

[2] On quite different grounds some philosopher mentioned but not named by Aristotle (Physics, 1.2.185b28) proposed to replace, for example, "The man is white" by "The man whites," coining a verb for the purpose if need be.

teenth and eighteenth centuries would have been anecdotal—
"I collected sea anemones at low tide"—the nineteenth and
twentieth centuries would cast the reporting subject into the
shadow of implicitness: "Sea anemones were collected at low
tide." Another way to avoid personality is to avoid finite
verbs altogether, by nominalizing.

c. Nominality offers another advantage to the scientific
writer. The finite verb has not only person but also number
and (as does the participle) tense. Of these three dimensions
tense is widely felt to be the most fundamental; similarly
Aristotle distinguishing the Greek verb from the Greek noun
does it on the basis of having or lacking tense (*On Interpretation*, 2.16a19, 3.16b6). Now to the extent that a writer can
avoid finite verbs and participles (including forms of the verb
"to be"), he can avoid commitments as to tense. Indeed, it is
partly because of this fact that the pairing of nominalizing
and verbalizing sentences is a fiction. "At the time of our
arrival" has not one verbal counterpart but two, "when we
arrived" and "when we arrive."

d. The very fact that nominality is contrary to conver-
sational style has its value. It sets off the writing as esoteric,
specialized, technical. Nominal style in English can be used to
play the role (although much less conspicuously and effectively) that Latin played until several hundred years ago.

Certain neutral remarks can be made about these judgments. Those who approve nominal style and those who dis-
approve it are not in utter disagreement. Its advocates do not
claim that it is graceful or elegant, and its critics do not
deny that it achieves impersonality and the rest. But after
the mutual concessions, a residue of disagreement remains. It
is admitted by all that verbal style is harder to write than
nominal style; is it *worth* the trouble? This would raise the
broader question whether good style is being urged for its
own sake (i.e., as an end), or as a means to some other
end, or on both grounds. Advocates of nominal style usually
defend it as a means to an end; its attackers might argue that
it does not achieve its end, and that for the very same end
verbal style is more effective. In that case, verbal style would
be preferable to nominal both as an end and as a means.

Aphasia: The Metaphoric and Metonymic Poles

ROMAN JAKOBSON

THE VARIETIES OF aphasia [pathological language disorder] are numerous and diverse, but all of them oscillate between the two polar types. . . . Every form of aphasic disturbance consists in some impairment, more or less severe, either of the faculty for selection and substitution or for combination and contexture. . . . The relation of similarity is suppressed in the former, the relation of contiguity in the latter type of aphasia. Metaphor is alien to the similarity disorder, and metonymy to the contiguity disorder.

The development of a discourse may take place along two different semantic lines: one topic may lead to another either through their similarity or through their contiguity. The metaphoric way would be the most appropriate term for the first case and the metonymic way for the second, since they find their most condensed expression in metaphor and metonymy respectively. In aphasia one or the other of these two processes is restricted or totally blocked—an effect which makes the study of aphasia particularly illuminating for the linguist. In normal verbal behavior both processes are continually operative, but careful observation will reveal that under the influence of a cultural pattern, personality, and verbal style, preference is given to one of the two processes over the other.

In a well-known psychological test, children are confronted with some noun and told to utter the first verbal response that comes into their heads. In this experiment two opposite linguistic predilections are invariably exhibited: the response is intended either as a substitute for, or as a complement to the simulus. In the latter case the stimulus and the response together form a proper syntactic construction, most usually a sentence. These two types of reaction have been labeled substitutive and predicative.

To the simulus *hut* one response was *burnt out;* another, *is a poor little house*. Both reactions are predicative; but the first creates a purely narrative context, while in the second there is a double connection with the subject *hut*: on the one

From **Fundamentals of Language** by Roman Jakobson and Morris Halle. Moulton and Co., 1956. Reprinted by permission of the author.

hand, a positional (namely, syntactic) contiguity, and on the other a semantic similarity.

The same stimulus produced the following substitutive reactions: the tautology *hut;* the synonyms *cabin* and *hovel;* the antonym *palace,* and the metaphors *den* and *burrow.* The capacity of two words to replace one another is an instance of positional similarity, and, in addition, all these responses are linked to the stimulus by semantic similarity (or contrast). Metonymical responses to the same stimulus, such as *thatch, litter,* or *poverty,* combine and contrast the positional similarity with semantic contiguity.

In manipulating these two kinds of connection (similarity and contiguity) in both their aspects (positional and semantic) —selecting, combining, and ranking them—an individual exhibits his personal style, his verbal predilections and preferences.

In verbal art the interaction of these two elements is especially pronounced. Rich material for the study of this relationship is to be found in verse patterns which require a compulsory parallelism between adjacent lines, for example in Biblical poetry or in the West Finnic and, to some extent, the Russian oral traditions. This provides an objective criterion of what in the given speech community acts as a correspondence. Since on any verbal level—morphemic, lexical, syntactic, and phraseological—either of these two relations (similarity and contiguity) can appear—and each in either of two aspects—, an impressive range of possible configurations is created. Either of the two gravitational poles may prevail. In Russian lyrical songs, for example, metaphoric constructions predominate, while in the heroic epics the metonymic way is preponderant.

In poetry there are various motives which determine the choice between these alternants. The primacy of the metaphoric process in the literary schools of romanticism and symbolism has been repeatedly acknowledged, but it is still insufficiently realized that it is the predominance of metonymy which underlies and actually predetermines the so-called "realistic" trend, which belongs to an intermediary stage between the decline of romanticism and the rise of symbolism and is opposed to both. Following the path of contiguous relationships, the realistic author metonymically digresses from the plot to the atmosphere and from the characters to the setting in space and time. He is fond of synecdochic details. In the scene of Anna Karenina's suicide Tolstoy's artistic attention is focused on the heroine's handbag; and in *War and Peace* the synecdoches "hair on the upper lip" or "bare shoulders" are used by the same writer to stand for the female characters to whom these features belong.

The alternative predominance of one or the other of these two processes is by no means confined to verbal art. The same oscillation occurs in sign systems other than language. A salient example from the history of painting is the manifestly metonymical orientation of cubism, where the object is transformed into a set of synecdoches; the surrealist painters responded with a patently metaphorical attitude. Ever since the productions of D. W. Griffith, the art of the cinema, with its highly developed capacity for changing the angle, perspective and focus of "shots," has broken with the tradition of the theater and ranged an unprecedented variety of synecdochic "close-ups" and metonymic "set-ups" in general. In such pictures as those of Charlie Chaplin, these devices in turn were superseded by a novel, metaphoric "montage" with its "lap dissolves"—the filmic similes.[1]

The bipolar structure of language (or other semiotic systems), and, in aphasia, the fixation on one of these poles to the exclusion of the other require systematic comparative study. The retention of either of these alternatives in the two types of aphasia must be confronted with the predominance of the same pole in certain styles, personal habits, current fashions, etc. A careful analysis and comparison of these phenomena with the whole syndrome of the corresponding type of aphasia is an imperative task for joint research by experts in psychopathology, psychology, linguistics, poetics, and semiotics, the general science of signs. The dichotomy here discussed appears to be of primal significance and consequence for all verbal behavior and for human behavior in general.[2]

To indicate the possibilities of the projected comparative research, we choose an example from a Russian folktale which employs parallelism as a comic device: "Thomas is a bachelor; Jeremiah is unmarried" (*Fomá xólost; Erjóma*

---

[1] Cf. B. Balazs, *Theory of the film* (London, 1952).

[2] For the psychological and sociological aspects of this dichotomy see Bateson's views on "progressional" and "selective integration" and Parsons' on the "conjunction-disjunction dichotomy" in children's development: J. Ruesch and G. Bateson, *Communication, the social matrix of psychiatry* (New York, 1951), pp. 183ff.; T. Parsons and R. F. Bales, *Family, socialization and interaction process* (Glencoe, 1955), pp. 119f.

nezenát). Here the predicates in the two parallel clauses are associated by similarity: they are in fact synonymous. The subjects of both clauses are masculine proper names and hence morphologically similar, while on the other hand they denote two contiguous heroes of the same tale, created to perform identical actions and thus to justify the use of synonymous pairs of predicates. A somewhat modified version of the same construction occurs in a familiar wedding song in which each of the wedding guests is addressed in turn by his first name and patronymic: "Gleb is a bachelor; Ivanovič is unmarried." While both predicates here are again synonyms, the relationship between the two subjects is changed: both are proper names denoting the same man and are normally used contiguously as a mode of polite address.

In the quotation from the folk tale the two parallel clauses refer to two separate facts, the marital status of Thomas and the similar status of Jeremiah. In the verse from the wedding song, however, the two clauses are synonymous: they redundantly reiterate the celibacy of the same hero, splitting him into two verbal hypostases.

The Russian novelist Gleb Ivanovič Uspenskij (1840–1902) in the last years of his life suffered from a mental illness involving a speech disorder. His first name and patronymic, *Gleb Ivanovič*, traditionally combined in polite intercourse, for him split into two distinct names designating two separate beings: Gleb was endowed with all his virtues, while Ivanovič, the name relating the son to the father, became the incarnation of all Uspenskij's vices. The linguistic aspect of this split personality is the patient's inability to use two symbols for the same thing, and it is thus a similarity disorder. Since the similarity disorder is bound up with the metonymical bent, an examination of the literary manner Uspenskij had employed as a young writer takes on particular interest. And the study of Anatolij Kamegulov, who analyzed Uspenskij's style, bears out our theoretical expectations. He shows that Uspenskij had a particular penchant for metonymy, and especially for synecdoche, and that he carried it so far that "the reader is crushed by the multiplicity of detail unloaded on him in a limited verbal space, and is physically unable to grasp the whole, so that the portrait is often lost." [3]

[3] A. Kamegulov, *Stil' Gleba Uspenskogo* (Leningrad, 1930), pp. 65, 145. One of such disintegrated portraits cited by the monograph: "From underneath an ancient straw cap with a black

To be sure, the metonymical style in Uspenskij is obviously prompted by the prevailing literary canon of his time, late nineteenth-century "realism"; but the personal stamp of Gleb Ivanovič made his pen particularly suitable for this artistic trend in its extreme manifestations and finally left its mark upon the verbal aspect of his mental illness.

A competition between both devices, metonymic and metaphoric, is manifest in any symbolic process, either intrapersonal or social. Thus in an inquiry into the structure of dreams, the decisive question is whether the symbols and the temporal sequences used are based on contiguity (Freud's metonymic "displacement" and synecdochic "condensation") or on similarily (Freud's "identification and symbolism").[4] The principles underlying magic rites have been resolved by Frazer into two types: charms based on the law of similarity and those founded on association by contiguity. The first of these two great branches of sympathetic magic has been called "homoeopathic" or "imitative," and the second, "contagious magic." This bipartition is indeed illuminating. Nonetheless, for the most part, the question of the two poles is still neglected, despite its wide scope and importance for the study of any symbolic behavior, especially verbal, and of its impairments. What is the main reason for this neglect?

Similarity in meaning connects the symbols of a metalanguage [5] with the symbols of the language referred to. Similarity connects a metaphorical term with the term for which it is substituted. Consequently, when constructing a metalanguage to interpret tropes, the researcher possesses more homogeneous means to handle metaphor, whereas metonymy, based on a different principle, easily defies interpretation. Therefore nothing comparable to the rich literature on metaphor can be cited for the theory of metonymy. For the same reason, it is generally realized that romanticism is closely linked with metaphor, whereas the equally intimate ties of realism with metonymy usually remain unnoticed. Not only

---

spot on its shield, there peeked two braids resembling the tusks of a wild boar; a chin grown fat and pendulous definitively spread over the greasy collars of the calico dicky and in thick layer lay on the coarse collar of the canvas coat, firmly buttoned on the neck. From below this coat to the eyes of the observer there protruded massive hands with a ring, which had eaten into the fat finger, a cane with a copper top, a significant bulge of the stomach and the presence of very broad pants, almost of muslin quality, in the broad ends of which hid the toes of the boots."

[4] S. Freud, *The Interpretation of Dreams.* (Vienna, 1950).

[5] A way of talking about language. *Ed.*

the tool of the observer but also the object of observation is responsible for the preponderance of metaphor over metonymy in scholarship. Since poetry is focused upon sign, and pragmatical prose primarily upon referent, tropes and figures were studied mainly as poetical devices. The principle of similarity underlies poetry; the metrical parallelism of lines or the phonic equivalence of rhyming words prompts the question of semantic similarity and contrast; there exist, for instance, grammatical and anti-grammatical but never agrammatical rhymes. Prose, on the contrary, is forwarded essentially by contiguity. Thus, for poetry, metaphor, and for prose, metonymy is the line of least resistance and, consequently, the study of poetical tropes is directed chiefly toward metaphor. The actual bipolarity has been artificially replaced in these studies by an amputated, unipolar scheme which, strikingly enough, coincides with one of the two aphasic patterns, namely with the contiguity disorder. [6]

Linguistic Aspects of Yokuts Style

STANLEY S. NEWMAN

TO THE EXTENT that language is a medium for communicating ideas and for recording experience, appropriate equivalents in one language can always be supplied for those of another. On this colorless level a language has no style; it is merely what a dictionary implies it is—a bundle of lexical units for referring to things and events and relations, an instrument for conveying the brute content of experience.

But we are intuitively aware that our own native tongue, at least, is more than a group of speech symbols for referring to chairs and tables. We know, for instance, that there are a number of ways of saying essentially the same thing, that similar notions can be expressed by different stylistic uses of the language. Our intimate association with our native mode of expression has made us so acutely sensitive to these minute

[6] Thanks are due to Hugh McLean for his valuable assistance and to Justinia Besharov for her original observations on tropes and figures.

From **Yokuts and Western Mono Myths** by A. H. Gayton and Stanley S. Newman. University of California Publications, Anthropological Records, Volume 1, Berkeley, 1940. Reprinted by permission of University of California Press.

differences of style that we can frequently identify speakers or writers by the manner in which they draw upon the resources of the language. But our ability to make such fine discriminations within one language medium carries with it the seeds of an illusion, for inevitably we get the feeling that there is no limit to the potential variations of style in our language. And we are encouraged in this illusion by literary artists, whose task it is to convince us that they are working with a perfectly flexible medium that can be molded to any desired shape.

The process of translation helps to correct such illusions. In translating we come to the unhappy realization that each language, instead of shaping itself to our will, governs and directs the trend of our expression. We are sharply reminded that languages have an inner resistance. Their materials are already shaped into a system of formal and conceptual patterns. Within the patterns of a language other than our own, we are forced to make uncongenial distinctions and to ignore other distinctions that seem imperative to us. In Yokuts, for example, it is necessary to discriminate in all tenses an event which is in the process of transpiring from one that has already taken place and exists only as a resultant state or condition: a fundamental contrast is expressed in "he is walking" as against "he is in a condition subsequent to walking." Such a distinction is pedantic in English. Plurality need not be expressed in most nouns unless there is some special point to it; the form "house" can do the work of referring to the plural as well as the singular.

These patterns, however, are merely the potentialities of style. A grammar deals with them directly, describing their forms and their conceptual functions. It is not concerned with the selective tendencies operating in actual usage to favor certain potentialities and to neglect others. It tells what a language can do but not what it considers worthwhile doing. To the native a grammar is always unconvincing, for it ignores the most vital and intimate part of his language—the intricate network of values, of attitudes and expectancies that guides his selection of expressive tools.

It would be a sentimental presumption to suppose that we, as outsiders, can respond significantly to the values locked within the Yokuts language. The values and anticipations that we have developed in our own language will not be satisfied in Yokuts. In spite of this, we can escape our bias to some degree by following the selective trends of Yokuts as manifestations of the stylistic values proper to that language and by examining the manner in which Yokuts arrives at an integrated style through the exploitation of certain of its latent resources and the rejection of others.

A striking uniformity of style is to be found in Yokuts, and the personal narratives collected in the field show the same stylistic qualities as the myths and tales. In these stories there is no tendency to indulge in the elaboration of concrete details. The notions expressed remain on a highly generalized level. This bareness and simplicity of expression can be traced to a number of grammatical factors. Suffixation is practically the only grammatical technique of Yokuts that augments the meaning of word roots. The addition of a suffix, however, sets in motion a chain of formal operations. Principal among these are the vowel processes: in addition to occasional vowel changes that occur under special conditions, the root vowels undergo constant changes dictated by an intricate system of vowel classes; and the vowels of the suffix itself must then be changed to harmonize with the vowels of the root. To add the durative present—*?an,* for example, the roots *?e:pi,* "swim," and *de:yi,* "lead, take the lead," change their vowels in the stems *?ipa:–?an,* "he is swimming" and *diya:–?an,* "he is leading." But the suffix must also change its vowel when it is appended to a stem of the "o" class: parallel to the forms quoted above, the root *yo:wo* "go home," undergoes vowel changes and also affects the vowel of the suffix in *yowo:—?on,* "he is going home."

But all of this shifting and balancing of vowels is completely devoid of any referential function. The vowel changes have a purely formal relevance and carry with them no increments of meaning. They are not like our vowel changes in "sing, sang, sung" or in "man, men," which have a clearly assignable function. They resemble the nonfunctional vowel changes in the stressed syllables of "grateful, gratitude" or "volcano, volcanic." Whereas changes of this type affect only a minute portion of the English vocabulary, in Yokuts they are deeply embedded in the language system and accompany every process applied to the word.

In its organization of morphological elements, Yokuts shows the same disregard for external function. The tightly organized and interrelated classifications of word types and subtypes, of stems, and of suffixes are not based upon any rationale of their conceptual content. These elements are classified according to their phonetic form and the way they behave as morphological units, not according to their meaning.

Every language possesses a certain amount of formal machinery that does not generate meaning. Of this type are the occasional vowel changes of English, mentioned above, and some scattered consonant changes ("invade, invasion; equate, equation"). But there is a scrupulous and unremitting attention given to form for its own sake in Yokuts. Throughout its grammatical system Yokuts reveals a degree of neatness and consistency in organization, a formal balance and symmetry, that is rare among languages. Although this formal emphasis contributes feebly to the creation of meanings, it is by no means insignificant as a stylistic factor. Formal movements that take place below the level of tangible meanings carry their own esthetic satisfactions. But they are the most subtle and indigenous aspects of a language; they can never be captured in a translation.

The suffixing system, which bears the heaviest burden of functional work in Yokuts, does not provide the means for an elaborate development of concepts within the word. There are no more than a hundred suffixes in Yokuts. Although English possesses about the same number, it does not rely primarily upon suffixation; such techniques as word order, compounding, prefixation carry as much, if not more of the functional load. Yet, in spite of the fact that Yokuts depends almost exclusively upon suffixes, it is remarkably restrained in exploiting the possibilities of suffix combination. Every word in Yokuts, except the uninflected particle, must have at least one suffix, and the great majority of words occurring in the several volumes of text dictated by my informants do not go beyond this minimum requirement. Words containing two suffixes are fairly common; but words with three suffixes are relatively rare, and those with more than three are practically nonexistent in the texts. This is not a matter of mere statistics; it is a manifestation of selective forces in Yokuts that limit the free application of its grammatical resources. There is no analogous tendency in English to set upper and lower limits to the use of suffixation and to demand that a uniform degree of suffix elaboration be applied to words. As a matter of fact, English does not seek economy or uniformity in the use of any of its grammatical materials. In spite of the fact that we generally look outside the word unit to syntax for the creation of notional complexes, we feel no more strain in a lavishly suffixed word, such as "nationalistically" with its six suffixes, than in a suffixless word, such as "state."

An instructive exercise that I indulged in during my Yokuts field work was to construct words having four or five suffixes and to ask the informant for a translation. Although such words complied with the grammatical rules and could be translated by my informant without any difficulty, they seldom failed to provoke his amusement. It was obvious that these words were impossibly heavy and elaborate. To the Yokuts feeling for simplicity they were grammatical monstrosities.

The concepts expressed by the suffixes are abstract in nature. Yokuts does not possess the types of formative element, so familiar in many American Indian languages, that convey notions of concrete instrumentality, such as "with the hand" and "with a stick," or notions of specific location, such as "on the shore" and "in the house." The suffixes of Yokuts have more the character of algebraic symbols; their content is schematic rather than material. Among the verb suffixes, for example, are those defining an event as durative, continuative, repetitive, causative, reciprocal, passive, subordinate, undifferentiated past or present, future. The most common noun suffixes refer to case relations, marking the subject, direct object, and indirect object, or denoting possession, location, and the like. Particularized and concrete meanings are not expressed through the suffixes in Yokuts.

Even the stems, which are the only elements in Yokuts that can specify the material details of reference, show a strong tendency to carve out broad and comprehensive meanings from the referential field. The vocabulary of verb stems is largely made up of such diffuse and generalized notions as "come," "go," "walk," "run," "hear," "see," "smell." When suffixes with their abstract meanings are joined to stems whose referential content is so inclusive, the resulting words contain notions that are generalized. Although English is well stocked with words expressing notions of this kind, it also has an extensive vocabulary whose words are packed with delicate overtones of meaning. It can add subtle nuances to the general notion of "walk" by using such terms as "stroll," "saunter," "stride," "pace," "march," "tread," "plod," "hobble," "limp," "toddle." There is nothing like this in Yokuts. A book of Yokuts synonyms would be poor indeed. The language is not well equipped, either in its stems or in its formative elements, to build word units that are conceptually detailed or that express refinements and shadings of meaning.

Nor are the broad concepts of Yokuts words sharpened by special figurative uses. A stubborn literalness of reference invades the entire language. The shifts and extensions of meaning that add pungency and vigor to English play no part in Yokuts style. Such phrases as "to strike the eye," "to strike a bargain," "a sharp tongue," "a sharp appetite," "the family tree," "the tree of knowledge" illustrate the English genius for employing terms transferred from their literal sense. But in Yokuts a tree is a tree and nothing more. The language does not permit its words to cut metaphorical capers.

By exploiting the metaphorical possibilities of English words and by drawing upon our vocabulary of finely nuanced words, we can achieve variety and nicety of expression. Manuals of English style are merely underlining the potentialities inherent in the language when they encourage the student in his frantic efforts to avoid repetitions of the same word in close proximity. Although we may regard variety as an absolute virtue of style and repetition as a universal sin, it is obvious that Yokuts cannot be driven in this direction. The broad area of reference covered by Yokuts words gives them a wide range of application, and their literal significance holds them austerely within their proper boundaries of reference. It would be flying in the face of these forces in Yokuts to seek variety by ringing delicate changes upon a recurring notion. When a notion is to be repeated, there is no need to avoid verbal repetition. A passage such as, "and he walked home. And his friend also walked home. And the people walked home," however monotonous and slovenly it may appear to English sensibilities, is stylistically appropriate in Yokuts.

Yokuts possesses a special class of verbs which, in contrast to the generalized concepts typical of the language, express notions that are narrowly defined and specific. The following examples illustrate the kind of notions conveyed by this class of verbs.

k?ubwiyi	"strike a flat object to the ground"
wip?wiyi	"make a slow bending motion upward" (as branches bending upward in the wind)
bidinwiyi	"tumble from a high place"
xapapwiyi	"get spread out in a fanlike formation"
no:mno:mwiyi	"make puckering motions in and out"

The stylistic possibilities of these verbs for creating vivid images in a concentrated manner is obvious; but not so obvious to English feeling, which delights in flashes of sharp imagery, is the sense of violence and bizarreness which these verbs suggest to the Yokuts stylistic consciousness.

From the perspective of Yokuts, these verbs are linguistic freaks. Their grammatical form, as well as their content, is anomalous in the Yokuts system. These verbs are composed of two elements, a stem of the verb *wiyi*, "do, do thus," being added to another stem defining the nature of the activity. The technique of stem composition, displayed in these "do" verbs, occurs nowhere else in the language. Furthermore, a number of the "do" verbs, particularly those referring to specific sounds, contain a stem having an onomatopoetic force: *ga:gwiyi*, "cackle," *tuhwiyi*, "spit," *ʔuhwiyi*, "cough," *hikʔwiyi*, "make a hiccuping sound," *miwwiyi*, "whistle through the air." Such mimetic play with sounds is not only absent elsewhere in the language, but it is out of keeping with the severe formalism of Yokuts. In their meanings, in their form, and in their phonetic mimicry, these verbs seem to be cut to the pattern of a foreign idiom. They are like an ornate Byzantine mosaic set in a Calvinistic church.

It is a significant comment on the directive tendencies of historical drift in language that these eccentric "do" verbs have been leveled out of most of the modern Yokuts dialects. Only a few petrified noun derivatives are left in these dialects to indicate that the "do" verbs were formerly common throughout Yokuts. Only in one dialect, Yauelmani, have they been found as a fully operative and productive set of verbs. But they have a peculiar status in this dialect: they are regarded as the linguistic property of children. I did not become aware of this class of verbs until, after two or three weeks of field work, I overheard some remarks which my informant's eight-year-old son was addressing to himself. Only with the greatest difficulty could I coax my informant to explain the "do" verb which his child had used and to give me further examples of this class. It was evident that he regarded words of this type as being too silly for serious discussion and totally out of keeping with the essential sobriety of adulthood. Not until some time later did he tell me that these words were used primarily by children. But even after he had overcome his reluctance to discuss the "do" verbs, he was never able to treat them seriously. A spirit of facetiousness always accompanied our work with them.

The myths do not contain many examples of the "do" verbs. As a stylistic device these verbs are limited in their usefulness to contexts where an implication of startling and ludicrous extravagance is appropriate. In the story of Condor and Falcon only two examples occur. The first one describes the ineffectual booming sound made by Thunder in his efforts to move, the use of a "do" verb in this case suggesting not only the violence of the noise but its incongruity as coming from so helpless a person as Thunder. In the incident dealing with Crow, another "do" verb is employed to refer to his sudden transformation of color. Again the verb adds a touch of characterization, for Crow turns black as a result of stupidly gorging himself with black seeds. Stories dealing with Coyote as a trickster and a dupe offer the most favorable conditions for the use of these verbs. And yet, despite their effectiveness for describing the clownish antics of Coyote, they are not very frequent even in stories of this type. There still remains the feeling that the "do" verbs belong to a lunatic fringe of the language.

Something of the same flavor pervades the various sets of reduplicated words in English—"putt-putt" and "toot-toot," "pitter-patter" and "tittle-tattle," "piggy-wiggy" and "ducky-wucky." Like stem composition in Yokuts, reduplication is so exceptional and aberrant in English that it strikes the native form-feeling as a piece of ingenuous frivolity, proper to childish speech and appropriate on an adult level only when a frivolous reference is intended. But the values which color a grammatical technique are relative to the individual patterning of each language. To reverse the analogy, reduplication is felt as a thoroughly respectable technique in Yokuts, just as stem composition in English, as illustrated in "blackbird" or "noteworthy," has nothing of the outlandish character that it possesses in Yokuts. Even onomatopoeia, whose apparently spontaneous and direct symbolism might be expected to find a universal response, carries a different stylistic tone in the two languages: in Yokuts, it is associated only with the eccentric "do" verbs; in English, though it occurs in many of the low-caste reduplicated words, it is also found extensively throughout our vocabulary of image-creating words, such as "clink," "hush," "squeak," "squeal," where it serves to sharpen the vividness and specificity of reference.

Words are convenient but arbitrary units by means of which to examine the kinds of notions that a language expresses and the style of its expression. The limits of a word are determined by the morphological factors peculiar to each language, not by any notional criteria. Although Yokuts words, with the notable exception of the "do" verbs, tend to sketch only the bare and generalized outlines of a reference, the language possesses syntactic resources for combining words in such a way that its sentences could attain any degree of notional intricacy and richness. A passage of Macaulay's prose, with its long and involved periods, could be translated into grammatically correct Yokuts. But the result would be a grammarian's idle fancy, a distortion of the syntactic idiom of Yokuts. The language is as diffident in applying its means of elaboration in syntax as in suffixation.

Adjectival notions, for example, can be expressed by means of a simple syntactic device. A noun functions as an adjectival term augmenting or delimiting the meaning of any other noun by being linked in parallel series with it, and theoretically any number of such adjectival nouns can be juxtaposed to the noun they modify. The English predication, "he entered the small gray house," could be paraphrased in Yokuts: *go:binhin tew gudew p?ahlik?niw,* "he entered the house, the small one, the gray one." But one will search far in a body of Yokuts myths to find any such double use of adjectival terms modifying a noun. With the exception of demonstratives ("this one, that one") and quantifiers ("one, two, all, many"), even a single modifying term is rarely juxtaposed to a noun. Yokuts prefers to make separate sentences of its qualifications. More in line with the stylistic habits of Yokuts would be *go:binhin tew/ ?ama? ta guidi? / ?ama? ta yow p?ahlik?in,* "he entered the house. And that one was a small one./ And that one was also a gray one."

In the same spirit Yokuts avoids expressing subordinate and superordinate relations between its predications. It possesses particles indicating temporal and modal subordination, such as "when" and "if," and suffixes forming subordinate verbs, but these are syntactic tools that Yokuts employs only on rare occasions. Its favorite device for relating predications to one another is the particle *?ama?,* that can best be translated as "and" or "and then," an element that achieves only the loosest and most ambiguous type of coordination. The great majority of sentences in a Yokuts text begin with this feeble coordinator. Occasionally a tighter cohesion is attained by the use of another particle meaning "also, again." But the language seldom goes beyond this in its efforts to connect and relate its predications.

These items of syntactic behavior reflect the general tendency in Yokuts to demand a severe simplicity of content from its units of expression. In contrast to English, Yokuts does not pack its individual words with a wealth of meaning, nor does it compensate for the conceptual thinness of its words by an elaborate display of syntactic processes. Notions are sparsely distributed over a sequence of predications, and the predications themselves are broken up into independent, loosely joined sentences.

To the English imagination, rooted in its own habits of expression, the total effect of Yokuts style is anything but stimulating. The mode of expression undoubtedly appears drab, colorless, monotonous. Instead of a sentence structure that is varied, that presents smooth contours in passing from one predication to another, the progression is a series of bumps and jerks; statements are made in the abrupt manner of a telegram. The brevity of the sentences suggests a cryptic style, but one searches in vain for evidences of concentrated expression, for latent implications, for subtle metaphors playing beneath the surface of overt meanings. The broadly generalized notions have a literal reference. But the absence of nicety and richness of expression in Yokuts is not the symptom of meager grammatical resources; it is, rather, the result of willful selective forces within the language, for those resources which are the most powerful for the creation of meanings and for the development of notional complexes in words and in sentences are employed the most sparingly.

But by the same token, the stylistic features of English cannot appeal to the intuitions of a Yokuts native. To him English must appear erratic, lacking in those qualities of restraint and consistency which he finds in his own language. He will see no uniformity in the pattern of English sentences: some are short, and some are tediously long; some are lucid and immediately comprehensible, and some are so overloaded with subordinated and sub-subordinated notions, with qualifications and involutions of meaning, that the mind is wearied in trying to follow the labyrinthine twists and turns. Behind this unevenness of expression there seems to be a strident and feverish energy, obsessed with the need of expressing nuances that could best be left to contextual inference. To the native accustomed to the casual and quiet dignity of Yokuts style, English hammers too insistently upon the sensibilities with its succession of garish images, its interminable sleight-of-hand tricks with meanings that pass through sudden metaphorical changes, its insatiable taste for onomatopoetic mimicry. The language lacks balance and symmetry even in its grammatical system, which is a tangle of sprawling patterns. And English practices no economy in exploiting its motley resources; it draws upon its forms of expression with a prodigal hand.

Each of these appraisals is based upon the use of an irrelevant frame of values. It is no more valid than applying the principles of realistic painting to geometric art. Each language is like a particular art form in that it works with a limited range of materials and pursues the stylistic goals that have been and are constantly being discovered in a collective quest. Yokuts is a type of collective expression that values balance of inner form and restraint in the representation of meanings. In spite of the spurious impression that can hardly be avoided in an English translation, Yokuts is not a peculiar and imperfect kind of English.

VII. EPILOGUE

The Problem of Form

J. V. CUNNINGHAM

I SHALL STIPULATE that there is a problem of form in the poetry of our day, but I shall treat *form*, for the moment, as an undefined term, and I shall not until later specify the nature of some of the problems. I am, at the outset, interested in pointing to certain generalities, and to certain broad, simpleminded, pervasive attitudes and dualisms, of which the problem in poetry is to a large extent only a localization. These will give in outline the larger context of the problem.

To begin with, it is apparent that in our society we have too many choices. When we ask the young what they are going to do when they grow up, we should not be surprised or amused that the answers are whimsical and bewildered. The young poet today has a large and not too discriminated anthology of forms to realize; only illiterate ignorance or having made the pilgrimage to Gambier or to Los Altos will reduce the scope of options to manageable size—and even then there will be a hankering for further options. On the other hand, the young poet 250 years ago had it easy in this respect. He wrote octosyllabic or decasyllabic couplets, and the rhetoric and areas of experience of each were fairly delimited. For recreation he wrote a song in quatrains, and once or twice in a lifetime a Pindaric ode.

We come now to those attitudes and dualisms that make the problem of particular forms peculiarly our problem. We are a democratic society and give a positive value to informality, though some of the ladies still like to dress up. We will have nothing to do with the formal language and figured rhetoric of the *Arcadia*, for that is the language and rhetoric of a hierarchical and authoritarian society in which ceremony and formality were demanded by and accorded to the gov-

From **The Journal of John Cardan** by J.V. Cunningham. Reprinted by permission of the publisher, Alan Swallow, Denver. Copyright © 1964 by J.V. Cunningham.

erning class. We are reluctant to salute an officer. Instead, we praise, especially in poetry, what we call the accents of real speech—that is, of uncalculated and casual utterance, and sometimes even of vulgar impropriety. Now, if this attitude is a concomitant of the democratic revolution, the value we give to antiformality, to the deliberate violation of form and decorum, is a concomitant of its sibling, the romantic revolution. The measured, the formal, the contrived, the artificial are, we feel, insincere; they are perversions of the central value of our life, genuineness of feeling. "At least I was honest," we say with moral benediction as we leave wife and child for the sentimental empyrean.

If informality and antiformality are positive values, then the problem of form is how to get rid of it. But to get rid of it we must keep it; we must have something to get rid of. To do this we need a method, and we have found it in our dualisms of science and art, of intellectual and emotional, of regularity and irregularity, of norm and variation. We have been convinced, without inquiry or indeed adequate knowledge, that the regularities of ancient scientific law, of Newton's laws of motion, are regularities of matter, not of spirit, and hence are inimical to human significance. And so we embrace the broad, pervasive, simpleminded, and scarcely scrutinized proposition that regularity is meaningless and irregularity is meaningful—to the subversion of form. For one needs only so much regularity as will validate irregularity. But form is regularity.

So we come to definition. The customary distinctions of form and matter, or form and content, are in the discussion of writing at least only usable on the most rudimentary level. For it is apparent to any poet who sets out to write a sonnet that the form of the sonnet is the content, and its content the form. This is not a profundity, but the end of the discussion. I shall define form, then, without a contrasting term. It is that which remains the same when everything else is changed. This is not at all, I may say, a Platonic position. It is rather a mathematical and, as it should be, linguistic notion. a^2-b^2 is equal to $(a+b)$ $(a-b)$ through all the potentialities of a and b. The form of the simple declarative sentence in English is in each of its realizations.

It follows, then, that form is discoverable by the act of substitution. It is what has alternative realizations. And the generality or particularity of a form lies in the range or restriction of alternatives. It follows, also, that form precedes its realization, even in the first instance, and that unique form, or organic form in the sense of unique form, is a contradiction in terms. For it is the essence of form to be repetitive, and the repetitive is form. It follows, further, that there may be in a given utterance simultaneously a number of forms, so that the common literary question, "What is the form of this work?" can only be answered by a tacit disregard of all the forms other than the one we are momently concerned with.

It is time for illustration. Donne has a little epigram on Hero and Leander:

> Both robbed of air, we both lie in one ground,
> Both whom one fire had burnt, one water drowned.

What are the forms of this poem? First, both lines are decasyllabic in normal iambic pattern. Second, they rhyme. Third, it is phrased in units of four and six syllables in chiasmic order. Fourth, there are three *boths* and three *ones* in overlapping order. Fifth, the whole story of the lovers is apprehended, summarized, and enclosed in the simple scheme or form of the four elements. Finally, it is recognizably an epigram. Now Sir Philip Sidney, a few years earlier, in one of the *Arcadia* poems has the following lines:

> Man oft is plagued with air, is burnt with fire,
> In water drowned, in earth his burial is . . .

The lines are decasyllabic in normal iambic pattern. The adjacent lines do not rhyme, for the form of the poem is *terza rima*, an alternative form. It is phrased in units of six and four in chiasmic order. The first line repeats *with*, the second *in*. Man, not Hero and Leander, is apprehended in the scheme of the four elements, and in both cases the order of the elements is not formally predetermined. Finally, it is not an epigram, but part of an eclogue.

I have illustrated in these examples and in this analysis something of the variety of what may be distinguished as form: literary kind, conceptual distinctions, and all the rhetorical figures of like ending, equal members, chiasmus, and the various modes of verbal repetition. That some of the forms of Sidney's lines are repeated in Donne's, with the substitution of Hero and Leander for man, shows they have alternative realizations, and that so many operate simultaneously shows, not that a literary work has form, but that it is a convergence of forms, and forms of disparate orders. It is the coincidence of forms that locks in the poem.

Indeed, it is the inherent coincidence of forms in poetry, in metrical writing, that gives it its place and its power—a claim for poetry perhaps more accurate and certainly more modest than is customary. For this is the poet's *Poetics:* prose is written in sentences; poetry in sentences and lines. It is encoded not only in grammar, but also simultaneously in meter, for meter is the principle or set of principles, whatever they may be, that determine the line. And as we perceive of each sentence that it is grammatical or not, so the repetitive perception that this line is metrical or that it is not, that it exemplifies the rules or that it does not, is the metrical experience. It is the ground bass of all poetry.

And here in naked reduction is the problem of form in the poetry of our day. It is before all a problem of meter. We have lost the repetitive harmony of the old tradition, and we have not established a new. We have written to vary or violate the old line, for regularity we feel is meaningless and irregularity meaningful. But a generation of poets, acting on the principles and practice of significant variation, have at last nothing to vary from. The last variation is regularity.

A Note on the Authors

Aristotle, Cicero, Swift, and Wordsworth, among others, need no introduction.

The Century Dictionary and Cyclopedia (1891) is one of the great, and neglected, monuments of American scholarship.

Paul Valéry (1871-1945) is generally thought to be the greatest European poet of the last hundred years.

Meyer Schapiro (1904-) is Professor of Art History at Columbia.

René Wellek (1903-) is Professor of Comparative Literature at Yale.

Longinus: Nothing is known of the author of *On the Sublime,* not even that his name is Longinus, but we may as well call him that.

Erich Auerbach (1892-1957), a German exile, was at the time of his death Professor of French and Romance Philology at Yale.

Morris Croll (1872-1947) was Professor of English at Princeton.

Pierre Nicole (1625-95), French Jansenist, taught at Port-Royal, where one of his students was Racine.

James Sledd (1914-) is Professor of English at the University of Texas.

Benedetto Croce (1866-1952), Italian philosopher, historian, and critic.

George Philip Krapp (1872-1934) was Professor of English at Columbia.

Charles Sanders Peirce (1839-1914), about whose views James Feibleman (1904-) writes, is one of the seminal minds of modern philosophy.

Sir Walter Raleigh (1861-1922) was Professor of English Literature at Oxford.

William Allan Neilson (1869-1946) was President of Smith College.

Ashley Horace Thorndike (1871-1933) was Professor of English at Columbia.

E. K. Chambers' (1866-1954) *William Shakespeare: A Study of Facts and Problems* is the standard work.

Lane Cooper (1875-1959) was Professor of English at Cornell.

Bergen Evans (1904-   ) is Professor of English at Northwestern University.

Frank Sullivan (1892-   ) first presented "The Cliché Expert" in *The New Yorker* in 1945.

Denys Page (1908-   ) is Professor of Greek at Cambridge University.

Rulon Wells (1919-   ) is Professor of Linguistics and Philosophy at Yale.

Roman Jakobson (1896-   ) is Professor of Slavic Languages and Literature at Harvard.

Stanley S. Newman (1905-   ) is Professor of Anthropology at the University of New Mexico.

Bibliography

SECTION I OF the following selective bibliography lists classic writings on style in roughly chronological order followed by several collections of essays. Section II lists general works on style; section III lists more particular works.

I

Aristotle, *Poetics,* tr. Thomas Twinning, 1789; tr. Ingram Bywater, 1909.

Aristotle, *Rhetoric,* ed. E.M. Cope and J.E. Sandys, 1867; tr. J.E.C. Welldon, 1886; tr. R.C. Jebb, 1909; tr. W.Rhys Roberts, 1924; tr. J.H. Freese, 1926; tr. Lane Cooper, 1932; E.M. Cope, *An Introduction to Aristotle's "Rhetoric,"* 1867.

Demetrius, *On Style,* tr. T.A. Moxon, 1934; tr. W. Rhys Roberts, 1902.

Cicero, *On the Orator (De Oratore),* Book III, tr. J.S. Watson, 1856; tr. H. Rackham, 1942.

Cicero, *The Orator (Orator)* tr. H.M. Hubbell, 1952.

Dionysius of Halicarnassus, *On Literary Composition,* ed., tr. W. Rhys Roberts, 1910.

Quintilian, *The Institutes of Oratory,* tr. J.S. Watson, 1875; tr. H.E. Butler, 1921-2.

Longinus, *On the Sublime,* tr. W. Rhys Roberts, 1899; tr. W. Hamilton Fyfe, 1927; tr. Benedict Einarson, 1945.

St. Augustine, *On Christian Doctrine,* Book IV, tr. J.F. Shaw, 1952; tr. D.W. Robertson, Jr., 1958.

Dante, *On the Vernacular,* tr. in Temple Classics, 1904.

Puttenham, George, *The Arte of English Poesie,* 1589, ed. Gladys D. Willcock and Alice Walker, 1936.

Hoskyns, John, *Directions for Speech and Style,* ca. 1599, ed. Hoyt H. Hudson, 1935.

Sprat, Thomas, *History of the Royal Society,* 1667, ed. Jackson I. Cope and Harold Whitmore Jones, St. Louis, 1958, pp. 111 ff.

Swift, Jonathan, *A Letter to a Young Clergyman Lately*

Enter'd into Holy Orders, London, 1721; *Prose Works,* ed. Temple Scott, London, 1898.

Hume, David, "Of Eloquence," "Of Simplicity and Refinement in Writing," *Essays, Moral, Political, and Literary,* London, 1742.

Chesterfield, Philip Dormer Stanhope, 4th Earl of, "Letter to his Son," 24 Nov. 1749, *Works,* New York, 1838.

Buffon, M. De, "Discours sur le Style," 1753, tr. from sophique, *Oeuvres de Voltaire,* Paris, 1879, by Lane Cooper, *Theories of Style,* New York, 1907.

Johnson, Samuel, "Style," *The Critical Opinions of Samuel Johnson,* ed. Joseph E. Brown, Princeton, 1926.

Voltaire, "Style," 1771-1774, tr. from *Dictionnaire Philosophique, Oeuvres de Voltaire,* Paris, 1879, by Lane Cooper, *Theories of Style,* New York, 1907.

Campbell, George, *Philosophy of Rhetoric,* London, 1776.

Diderot, Denis, *Thoughts on Art and Style,* selected and tr. by Beatrix Tollemache, London, 1893.

Blair, Hugh, *Lectures on Rhetoric and Belles Lettres,* Edinburgh, 1783.

Coleridge, Samuel Taylor, Chapters XIV, XVII, XVIII, XX, XXII, *Biographia Literaria,* 1817.

Hazlitt, William, "On Familiar Style," Essay XXIV, *Table Talk, or Original Essays,* London, 1822.

Whately, Richard, Part III, *Elements of Rhetoric,* London, 1828.

DeQuincey, Thomas, "Rhetoric," *Blackwood's Magazine,* Dec., 1828; "Style," *Blackwood's Magazine,* July, Sept., Oct., 1840 and Feb., 1841; "Language," 1858; all in *Collected Writings,* ed. D. Masson, Edinburgh, 1890.

Schopenhauer, Arthur, "On Style," 1851, tr. T. Bailey Saunders, *The Art of Literature, A Series of Essays,* London, 1891.

Spencer, Herbert, "Philosophy of Style," *Westminster Review,* NS, 58 (Oct., 1852); *Essays: Moral, Political, and Aesthetic,* New York, 1864.

Ruskin, John, "Pathetic Fallacy," *Modern Painters,* London, 1856.

Arnold, Matthew, "The Grand Style," *On Translating Homer,* 1861, *On Translating Homer: Last Words,* 1862.

Bagehot, Walter, "Wordsworth, Tennyson, and Browning; or Pure, Ornate, and Grotesque Art in English Poetry," *National Review,* Nov. 1864; *Literary Studies,* ed. Richard Holt Hutton, London, 1879.

Lewes, George H., "The Principles of Success in Literature," *Fortnightly Review,* Sept. and Nov., 1865; ed. T.S. Knowlson, 1898.

Stevenson, Robert L., "A Note on Realism," *Magazine of Art,* Nov., 1883; "On Some Technical Elements of Style in Literature," *Contemporary Review,* 47 (April, 1885); *The Works of Robert Louis Stevenson,* New York, 1898.

Pater, Walter, "Style," *Fortnightly Review,* Dec. 1, 1888; *Appreciations With An Essay on Style,* 1889.

Earle, John, Chapter IX, *English Prose: Its Elements, History and Usage,* London, 1890.

Raleigh, Sir Walter, *Style,* London, 1897.

Harrison, Frederic, "On Style in English Prose," *Nineteenth Century,* 43 (1898); in *Tennyson, Ruskin, Mill, and Other Literary Estimates,* London, 1900.

Brewster, William T., ed. *Representative Essays on the Theory of Style,* New York, London, 1905.

Brewster, William T., ed. *Studies in Structure and Style,* New York, 1896.

Cooper, Lane, *Theories of Style,* New York, 1907.

II

Auerbach, Erich, *Mimesis: The Representation of Reality in Western Literature,* tr. by Willard Trask, Princeton, 1953.

Barfield, Owen, *Poetic Diction: A Study in Meaning,* London, 1925.

Dobrée, Bonamy, *Modern Prose Style,* Oxford, 1934.

Enkvist, Nils Erik, John Spencer, and Michael J. Gregory, *Linguistics and Style,* London, 1964.

Fowler, H.W., *A Dictionary of Modern English Usage,* 2nd ed., revised by Sir Ernest Gowers, New York, 1965.

Graves, Robert, *The Reader over Your Shoulder,* New York, 1944.

Hulme, Thomas Ernest, *Notes on Language and Style,* ed. Herbert Read, Seattle, 1929.

Lucas, Frank L., *Style,* London, 1955.

Quiller-Couch, Sir Arthur, *The Art of Writing,* Cambridge, 1916.

Read, Sir Herbert, *English Prose Style,* London, 1928.

Rouse, W.H.D., "Style," *Essays and Studies,* XXVII (1941).

Saintsbury, George, "English Prose Style," *Miscellaneous Essays,* New York, 1892.

Sebeok, Thomas A., ed., *Style in Language,* Cambridge, Mass., 1960.

Smith, Logan Pearsall, *Fine Writing,* Oxford, 1936.

Spitzer, Leo, *Linguistics and Literary History: Essays in Stylistics,* Princeton, 1948.

Sutherland, James, *On English Prose,* Toronto, 1957.

Ullmann, Stephen, *Language and Style,* New York, 1964.

Wimsatt, W.K., *The Verbal Icon,* Lexington, 1954.

III

Alonso, Amado, "The Stylistic Interpretation of Literary Texts," *MLN,* LVII (1942).

Auerbach, Erich, *Literary Language and Its Public in Late Latin Antiquity and in the Middle Ages,* tr. by Ralph Manheim, New York, 1965.

Barish, Jonas A., "Baroque Prose in the Theater: Ben Jonson," *PMLA,* LXXIII (1958).

Barish, Jonas A., "The Prose Style of John Lyly," *ELH,* XXIII (1956).

Barkas, Pallister, *A Critique of English Prosody, 1880-1930,* Halle, 1934.

Bate, Walter Jackson, *The Stylistic Development of Keats,* New York, 1954.

Bradbrook, Frank W., "Style and Judgment in Jane Austen's Novels," *Cambridge Journal,* IV (1951).

Burke, Kenneth, "Four Master Tropes," *A Grammar of Motives,* New York, 1946.

Burke, Kenneth, "Style," *Permanence and Change: An Anatomy of Purpose,* revised ed., Los Altos, 1954.

Clark, A.C., *Prose Rhythm in English,* Oxford, 1913.

Croll, Morris W., Introduction to Harry Clemons' edition of Lyly's *Euphues,* London, 1916.

Croll, Morris W., *Style, Rhetoric, and Rhythm,* ed. J.M. Patrick, Princeton, 1965.

Elton, Oliver, "English Prose Numbers," *A Sheaf of Papers,* London, 1922.

Elton, Oliver, "Style in Shakespeare," *Proceedings of the British Academy,* XXII (1936).

Hatzfeld, Helmut, "Stylistic Criticism as Art-minded Philology," *Yale French Studies,* II (1949).

Hatzfeld, Helmut, *A Critical Bibliography of the New Stylistics Applied to the Romance Literatures, 1900-1952,* Chapel Hill, 1953.

Havens, R.D., "The Poetic Diction of the English Classicists," *Kittredge Anniversary Papers,* Boston, 1913.

Herdan, Gustav, *Language as Choice and Chance,* Groningen, 1956.

Hornstein, Lillian H., "Analysis of Imagery: A Critique of Literary Method," *PMLA,* LVII (1942).

Jones, Howard Mumford, "American Prose Style: 1700-1770," *Huntington Library Bulletin,* VI (1934).

Jones, Richard F., "Science and English Prose Style in the Third Quarter of the Seventeenth Century," *PMLA,* XLV (1930).

Joos, Martin, "The Isolation of Styles," *Georgetown University Monograph Series on Language and Linguistics,* XII (1960).

Levin, Harry, *Contexts in Criticism,* Cambridge, Mass., 1957.

[Levin, Harry] "Expressive Voices: The Emergence of a National Style," *Times Literary Supplement,* Sept. 17, 1954.

Lord, Albert B., *The Singer of Tales,* Cambridge, Mass., 1960.

MacDonald, Dwight, *Parodies: An Anthology from Chaucer to Beerbohm and After,* New York, 1960.

Magoun, Francis P., Jr., "Oral-Formulaic Character of Anglo-Saxon Narrative Poetry," *Speculum,* 28 (1953).

Martin, Harold C., ed. *Style in Prose Fiction,* New York, 1959.

Miles, Josephine, *The Continuity of Poetic Language,* Berkeley, 1951.

Miles, Josephine, *The Vocabulary of Poetry,* Berkeley, 1946.

Moore, Arthur K., "Rhetoric's Wrung Neck," *Western Humanities Review,* XVII (1963).

Murray, J. Middleton, "Metaphor," *Countries of the Mind,* second series, London, 1931.

Parry, Milman, "The Traditional Metaphor in Homer," *Classical Philology,* XXVIII (1933).

Ohmann, Richard M., "Prolegomena to the Analysis of Prose Style," *Style in Prose Fiction,* ed. Harold C. Martin, New York, 1959.

Pound, Louise, "The Dialect of Cooper's Leatherstocking," *American Speech,* II (1927).

Quayle, Thomas, *Poetic Diction: A Study of Eighteenth Century Verse,* London, 1924.

Reynolds, W.V., "Johnson's Opinions on Prose Style," *RES,* XI (1935).

Ricks, C.B., *Milton's Grand Style,* Oxford, 1963.

Riffaterre, Michael, "Criteria for Style Analysis," *Word,* XV (1959).

Shipley, Joseph T., ed. *Dictionary of World Literature,* rev. ed., 1953. Particularly articles signed: J.C. La D.

Spalding, William, *A Letter on Shakespeare's Authorship*

of "The Noble Kinsmen" and on the Characteristics of Shakespeare's Style . . . 1833, reprinted London, 1876.

Spedding, James, "On the Several Shares of Shakspere and Fletcher in the Play of *Henry VIII*," *Gent. Mag.*, XXXIV (1850) *Trans. I New Shakspere Soc.* (1874).

Spitzer, Leo, *A Method of Interpreting Literature*, Northampton, Mass., 1949.

Spurgeon, Caroline, *Shakespeare's Imagery and What It Tells Us*, Cambridge, 1935.

Stutterheim, C.F.P., "Modern Stylistics," Part I, *Lingua*, I (1947-48), Part II, *Lingua*, III (1952-53).

Sutherland, James, "Some Aspects of Eighteenth-Century Prose," *Essay on the Eighteenth Century: Presented to David Nichol Smith in Honour of His Seventieth Birthday*, Oxford, 1945.

Thompson, E.N.S., "Milton's Prose Style," *PQ*, XIV (1935).

Tillotson, Geoffrey, "Eighteenth Century Poetic Diction," *Essays in Criticism and Research*, Cambridge, 1942.

Trager, George L., "Paralanguage: A First Approximation," *Studies in Linguistics*, XIII (1958).

Ullmann, Stephen, *Style in the French Novel*, Cambridge, 1957.

Wellek, René and Austin Warren, "Style and Stylistics," *Theory of Literature*, New York, 1942.

Williamson, George, *The Senecan Amble: A Study in Prose Form from Bacon to Collier*, London, 1951.

Wimsatt, W.K., Jr., "One Relation of Rhyme to Reason," *MLQ*, V (1944), reprinted in *The Verbal Icon*, Lexington, 1954.

Wimsatt, William K., *The Prose Style of Samuel Johnson*, New Haven, 1941.

Winter, Werner, "Styles as Dialects," *Preprints of Papers for the Ninth International Congress of Linguists*, Cambridge, Mass., 1962.

Winters, Yvor, "The 16th Century Lyric in England," *Poetry* (Chicago), LIII-LIV (February, March, April, 1939).

Wyld, H.C., *Some Aspects of the Diction of English Poetry*, Oxford, 1933.

Yule, G.U., "On Sentence Length as Statistical Characteristics of Style in Prose," *Biometrika*, XXX (1939).

Yule, G.U., *The Statistical Study of Literary Vocabulary*, Cambridge, 1944.